ostensibly....

Hamass fund raisers in the U.S.
Holy Land Foundation in texas - front
for funding for H

Fatah was a terrorist
renounced violence - critical
Israel recognized PLO as principle rep. of Palestinians.

TERRORISM IN AMERICA

ABOUT THE AUTHOR

Harvey W. Kushner received a B.A. degree in political science from Queens College and an M.A. degree and Ph.D. in political science from New York University. He currently is Professor and Chair of the Department of Criminal Justice and Security Administration at Long Island University.

An internationally recognized expert on terrorism, antigovernment violence, and extremism, in recent years Professor Kushner has conducted workshops on the mind-set of the terrorist for a variety of state and federal agencies, including the Federal Aviation Administration, the Federal Bureau of Investigation, and the U.S. Federal Probation Department.

Professor Kushner's opinions and criticisms are much sought after by the media. His commentary has appeared on Voice of America, Cable News Network (CNN), and the Canadian Broadcasting Corporation (CBC), and in Associated Press articles, *Time*, *Newsweek*, and other magazines and newspapers worldwide. Advocacy groups, as well as victims, also rely on his expertise. He most recently was the plaintiff's expert witness in the civil litigation arising from the bombing of the World Trade Center in New York.

Professor Kushner's writings on terrorism have appeared in academic, professional, and trade publications such as *Studies in Conflict and Terrorism*, *Counterterrorism & Security International*, and *Security Management*. His most recent book is *The Future of Terrorism: Violence in the New Millennium* (1998). He also writes a monthly column on aviation security for *Airport Press*.

TERRORISM IN AMERICA

A Structured Approach to Understanding the Terrorist Threat

By

HARVEY W. KUSHNER, Ph.D.

CHARLES C THOMAS • PUBLISHER, LTD.
Springfield • Illinois • U.S.A.

Published and Distributed Throughout the World by

CHARLES C THOMAS · PUBLISHER, LTD.
2600 South First Street
Springfield, Illinois 62794-9265

© *1998 by* CHARLES C THOMAS · PUBLISHER, LTD.

ISBN 0-398-06894-1 (cloth)
ISBN 0-398-06895-X (paper)

Library of Congress Catalog Card Number: 98-27285

With THOMAS BOOKS *careful attention is given to all details of manufacturing
and design. It is the Publisher's desire to present books that are satisfactory as to their
physical qualities and artistic possibilities and appropriate for their particular use.*
THOMAS BOOKS *will be true to those laws of quality that assure a good name
and good will.*

Printed in the United States of America
SM-R-3

Library of Congress Cataloging in Publication Data

Kushner, Harvey W.
    Terrorism in America : a structured approach to understanding
the terrorist threat / Harvey W. Kushner.
        p.   cm.
    Includes bibliographical references and index.
    ISBN 0-398-06894-1 (cloth). -- ISBN 0-398-06895-X (pbk.)
    1. Terrorism--United States. I. Title.
HV6432.K87   1998
364.1--dc21   98-27285
                                                                         CIP

FOR THE GIRLS IN MY LIFE

Sara
Meredith Hope
Patches
Candy

PREFACE

Most books devoted to the study of terrorism avoid discussions that require the author to make a call about some event that has not been categorized by the authorities as a terrorist incident. Sometimes, social scientists are unwilling to interject their own opinions for fear of being labeled biased. They would rather let some federal agency tell them what is a terrorist event. At other times, these same social scientists hide behind a morass of minutia about, for example, some terrorist organization. Their admittedly interesting descriptive analyses do little to further the understanding of today's terrorism. At still other times, they undertake abstract quantitative analyses that wind up showcasing the method, rather than explaining terrorism. Besides, can data pertaining to the number of people killed or injured by a terrorist attack be added and subtracted in the same way demographers crunch numbers? And how does one compare the World Trade Center bombing that killed six and injured many more with the recorded act of a radical animal rights terrorist who scribbled some graffiti on the wall of a butcher shop? In both cases, the answer is you cannot.

In this work, I have intentionally avoided descriptions of some past terrorist incidents and opted instead to stress the present. This is not a sourcebook for looking up everything you ever wanted to know about terrorism but were afraid to ask. I have also purposely stayed away from using tables and graphs to compare terrorist incidents across different time periods. Of course, some might disagree with my omissions. With caveats in full display, I ask these critics to forgive these omissions and to consider my structured approach to understanding the current terrorist threat. In this way, the reader will come to know the evil within—terrorism in America.

H. W. K.

ACKNOWLEDGMENTS

Many people assisted in the development of this project—some by offering their insightful comments, and others by providing data on extremists, terrorists, and assorted crazies. They all share in making this a better book. Of course, any mistakes are mine. With this said, I proudly reveal all those individuals and organizations that unselfishly answered my calls for assistance: Brian Levin, Moorhead Kennedy, Jerome Glazebrook, Hal Mansfield, Judge Robin D. Smith, the Anti-Defamation League, the Southern Poverty Law Center, the American Jewish Committee, and the Coalition for Human Dignity.

My sincerest thanks to Michael Payne Thomas of Charles C Thomas, Publisher. His patience is appreciated in an age when developmental editors e-mail authors about their forthcoming deadlines. My graduate research assistant at Long Island University, Jeff Liss, deserves my gratitude for not depleting my Lexis account looking up the anniversary of some terrorist event. Kudos to my copy editor, Linda Poderski, who always provides invaluable guidance and attention to detail; whoever thinks one cannot make a silk purse out of a sow's ear has not seen Linda weave straw into gold.

To Meredith, my beautiful and talented daughter, may she always be Merry Hope. My significant other, Sara, was always there to listen to my explanation of why a certain event was an act of terrorism even though the politicians were saying something else. Her advice was always taken. Her support and love are most appreciated. My father, Albert, taught me to bring politics to the dinner table. As I grow older, I better understand his plan. Love ya, Pop. Last, but certainly not least, I thank my feline companions, Patches and Candy. Both gave up comfortable spots on the sofa to keep me company atop my computer keyboard. My thanks, Girls, for allowing the mouse to live long enough for me to finish this project.

CONTENTS

		Page
Preface		vii

Chapter
1. TERRORISM: THE CONCEPT   3
   The Search for the Perfect Definition   3
   The Search for the Perfect Typology   6
   No Search at All   7
   A Definition of Terrorism   8
2. INTERNATIONAL TERRORISM   11
   The Threat From Outside   11
   Out With the Old   13
       The Soviet Union and Terrorism   13
       The Persian Gulf War and Yasir Arafat   17
       The Islamic Resistance Movement   19
       Arafat: Assassinations, Mortality, and the Peace Process   20
   In With the New   22
       Iran   22
       Sudan   25
       Boot Camps for Terror   27
         Sudan   27
         Afghanistan   28
   A New Terrorism   29
       Suicide Bombers   32
       Freelancers   33
   They're Here: Terrorist Groups and Their Ardent Supporters   35
       The Abu Nidal Organization   35
       Palestine Islamic Jihad   37
       Hamas   38
       Networking From Coast to Coast   40

        Good News, Bad News   42
    They're Here Too: The Freelancers   43
        Mir Aimal Kasi   43
        Rashid Baz   45
        Ali Hassan Abu Kamal   46
        Gazi Ibrahim Abu Maizer and Lafi Khalil   47
        Wanna-bes, Freelancers, or What?   48
    What It All Means   49
3. DOMESTIC TERRORISM   56
    The Threat From Within   56
    Christian Identity: The Belief That Binds   59
    Theory Into Practice: Posse Comitatus   64
    The Guru of the Extreme Right: William Pierce   68
    Tactical Training for Armageddon: Louis Beam   72
    Cyberspace: The Antigovernment Extremist's
            Road to High-Tech Communications   74
        The Internet   74
        The Usenet   75
        The World Wide Web   76
    Antigovernment Extremists Identified   79
    The New Domestic Terrorist   81
4. THE TIMES THEY ARE A-CHANGIN'   86
    Once Upon a Time   86
    Terrorist Groups of the Future   88
    The Day of the Freelancer   92
    What's a Law Enforcement Agency to Do?   94
5. TERRORIST AND EXTREMIST GROUPS
            IN THE UNITED STATES   99
    Taking Inventory   99
    Domestic Groups   100
        Animal Rights and Environmental Groups   100
        Common Law Courts   101
        Criminal Gangs   108
        Jewish Groups   109
        Klans   110
        Left-Wing Extremist Groups   114

Militias 116
Puerto Rican Groups 126
Right-Wing Extremist Groups 129
    Christian Identity 129
    Neo-Nazi 130
    Other 131
Skinheads 132
International Groups 135
    Afghani Groups 136
Armenian Groups 137
Cuban Groups 137
Irish Groups 138
Israeli Groups 140
Japanese Groups 140
Middle Eastern Groups 141
Pakistani Groups 143

6. CHRONOLOGICAL SUMMARY OF TERRORIST AND TERRORIST RELATED INCIDENTS IN THE UNITED STATES 145
7. ORGANIZATIONS TO CONTACT FOR INFORMATION ON TERRORISTS AND EXTREMISTS 194
The Sentinels 194
References 205
Index 211

TERRORISM IN AMERICA

Chapter 1

TERRORISM: THE CONCEPT

THE SEARCH FOR THE PERFECT DEFINITION

Many authors would agree that it is difficult to define terrorism (see, e.g., Atkins, 1992; Combs, 1997; Kidder, 1993; Sadler & Winters, 1996; Sederberg, 1993; Vetter & Perlstein, 1991; White, 1991). So did Alex Schmid, who in a comprehensive review of the literature identified 22 elements that appeared in more than 100 competing definitions of terrorism provided by writers between 1936 and 1983. In an effort to summarize, if not synthesize, Schmid developed a definition of terrorism that incorporated 16 of these elements:

> Terrorism is an anxiety-inspiring method of repeated violent action, employed by (semi-) clandestine individual, group, or state actors, for idiosyncratic, criminal, or political reasons, whereby—in contrast to assassination—the direct targets of violence are not the main targets. The immediate human victims of violence are generally chosen randomly (targets of opportunity) or selectively (representative or symbolic targets) from a target population, and serve as message generators. Threat- and violence-based communication processes between terrorist (organization), (imperiled) victims, and main target (audience(s)), turning it into a target of terror, a target of demands, or a target of attention, depending on whether intimidation, coercion, or propaganda is primarily sought. (1983, p. 28)

One glimpse at this lengthy definition indicates that Schmid's Herculean effort neither solved the definitional problem nor ended the proliferation of definitions. Actually, by the time Schmid published a second edition of *Political Terrorism: A Research Guide to Concepts, Theories, Data Bases, and Literature* in 1988, more definitions had been proffered, ironically, in part in response to a survey on the definitional problem he conducted.[1]

Brian Jenkins (1985) best represents all those authors who could easily obfuscate a concept with a morass of verbiage but who instead choose to define terrorism in the most simplistic of terms. Terrorism, wrote this erudite terrorism expert, is the threatened use of force designed to bring about political change. Walter Laqueur, in his widely read and extraordinarily detailed *Age of Terrorism* (1987), offers a similar definition. Laqueur writes that terrorism constitutes the illegitimate use of force against innocent people in order to achieve a political objective. These two well-respected terrorism experts are certainly aware of the problems with simple definitions. They would argue, however, that to move beyond them would not prove fruitful because the concept itself is so controversial.

Schmid's definition given above is a perfect example of a complex definition of terrorism. The definition's length, as well as complexity, makes it exceedingly hard to follow. Other authors as diverse as U.S. Department of State analyst Thomas P. Thornton (1964), social scientist Martha Crenshaw (1983), and senior criminologist with the Australian Institute of Criminology in Canberra, Australia, Grant Wardlaw (1989) are also partial to detailed definitions. Consider, for example, Wardlaw's definition:

> Political terrorism is the use, or threat of use, of violence by an individual or a group, whether acting for or in opposition to established authority, when such action is designed to create extreme anxiety and/or fear-inducing effects in a target group larger than the immediate victims with the purpose of coercing that group into acceding to the political demands of the perpetrators. (p. 16)

Certainly, this definition is not as complex as Schmid's. Still, one would not call it succinct.

Other authors skirt the simplicity/complexity issue only to create definitions that have their own shortcomings. Consider, for example, definitions of terrorism that concentrate on the use of motivational violence to achieve a political end. Although they manage to distinguish between terrorism and criminal activity, they do not distinguish between a terrorist hijacking and a military battle. Authorities whose works have a tendency to conflate terrorism with a variety of other forms of coercion include Brian Crozier (*Terrorist Activity*, 1974) and James Lodge (1981).

Neil Livingstone (Livingstone & Arnold, 1986) and Benjamin Netanyahu (1986; 1995) offer yet another direction in defining terrorism. These authors, notwithstanding their well-documented political positions, claim that terrorism represents a cheap and effective weapon of warfare against the United States and Western civilization itself. Gerardo Jorge Schamis (1980) takes a somewhat less ethnocentric position and argues that terrorism now constitutes a new form of warfare that has been sponsored by underdeveloped countries to fight against militarily stronger ones. And for the noted French terrorism expert Gerard Chaliand (1987), terrorism is a natural outgrowth of the anticolonial struggle; it is merely another weapon of revolutionary guerrillas in their campaign of psychological warfare. Donald Hanle (1989) also links the theory of terrorism to warfare. For this career U.S. Air Force officer, terrorism is a form of war based on the manipulation of force to meet political objectives. All forms of terrorism, Hanle argues, employ force as a form of war.

Edward Herman (1983) and Jeffrey Ian Ross (1995) eschew the military approach to explaining terrorism in favor of defining terrorism in much the same way Hannah Arendt did in her classic *Origins of Totalitarianism* (1951). For Herman and Ross, terrorism is something a state does to its citizens to maintain political power, which for Arendt meant state control from the "cradle to the grave." For others, like David Claridge (1996) and Roberta Goren (1984), terrorism is something defined and practiced by a state against people for a variety of reasons as diverse as struggles of liberation and pacifications of populations after annexation. Many proponents of this approach label the policies of Israeli, as well as of the former South African regime, terroristic. Noam Chomsky (1986) would even argue that the United States itself conducts terrorist activities against selected targets while attacking other counties for promoting terrorist activities. Although controversial, Chomsky's viewpoint is shared by many radical academicians. Still others look toward the state and its agents to provide definitions of terrorism, an approach favored by Brent Smith (1994) in his informative *Terrorism in America: Pipe Bombs and Pipe Dreams.*

Probably the most widely used method of defining terrorism involves those authors who have tried to come to terms with the concept through writing about the psychological causes of terrorism. Some of these authors have created their psychological definitions through the study of individual terrorists (see, e.g., Cooper, 1977; Kellman, 1983; Morf, 1970; Post, 1984). Other authors have turned to the terrorist groups themselves (see, e.g., Clark, 1983; McCauley & Segal, 1987; Morf, 1970) or the region in which these terrorist groups operate for their theories (see, e.g., Ferracuti & Bruno, 1981; Heskin, 1984). Still other authors and theorists have developed broad psychological theories for explaining the causes of terrorism (see, e.g., Crenshaw, 1990; Gurr, 1970; Kaplan, 1978; Ross, 1996; Weinberg & Davis, 1989).

THE SEARCH FOR THE PERFECT TYPOLOGY

Definitions are indeed important tools of social research, but they fail to capture the complexity of the dynamics and consequences of terrorist acts. Typologies offer yet another approach. They allow for the concept of terrorism to be subdivided into related categories of some type of classification system.

One of the first to employ this approach was Paul Wilkinson, the noted Scottish scholar. In 1974, Wilkinson wrote that terrorism should be classified according to type of terrorist action: revolutionary terrorism, subrevolutionary terrorism, and repressive terrorism. *Revolutionary terrorism*, writes Wilkinson, is the use of "systematic tactics of terroristic violence with the objective of bringing about political revolution" (p. 36). Whereas revolutionary terrorism seeks total change, the second category in Wilkinson's typology, *subrevolutionary terrorism*, is terror used "for political motives other than revolution and governmental repression" (p. 38). Wilkinson's third category, *repressive terrorism*, is defined as "the systematic use of terroristic acts of violence for the purposes of suppressing, putting down, quelling, or restraining certain groups, individuals or forms of behaviour deemed to be undesirable by the oppressor" (p. 40).

About the same time that Wilkinson published *Political Terrorism*, J. Bowyer Bell (1975) settled on a sixfold classification scheme related to the motivation of the terrorist: psychotic, criminal, vigilante, endemic, authorized, and revolutionary. According to Bell, the *psychotic* terrorist's purpose was psychological gratification, the *criminal* sought profit, the *vigilante* wanted to retaliate, the *endemic* acted out of internal struggles, the *authorized* represented state repression, and the *revolutionary* aimed at bringing about change through fear. Frederick Hacker (1977), a psychiatrist, followed with a similar classification system for terrorists that is also the title of his popular book, *Crusaders, Criminals, and Crazies*.

The typologies of Wilkinson, Bell, and Hacker complement one another and have served as the basis for further classification in recent years. None of the classification schemes emanating from their pioneering work, however, from the simplest to the most complex, prove complete. On the one hand, efforts to create a typology with categories that are independent, mutually exclusive, and exhaustive usually result in a typology with categories that fit only single terrorist groups (see, e.g., Gross, 1990). On the other hand, a typology that reduces terrorist groups to two or three categories tends to blend important distinctions between terrorists and terrorist groups (see, e.g., Crenshaw, 1973).

Peter Fleming and Michael Stohl (1988), aware of the problem inherent in the search for the perfect typology, set out to identify the best typologies from almost 50 different ones that attempt to categorize the varieties of terrorism. Their efforts identified four major types: (a) those based on the motivation of the terrorist, (b) those based on the historical origin of the terrorist group, (c) those based on the terrorist group, and (d) those based on the type of targets or method of operation selected by the terrorist group. Their effort, reminiscent of the earlier Schmid work on definitions, neither solved the problem inherent in developing the ideal typology nor ended the ever-expanding universe of different typologies. Also like Schmid, they may have inadvertently contributed to the problem by calling attention to the problem itself. Actually, typologies of organizational structures, aims, motives, or ideologies, like definitions, do little if anything to eliminate the controversy surrounding the concept of terrorism.

NO SEARCH AT ALL

Some authors take pride in writing how they will not take time to define terrorism because attempts to define the term only add to the sense of confusion surrounding it. One author even goes as far as to suggest that "[t]he more disagreements there are on defining terrorism, the more terrorists can benefit by the added confusion on the issue" (Simon, 1994, p. 385). These authors approach the subject by dealing with the tactics of terrorists–hijackings, sabotage of aircraft, hostage-taking–rather than with what exactly constitutes "terrorism."

A surprising number of authors, however, fail even to mention that they are not going to define terrorism. In other words, they write about terrorism and expect everybody to know what they mean.

Consider, for example, *The Terrorism Reader* (1987), edited by Walter Laqueur and Yonah Alexander. In this historical anthology, these renowned experts on terrorism cover everything from the Greek origin of tyranny to the possibility of terrorists going nuclear. Nowhere, however, is an attempt made at offering a working definition of terrorism.

Nowhere is the lack at an attempt to define terrorism more evident than in the works of those authors who write about the very individuals and groups purported to have terrorist inclinations. Consider, for example, the Samuel Katz (1993) biography of one of the world's most notorious terrorists, Ahmed Jibril. In this important work, Katz painstakingly documents a series of brutal terrorist firsts instituted by Father Holy War, the nom de guerre of Jibril. Never once, however, in this riveting biography does Katz define what he means by terrorism. It is assumed that the detailed discussions of the act itself are enough to define the concept. Or, as one expert writing about modern aviation security put it, "Terrorism! The word defines itself" (Moore, 1991, p. 21). This makes about as much sense as the remark made by Associate Justice of the U.S. Supreme Court Potter Stewart, who offered no definition for obscenity but quipped, "I know it when I see it."

A DEFINITION OF TERRORISM

It should be apparent to all who peruse the literature on terrorism that the number of approaches to dealing with the concept of terrorism is limited only by those interested in its study. The same can also be said of the number of approaches that inventory the types of approaches (compare, e.g., Cooper, 1973; Schmid, 1983; Wardlaw, 1989). Adding to the confusion are those authors who try to explain in great detail the different definitions and typologies used to explain terrorism (see, e.g., Combs, 1997, pp. 3-19; Vetter & Perlstein, 1991, pp. 3-28; White, 1991, pp. 3-20).

The term *terrorism* means different things to different people. This is why trying to define or classify terrorism to everyone's satisfaction proves impossible. Whereas some blame it on politics, others attribute the difficulty on the popular aphorism, "One man's terrorist is another man's freedom fighter." Some would use this logic to label George

Washington a terrorist and Yasir Arafat a freedom fighter. Suffice it t
say that comparing the first president of the United States with the first
president of the Palestinian Authority might not raise eyebrows in the
22nd century. For now, however, the comparison is ludicrous.

As the noted British terrorism expert Richard Clutterbuck (1994)
suggests, mumbling about freedom fighters betrays a lack of understanding of what terrorism is. Terrorism against unarmed victims–
killing without due process in order to force a government or civilian
population into compliance–is never justifiable. These are the actions
of criminals, not freedom fighters.

The terrorist/freedom fighter controversy aside, definitions offered
by some very different sources exhibit some striking similarities:

> *American Heritage College Dictionary of the English Language:* The unlawful use
> or threatened use of force or violence by a person or organization against
> people or property with the intention of intimidating or coercing societies
> or governments, often for ideological or political reasons. (1996, p. 1854)

> *FBI Terrorist Research and Analytical Center:* The unlawful use of force or vio-
> lence against persons or property to intimidate or coerce a Government, the
> civilian population, or any segment thereof, in furtherance of political or
> social objectives. (1991, p. 25)

> *Grant Wardlaw:* Political terrorism is the use, or threat of use, of violence by
> an individual or a group, whether acting for or in opposition to established
> authority, when such action is designed to create extreme anxiety and/or
> fear- inducing effects in a target group larger than the immediate victims
> with the purpose of coercing that group into acceding to the political
> demands of the perpetrators. (1989, p. 16)

The definitions given by *The American Heritage College Dictionary of
the English Language* and the Federal Bureau of Investigation are not
unlike those used by academicians such as the Australian criminologist
Grant Wardlaw. Each definition includes three distinct elements: (a)
the *method* (force or violence), (b) the *target* (governments and civilian
populations), and (c) the *purpose,* which is twofold (to bring about fear
and to bring about political or social change). Beyond this point, lex-
icographers, government agencies, and academicians differ in their
focus on the various aspects or dimensions of terrorist events and the
individuals, groups, or organizations involved in their perpetration.
Compare, for example, the definition from the FBI with the following
one from the U.S. Department of State: "Terrorism is premeditated,
politically motivated violence against noncombatant targets by subna-
tional groups or clandestine agents, usually intended to influence an

audience." Unlike the department's definition, the bureau's includes that the terrorist act can be done by an individual or group of two or more individuals for political as well as social objectives. Because of this broader definition, the FBI can then include in its annual reports on terrorism in the United States acts such as assaults, bombings, and hijackings committed by individuals who may be suspected of associating with antigovernment groups, foreign terrorist cells, and others.

These definitional distinctions aside, adapting all three elements from above provides the following simple definition that allows an intelligent discussion of terrorism to go forward:

> *Terrorism is the use of force (or violence) committed by individuals or groups against governments or civilian populations to create fear in order to bring about political (or social) change.*

This rather straightforward definition allows the forthcoming analysis to include in it terrorist acts committed by individuals or groups of two or more individuals for social as well as political gain. Unfortunately, it will not solve the definitional problem or please everyone. No definition can. Yet, to argue that terrorism cannot be studied without a comprehensive definition is patently absurd. The approach taken here rescues the discussion of terrorism from those involved in endless debate over definitions and extends it beyond those who mumble about freedom fighters while wrapping themselves in a cloak of political correctness. Those who do are simply industrious tailors to a naked emperor. Instead, this study exposes itself to possible criticism by addressing terrorism in America to uncover the evil within.

ENDNOTES

1. Schmid's new edition is entitled *Political Terrorism: A New Guide to Actors, Authors, Concepts, Data Bases, Theories, and Literature* (1988).
2. Anyone interested in polemics should consult H. A. A. Cooper's appropriately titled publication "Terrorism: The Problem of the Problem Definition" (1978), Wardlaw's *Political Terrorism: Theory, Tactics, and Counter-Measures* (1989), and the definitional debate that takes place from time-to-time in the journal *Terrorism and Political Violence* (see, e.g., Silke, 1996, pp. 12-28).

Chapter 2

INTERNATIONAL TERRORISM

THE THREAT FROM OUTSIDE

O n Friday, February 26, 1993, at 12:18 p.m., a massive explosion occurred in the subterranean garage of the Vista Hotel, located at the World Trade Center complex in New York City. Had the terrorists accomplished what they intended to do, they would have toppled one of the 110-story towers into the other and killed many of the approximately 50,000 people who were in the complex at the time of the blast. Or had the sodium cyanide in the terrorists' bomb not vaporized instead of burning, cyanide gas would have been sucked into the north tower and killed thousands.

Ramzi Ahmed Yousef (a.k.a. Abdul Basit Mahmoud Abdul Karim), found guilty for plotting against U.S. airlines in East Asia in 1995, was what prosecutors called the "architect of the bombing." He told Secret Service Agent Brian Parr on a flight to New York from Islamabad, Pakistan, after his arrest in 1995 that his only regrets were that the casualties and destruction had not been greater and that if he had had more money he could have built a bigger, "more effective" bomb. The agent also related that Yousef watched in disappointment from the Jersey City side of the waterfront as smoke poured from the still-upright towers in lower Manhattan.

Miscalculations and evil intentions aside, the terrorists' bomb, consisting of approximately 1,200 pounds of explosives, caused $500 million in damage, cut short the lives of 6 innocent people, and injured more than 1,000 others. Not since the Civil War has the United States seen such a patient-producing event. The largest act of terrorism on U.S. soil in history made people skittish for months to come.

In a typical textbook of the early 1990s, *Perspectives on Terrorism*, Harold Vetter and Gary Perlstein (1991) argue that the continental United States should remain relatively "free from much of the violence

11

that seems to be endemic to other parts of the world" (p. 50). For Vetter and Perlstein, "Political terrorism of the kind that is familiar to the people of Europe and Latin America has not posed a serious danger to the public order in the U.S." (p. 64). Jonathan White (1991) agrees. Terrorism, writes White in *Terrorism: An Introduction,* "is something that happens in other places" (p. 163). "When Americans speak of terrorism," says White, "they are usually referring to incidents far from American shores. Americans may be victimized frequently by terrorist acts, but these incidents generally occur overseas. . . . Many people believe that terrorism is not an internal problem for the United States" (pp. 162-163).

Even a book devoted to terrorism in America that had the advantage of being published just short of 1 year after the World Trade Center bombing, Brent Smith's *Terrorism in America: Pipe Bombs and Pipe Dreams* (1994), devotes precious little space to why foreign terrorists were able to strike inside the United States. Only Smith's mention of the capture of Japanese Red Army member Yu Kikumura at a rest stop on the New Jersey Turnpike in 1988 addresses the reality of international terrorism coming to America. His discussions of the Irish Republican Army's (IRA) fund-raising activities and Omega 7's bombings and assassinations do not. Consider, for example, the exploits of Omega 7, which targeted anyone or anything that supported Fidel Castro (that usually meant the Soviet Union). This unhappy group of expatriated Cubans' disdain for the Soviets made their actions appear justified to a considerable portion of U.S. society at war with the Kremlin.

Clearly, these textbook writers were not overly concerned with foreign nationals committing acts of terrorism on U.S. soil. Others, however, were more focused on the threat. They knew that "the times are a-changin'." Consider, for example, Robert Kupperman and Jeff Kamen's admonition in their book *Final Warning* (1989): "Spilling blood on U.S. soil was probably perceived not only as problematic logistically but also too risky in terms of provoking a devastating reaction. But events would gradually discourage that caution and lead terrorists to consider strikes directly into the heart of America" (p. 6). Steven Emerson and Christina Del Sesto were also busy documenting the terrorist threat to the United States in their book *Terrorist* (1991).

Reports published by the U.S. Department of State, *Patterns of Global Terrorism* (see, e.g., 1991 through 1994), and the FBI Terrorist

Research and Analytical Center, *Terrorism in the United States* (see, e.g., 1991 through 1994), also warned of the potential for a new wave of terrorism. In *Terrorism in the United States: 1991*, for example, the FBI (1992) writes that even though "the United States did not evidence an international terrorist attack within its borders during [the Persian Gulf War] . . . the threat was not eliminated. . . . [And] given the present state of global affairs, and . . . the potential for terrorism inside the United States, we must remain alert to the possibility of terrorism" (pp. 20-21).

Because the study of terrorism involves the study of changing global politics and violence, most scholars believe that journalists like Emerson and Kamen, and government bureaucracies like the U.S. Department of State and the FBI, have trouble being objective, albeit scientific, about their analyses. Are academicians immune from doing the same? Clearly, they are not. As a matter of fact, textbook writers like Vetter, Perlstein, White, and Smith should have followed the lead of investigative reporters like Emerson and Kamen, as well as reports from the U.S. Department of State (1991, 1992, 1993) and the FBI (1990, 1991, 1992), and paid closer attention to political and social occurrences that spelled trouble for the United States. Now let's look at all those events that made it possible for a new breed of foreign terrorists to bomb the World Trade Center, plot to bomb other landmarks in New York City, and pose an ongoing threat to law enforcement authorities because the terrorist groups are difficult to track, infiltrate, and intercept.

OUT WITH THE OLD

The Soviet Union and Terrorism

Throughout the late 1960s and the 1970s, many Middle Eastern terrorist groups sent their recruits to the Soviet Union for training in low-intensity warfare, which is a rather benign-sounding name for terrorism. Actually, the Soviets viewed terrorism as compatible with their efforts to support wars of national liberation even though they knew that violence against civilian populations was inconsistent with traditional Marxist-Leninist thinking on class struggle. The Soviets hoped that Palestinian terrorism against Israel would enhance their position within the Arab world and erode that of Israel's staunchest supporter, the United States.

Patrice Lumumba University in Moscow was where Palestinians would go to learn terrorist tactics. Their curriculum included liberal doses of Marxist ideology interspersed with demonstrations on how to handle Kalashnikov assault rifles and to make bombs. Some of the more promising students were recruited for more elaborate training by the Soviet secret police, the KGB.

Lumumba graduates would often return home to assume leadership roles in many of the Palestinian terrorist groups that sponsored their stay at the university, most notably the Palestinian Liberation Organization (PLO). Their duties included, among other things, the sharing of their newfound skills. Soon, Palestinian terrorist groups like the PLO were running their own terror academies.

An unidentified source in Turkey's Istanbul GUNES news service, on July 17, 1982, listed more than 40 terrorist organizations receiving training from the PLO in terrorist camps in Lebanon. Among the most frequent students were the Turkish terrorist groups: Dev-Sol (Revolutionary Left); Dev-Yol (Revolutionary Way); Turkish Communist Party-Marxist-Leninist (TKP-ML); Turkish Communist Workers Party (TKIP); Acilciler (The Swift Ones); Marxist-Leninist Armed Propaganda Union (or Unit) (MLSPB); Turkiye Devrimci Kommunist Partisi (Turkish Revolutionary Communist Party); Devirimci Halk Birligi (Revolutionary Turkish People's Union); Dev-Savas (Revolutionary Fight); Halkin Devirimci Conculeri (People's Revolutionary Pioneers); and Apolcular (Followers of the Abdyllah Ocal Group). The Red Brigades (RB); Basque Nation and Liberty (ETA); Irish Republican Army (IRA); Italian Marxist-Leninist Vanguard Organization; Corsican Separatists; Swiss Anarchists Union; German Red Army (RAF); Japanese Red Army; Secret Army for the Liberation of Armenia (ASALA); National Liberation Front of El Salvador; Argentine Montoneros guerrillas; Peronist Revolutionary Movement; Sri Lanka guerrillas; Dhofar Front guerrillas; and Nicaraguan Sandinista guerrillas all participated as well. Strange as it may seem, the Ku Klux Klan (KKK) and the WSG, known as the War Sports Group, representing the neo-Nazis, were also reported to have received training in these PLO camps, which as noted, passed on techniques learned from the Soviets (Mickolus, Sandler, & Murdock, 1989, p. 296).

For nearly a decade, Soviet-trained and -supported terrorism operated with impunity in the Middle East and, to a lesser extent, in Europe. The Soviets, as Roberta Goren (1984) notes, viewed terrorism as "indirect aggression" and a very useful instrument of political subversion. According to Goren, the Soviet Union was quick to support terrorist activities that could systematically "undermine a society with the ultimate goal of causing the collapse of law and order and the loss of confidence in the state" (p. 14). Terrorism, writes Ray Cline and Yonah Alexander in *Terrorism: The Soviet Connection* (1984), was simply another way to aid the Soviets in their efforts to destabilize the West.

As events in the Middle East or Europe would threaten to affect public opinion—or worse yet, U.S. intervention—Soviet leaders would rein in their client terrorists. The Soviets always kept their terrorists on the proverbial "short leash." Moreover, the Soviets never granted anything without strings attached, much less unconditional support for terrorists. In fact, conditional support of the Palestinian cause created considerable resentment against the Soviets within the very Palestinian terrorist groups they aided and abetted. Evidence does suggest, however, that, on occasion, Soviet authorities would ask the PLO for advice and were willing to defer to their wishes on matters of policy and tactics relating to the Middle East. The substance of a transcript of a conversation between Andrei Gromyko, the Soviet foreign minister, and Yasir Arafat, chairman of the PLO, on November 13, 1979, uncovered during an Israeli operation in Lebanon, bears this out:

Gromyko: Are you considering certain tactical concessions in return for getting recognition from the hostile camp? And are you also considering recognizing Israel's right to exist as an independent sovereign state? During the discussions with the Americans, we felt we were at a dead end. Here I would like to know what your opinion is and please regard it as a question only. . . .

Arafat: Knowing that we are the victim, we raised many possible solutions, while none of our enemies presented any. We said: A democratic state where Jews and Arabs will live. They said: This means the destruction of Israel. In 1974, we said we will establish the Palestinian state on every part of land that Israel withdraws from, or which will be liberated, and this is our right.

We have proposed all these things and they have offered nothing.

Gromyko: If there is a change in your position, I ask you notify us, since one cannot escape this issue. In every statement, the Americans say: How can we recognize an organization while they are not ready to recognize any-

thing? This is demagoguery, but we have to know how to deal with it. I ask
you to think about it and make your comments.

I thank you for the useful discussion. We think that we march with you
on the same path concerning the Middle East problem. The Soviet Union
is a friend of the Arabs and does not tend to change its friends. We hope
that the Arabs and the PLO feel the same way.

Arafat: The PLO has no doubts. (Adams, 1986, pp. 45-46)

Some actions of the more radical Middle Eastern terrorist groups
eventually caused the Soviets to become less enthusiastic about the
potential destabilizing benefits of low-intensity warfare. This especially was true whenever the Soviets were on the receiving end of a terrorist operation. The hijacking of an Antonov-24 airplane in which a
stewardess was killed and three passengers were wounded in October
1970 by two Lithuanian residents from the Soviet Central Asian republic of Uzbekistan even caused the Soviets to vote for the punishment
of hijackers. After a Soviet diplomat was shot and killed by an unidentified gunman on a motorcycle near the Soviet embassy in New Delhi
in 1985, the Soviets had had enough and proceeded to vote for a
strongly worded condemnation of terrorism in the United Nations.
Actually, the Soviets, according to Walter Laqueur (1987), always
opposed terrorist hijackings and attacks against diplomats. By the late
1970s, Soviet sponsorship of terrorism had lessened, but the Middle
Eastern terrorist groups had a life of their own. The evil genie that was
terrorism was out of the bottle, and there was no getting it back inside.

Nearly three decades after the Soviet Union trained its first batch
of Palestinian terrorists, the Soviets themselves began to sense their
own vulnerability to terrorism. In 1989, under the watch of Mikhail
Gorbachev, the Soviets, in what Galia Golan (1990) called a major
shift in policy, began to implement a counterterrorism policy. By the
next decade, the former Soviet Union and the United States actually
took steps toward resolving terrorist issues with the formation of a joint
task force to prevent international terrorism. Today, in fact, the
Russians are themselves faced with the threat of terrorism in Armenia,
Azerbaijan, and Chechnya. Separatist groups, such as the Chechens,
have already used terrorism to advance their cause. Still, until their
collapse, a somewhat less enthusiastic, notwithstanding more vulnerable, Soviet Union played the "terrorist" card and made money and
weapons available to terrorists by way of its client states.

The disintegration of the Soviet Union in 1991 deprived
Palestinian terrorist groups of a significant source of money, weapons,

and safe havens. The FBI Terrorist Research and Analytical Center also believes that the collapse affected left-wing extremist groups in the United States. "The transformation of the former Soviet Union also deprived many leftist groups [in the United States] of a coherent ideology or spiritual patron. As a result, membership and support for these groups waned" (FBI, 1996, p. 11).

German reunification also affected these Palestinian terrorist groups. It ended East Germany's role as an important supplier of money, weapons, and sanctuary for terrorists to hide after their operations. The training camp in Pankow, East Germany, had been particularly notorious for assisting these terrorists with arms, money, and intelligence. Aid from training camps inside Albania; Varna, Bulgaria; Ostrova and Karlovt Varv, Czechoslovakia; Lake Belaton, Hungary; Poland; and Rumania also dried up with the collapse of the Soviet-sponsored Warsaw Treaty of Friendship, Cooperation, and Mutual Assistance, better known as the Warsaw Pact. Even former Soviet client states Syria and Libya, which at times were independent sources of money, weaponry, and training, refrained from overt support of terrorism. Syrian training camps in the Bekaa Valley of Lebanon and Libyan training camps in Focra, Misurata, Res Hilal, and Sirte no longer advertise their wares as centers for terrorists to hone their skills. Instead, Tripoli and Damascus embarked on a series of covert actions in support of Palestinian terrorists because they could no longer get backing in any confrontation with the United States from a Soviet Bloc that no longer existed.

The Persian Gulf War and Yasir Arafat

The Persian Gulf War saw a dramatic increase in the number of international terrorist incidents. Yet, it only took 1 year for the U.S. Department of State to record one of the largest 1-year decreases in these occurrences since the United States began keeping such records. Attributing this decline to the destruction of Iraqi terrorist networks is as problematic as attributing the decrease to an increase of low-level terrorist events brought about by the Persian Gulf War itself. Furthermore, statistics gathered by organizations other than the U.S. Department of State may be based on different definitions of terrorism and, therefore, may show many more or less incidents of terrorism during the same time frame. Those interested in playing the numbers game can consult the U.S. Department of State's annual *Patterns of Global Terrorism* and compare it with, for example, the *Annual Risk Assessment* publication put out by Risk Assessment Services. Those interested in the impact of the war on the changing face of terrorism itself are asked to consider Yasir Arafat's tactical mistake of siding with Iraq before and during the Persian Gulf War in 1991.

Long before the war, Arafat, the man with the stubbly face and checkerboard kaffiyeh who personified terrorism itself, knew he could not run his PLO with the whimsical support of Libya's Moammar Gadhafi or the cash-and-carry conditional backing of the former Soviet Union. He set out to create alternative sources of funding that would give the PLO the stability it needed to carry on a protracted terrorist campaign. According to the British journalist James Adams (1986), a significant portion of this funding came in the form of protection money from the conservative and vulnerable oil states.

At the time of the Persian Gulf War, PLO assets were estimated to be in the neighborhood of $10 billion, with Saudi Arabia and the other oil-rich gulf states providing a large chunk of the PLO's annual operating budget. Khaled Abu Toameh (1993) estimates that, in the years leading up to the war, the annual donations of the Saudis and Kuwaitis were approximately $86 million and $50 million, respectively. Arafat's support of Saddam Hussein would shut down this extraordinary flow of oil money.

With the generous subsidies from the gulf sheiks and Saudi princes nothing more than a fleeting memory, the PLO found itself in the middle of its worst financial crisis since its inception in April 1964. Arafat, some said, trusted no one but himself on financial matters, and he alone would authorize and sign checks for large expenditures. At PLO headquarters in Tunis, staffed with MIT-trained computer experts, as well as throughout PLO offices around the world, where Harvard MBAs traded stocks and commodities, staff salaries were reduced and lifestyles strictly curtailed. Arafat was forced to sell off some valuable real estate holdings of the PLO and to close down its newspapers. He even agonized over investments as diverse as blue-chip stocks on Wall Street and cattle ranches in Somalia. The Fortune 500-like PLO, which was reputed to control enough Wall Street paper that it could move the Dow Jones, had a serious cash flow problem.

Further contributing to Arafat's financial woes was the decision by the United Nations Relief and Works Agency to curtail financial aid to

Palestinian refugees in the occupied territories. In addition, the *amwal al-sumud,* or "steadfastness funds," that Palestinians "outside" sent Palestinians living "inside" under Israeli occupation all but dried up when Saudi Arabia and Kuwait expelled Palestinians after the Persian Gulf War. Palestinians working in these countries would routinely have 5 percent of their salaries automatically deducted from their paychecks to contribute to these steadfastness funds. Rumor had it that the money that did make it to the territories was being pocketed by some prominent local Palestinians. But more serious than the financial woes of the PLO was a political crisis made worse when oil money went to Arafat's sworn opposition in the occupied territories–the shadowy terrorist group Hamas.

The Islamic Resistance Movement

Hamas is the Arabic acronym for Islamic Resistance Movement and means "zeal." It is a militant mass movement with solid support among Palestinians living in the West Bank, Gaza Strip, and East Jerusalem. Hamas was formed by Sheik Ahmed Yassin during the *intifada,* or uprising, against Israeli occupation of the territories on December 14, 1987, to stop stone-throwing Palestinian youths from joining the PLO. Its enemy is not only Israel but also the PLO and the Palestinian administration of Yasir Arafat. Why the difference? Why this antipathy?

It is important to recall that Islam is more than a faith. Its founder was a politician, as well as a visionary. Even the Israelis, usually so astute about their Arab environment, missed this reality. Even as they closed universities in the occupied territories, they encouraged Islamic seminary study. They hoped to turn the minds of their subject people away from Arab nationalism and support of the PLO toward the peaceful ways of religion.

Soon Israel found itself confronted by Hamas, which traces its roots to the Muslim Brotherhood founded in Egypt during the 1920s by Hassan al-Banna, championing the liberation of Palestine, not for the sake of nationalism, but of Islam. In contrast with a political movement like the PLO, which is willing to compromise with Israel as part of the peace process, Hamas is uncompromising and maximalist. It demands the total liberation of the sacred land of Palestine as demanded by God, who will repay martyrs for this cause with life everlasting.

The basic difference between the approach of the PLO and that of these militant Islamic fundamentalists, however, is how each views the West.

The PLO espouses an imitative Western-style nationalism complete with anthems and flags. Arab nationalism found its culmination in Gamal Abdel-Nasser, the Egyptian leader. Its low point came in 1967, with Abdel-Nasser's humiliating defeat by Israel. At that point, many Arabs, Palestinian and others, concluded that they had been following the wrong model. They could never succeed as imitation Westerners.

Instead, they seek their identity in their Islamic roots, which provide them with structure and self-confidence on the personal and ethnic levels. In the process, they reject the decadent West, with its recreational sex, its alcoholism, and its drug abuse. They reject Arafat for going outside the faith to marry the Sorbonne-educated, 28-year-old, Suha Tawil. The fact that she converted to Islam does not matter to her Islamic detractors. They reject the PLO leadership generally, Arafat specifically, for being reluctant to jeopardize their sizable fortune in support of the uprising against Israel. They accuse Arafat and the PLO of running an intifada on a "shoestring." Against the United States, their anger is particularly virulent because U.S. culture is so all-pervasive, so appealing, and so successful. The goals of Hamas are to destroy the peace process, Israel, and a PLO that it views as corrupted by the West.

It is important to remember that the astounding growth of Islamic fundamentalist groups like Hamas is not a result of its militancy, but of its good works. Hamas has taken to running its own educational systems, hospitals, and other services. In this way, mosques, schools, and hospitals are its weapons as much as bombs and automatic weapons. They are also popular and positive protests against incompetent, uncaring, Western-style governments and irresponsible wealth. For all these reasons, Islamic fundamentalism must be treated with great respect and an awareness of the strength underlying militant groups like Hamas.

Arafat: Assassinations, Mortality, and the Peace Process

Despite an occasional breakaway group, the PLO has long been acknowledged as the official voice of the Palestinian people, with

Arafat as its spokesman. Arafat has always been careful to surround himself in the PLO with friends from al-Fatah, the military wing of the PLO that Arafat and seven confederates founded in 1964, so leadership changes have been minimal. In recent years, however, Arafat has lost some of his top military, intelligence, and security aides. Specifically, a joint force of Israeli commandos and agents from Mossad, Israel's intelligence service, assassinated Khalil al-Wazir, the head of the PLO terrorist operations against Israel, in Tunis in April 1988. In January 1991, the rival Abu Nidal Organization (ANO), in a campaign of inter-Palestinian fratricide stemming from Saddam Hussein's invasion of Kuwait, assassinated Arafat's deputy in charge of PLO intelligence and a key figure in al-Fatah, Salah Khalef; and Hayil Abd al-Hamid, the security chief of al-Fatah. According to some estimates, several hundred moderate PLO leaders and supporters have been assassinated by order of Sadri al-Banna, better known to the world by his *nom de guerre* of Abu Nidal. Arafat's remaining associates openly criticized his rule for the first time in nearly 25 years, and PLO militants dropped out or turned to the fanatical Hamas.

In April 1992, 15 months after he lost his trusted deputy in charge of intelligence and security chief to ANO henchmen, Arafat suffered a serious head injury in an airplane crash in the Libyan desert. While recovering in a hospital, Arafat had time to ponder the loss of his comrades, as well as his own future. Arafat was said to have told close friends that the loss of his associates to assassins' bullets, coupled with his own mortality, moved him to seek peace with Israel.

Since the beginning of Arafat's historic Middle East peace talks in October 1991, which marked the first time Israelis and Palestinians had attended a conference together, and the signing of the 1993 Gaza-Jericho peace accord, Palestinian terrorist groups and radical Middle Eastern governments have rattled their sabers. These "rejectionists" threaten to use any means available, including violence, to impede the peace process. The threat posed to the United States, which has taken a lead in this peace initiative, is ever-present. Until now, such terrorists groups as Hamas and the Palestine Islamic Jihad (PIJ) have confined their terrorist activities to targets within Israel. There is no guarantee, however, that the United States will not be targeted in the future.

Whatever the reason behind the signing of the peace accord, Israel's Prime Minister Yitzhak Rabin, by shaking hands on a peace framework with Arafat, elevated him as the indisputable leader of the Palestinian state. Thus, Arafat had achieved the very objective for which his PLO and its offshoot terrorist organizations killed and maimed Israelis for more than four decades. Arafat was now, at least on the surface, locked into using politics as the means to achieving political change. Abdel-Rahman Abdel-Raout Arafat al-Qudwa Al-Husseini, known to the world as Yasir Arafat, would begin the process of shedding his image as the world's most recognizable terrorist. Only time will tell, however, whether he will wear the mantle of a statesman and, in turn, earn the title of freedom fighter. Clearly, his actions have changed the face of terrorism.

IN WITH THE NEW

Iran

The new terrorism began long before Arafat's miscalculation or the collapse of the Soviet Union. It can be traced, in part, to the Iranian Revolution of 1979, when Ayatollah Ruhollah Khomeini created Hezbollah (Party of God) as an extension of his Revolutionary Guards to purify the "revolution." The structure of Hezbollah, unlike that of the PLO, was informal and unknown to its mostly male members. The recruits of Hezbollah, drawn from the poorest segments of society, were not only interested in carrying out the goals of the revolution but also concerned with the social conditions of their fellow Shiites throughout the Middle East.

It is important to note that Iranians are not Arabs and that they practice a version of Islam—Shiism—that is somewhat distinct from orthodox practices. Suffice it to say that Shiites accept the spiritual authority of a divinely inspired imam (spiritual leader) descended directly from Ali, the Prophet Muhammad's cousin and son-in-law. Shiism derives its name from the words *Shiat Ali,* or partisans of Ali.[1]

In 1982, when the Israeli army invaded Southern Lebanon to destroy PLO bases, U.S. military forces were already there busy supporting Israeli-backed factions in a ragging Lebanese civil war. The military targets of U.S. actions were frequently Shiites, which further angered the Iranians, who blamed the West for corrupting Islam. By the end of the year, Hezbollah arrived in Lebanon to battle against the

"Great Satan" (the United States) and its Zionist partner (Israel).

Once in Lebanon, Hezbollah came under the direct control of Sheik Muhammed Hassan Fadlallah. This enterprising cleric helped solidify Iran's influence in the region through an outreach program to the Lebanese Shiites. His apocalyptic preaching attracted young followers who also believed that the enemies of Islam could be destroyed through martyrdom and suicide missions. Also under Fadlallah, Hezbollah spawned smaller terrorist groups, the most recognizable of which was the Islamic Jihad (Holy War).

In 1983, Islamic Jihad launched a devastating suicide bombing campaign against U.S. interests in the region. The first was on April 18, 1983, when a suicide bomber driving a van carrying approximately 400 pounds of explosives rammed the side of the U.S. Embassy in Beirut, killing 63 and injuring many more. Among the dead were several prominent U.S. officials. Six months later, on October 23, another Islamic Jihad suicide bomber drove a truck loaded with explosives into the U.S. Marine barracks at the Beirut Airport, killing 241 marines.

The use of suicide bombers so terrified and baffled the United States that it recalled its forces from Lebanon. But as Stephen Frederic Dale (1988) has noted, religiously sanctioned suicide attacks are not unique to the modern period or confined to the Middle Eastern region. Similar types of assaults are known to have occurred over a span of several centuries in three little-known Muslim communities of the Indian Ocean region: those of the Malabar coast of southwestern India, Atjeh in northern Sumatra, and Mindanao and Sulu in the southern Philippines. Although these earlier suicide attacks in Asia were not undertaken with the same political awareness that characterizes the organizers of the incidents in Beirut, they represent essentially the same phenomenon: protests against Western authority or colonial rule by Muslims who thought they had no other means of fighting against a superior military power.

The Beirut suicide bombers were merely performing acts of martyrdom that first took place 13 centuries ago after the death of Muhammad. The prophet's death in 632 left the Muslim community without a leader to watch over the faith. Several followers met to rectify this by selecting a *caliph*, a temporal authority to guide the Muslim community, but religion soon gave way to politics. Within 40 years after the prophet's demise, various caliphs had managed to assassinate

their way to power, and Islam had divided into two sects. The orthodox Sunnis accepted the reign of temporal leaders, whereas the Shiites
believed that their imams were the divinely inspired and infallible
descendants of Muhammad.

In 680, Hussein (or Husayn), the son of Ali (cousin of Muhammad)
and his wife Fatima (daughter of Muhammad), marched on the Sunnis
in what Hussein hoped would be a gesture of reconciliation. Hussein,
however, dreamed that no reconciliation was possible and that he and
his followers would die in a battle with the Sunnis. A badly outnum-
bered Hussein disregarded the premonition and knowingly marched
to his death near the village of Karbala, which is today in Iraq. To this
day, especially in Iraq and Iran, passion plays and mass processionals
are performed each year in commemoration of Karbala. These events
are sometimes marked by rites of self-flagellation. Young men scrape
their backs with hooks to draw blood, especially on Ashura, the 10th
day of the month of Muharram, the anniversary of Hussein's martyrdom.

Karbala is not an act of a suicide; Islam forbids the taking of one's
own life. Rather, it symbolizes the supreme willingness to submit to
the will of Allah with the understanding that rewards will come after
death. Islam emphasizes that life on earth is merely a transition to a
better life. A suicide bomber is making a transition that will put him
or her alongside the other heroes of Islam and next to Allah.

Members of such groups as the Arous Ad-Damm, the Brides of
Blood, sworn to avenge the death of Hussein through their own martyrdom, indicate their willingness to become martyrs, but the choice is
not theirs, just as it was not Hussein's. Actually, Allah selected
Hussein for martyrdom because of his "special merit." In the same
way, Allah's representatives here on earth, the *mullahs,* select whom to
honor with martyrdom. Here is the intimate link between the practice
of martyrdom in Islam–expressed in the act of suicide–and the official
structure of Islam as a political entity. Given no distinction between
church and the state in Islam, an act of religious devotion, such as suicide, becomes an instrument of state policy for the militant Muslim.

Viewing suicide as a form of religious devotion allows the uninformed to make sense of the bizarre features of the actions of these suicide bombers. Consider, for example, the affable smile worn on the
face of the bomber as he made his way into the compound to blow up
the U.S. Embassy in Beirut in 1983. This smile, known as the *bassamat*

al-Farah (smile of joy), symbolizes the joy of martyrdom. The notion of joy in the act of suicide is also evident in the videotape left behind by a 17- year-old female suicide bomber. On April 9, 1985, San'ah Muheidli drove her yellow Mercedes Benz laden with explosives into an Israeli military convoy in southern Lebanon, killing two soldiers and herself. On the tape, San'ah instructs her mother not to mourn her untimely death but, "Be merry, to let your joy explode as if it were my wedding day." A suicide bomber's death is described by Muslim militants as "the martyr's wedding," an occasion of joy and celebration.

Clearly, the United States was not used to Islamic Jihad's tactics, which are correctly characterized by Amir Taheri's book title *Holy Terror* (1987) and Robin Wright's *Sacred Rage* (1986). Until 1983, the U.S. Department of State reported that less than 9 percent of terrorist bombing victims from 1977 to 1983 were caused by terrorist bombers. Those terrorist deaths that did occur were largely thought to be the result of accidental explosions, rather than deliberate suicide missions (Office of Combating Terrorism, 1984).

Law enforcement and government officials within the United States were still used to the well-defined structure of the Palestinian groups and the state-sponsored terrorism brokered by the Soviet Bloc. Islamic Jihad, in contrast, with its indeterminate number of loosely structured semiautonomous cells that could not be clearly linked with any benefactor, was a puzzlement. Its structure and behavior were a harbinger of the new terrorism that became better defined through the Sudanese experience.

Sudan

Nearly a decade after the Iranian revolution, a military coup destroyed Sudan's inept democracy. The mastermind behind Sudan's Islamic counterreformation was a thin, rather ascetic looking, Sorbonne-educated Sheik Hassan Abdallah al-Turabi. Naysayers have called Turabi the Madison Avenue ayatollah because of his slick manners. Turabi sports a white turban and the whitest robes. Some say his shoes are unstained by the streets—no mean feat for anyone in Khartoum. The white Mercedes in which he motors around town is equally spotless. Nonetheless, the charismatic Turabi is a person of substance who has served as Sudan's attorney general and as dean of the law school at Khartoum. He is unabashedly committed to ending the bitter historic enmity that has separated Sunnis from Shiites since the seventh century. Turabi might just move the Muslim world a bit closer toward a much-feared militant Islamic monolith.

In April 1991, Sheik Turabi took the first step toward realizing his goal of Islamic reconciliation by hosting a 4-day meeting of Islamic politicians and intellectuals in the Sudanese capital of Khartoum. Among the participants were such notables as Gulbuddin Hekmatyar, the radical militant leader of Afghanistan's fundamentalist Hezb-i-Islami faction; Ibrahim Shukri, a chief of the Muslim Brotherhood of Egypt; Abassi Madani, then one of the two leaders of Algeria's ascendant Islamic Salvation Front (FIS); and, of course, high-ranking representatives of the Shiite Islamic Republic of Iran. Also in attendance at this event were terrorist leaders such as the notorious Dr. George Habash of the Popular Front for the Liberation of Palestine (PFLP) and Nayif Hawatmeh of the Democratic Front for the Liberation of Palestine (DFLP).

The group ultimately endorsed a 6-point manifesto containing Machiavellian prescripts for advancing extremist Islamic regimes throughout the Muslim world. Read in its entirety, the underlying message of the manifesto was that, in Islam's war against the West and the struggle to build Islamic states at home, the ends justify the means. This document, Judith Miller (1994) writes, represents the first time that an Islamic state defined a new world order with a strategy for achieving it. Moreover, writes Miller, the conference made progress toward Turabi's long-stated goal of overcoming the rift between Sunni Muslim states, like Sudan, and a Shiite state, like Iran.

Few serious observers of militant Islam would argue that the Khartoum conference represented the end of the animosity between Sunni and Shiite and the beginning of a reconciliation between divergent Islamic sects, much less a conspiracy led by Iran and Sudan. These two Islamic states have parted ways on too many occasions, such as during the gulf crisis when Khartoum refused to follow Tehran's lead in isolating Iraq and in turning against the PLO, to consider them part of some Islamic terrorist plot. Moreover, recent reports indicate a further widening since Iran has been less than generous in doling out financial aid to Sudan for capital building projects. Iran has even made the bankrupt Sudan pay market prices for Iranian crude. Fewer still think that the "Red Menace" of the Cold War era has been replaced by a monolithic "Green Peril," green being the color of Islam. Most knowledgeable observers of the Islamic world, including John Esposito (1992) and Judith Miller (1996), know that militant Islam is as diverse as the Arabs themselves and the countries in which it is taking hold. Despite their differences, Iran and Sudan are, and likely will remain, anti-Israel, anti-Western, and decidedly anti-American.

Boot Camps for Terror

Sudan

In August 1993, Sudan joined Iran on the U.S. Department of State's short list of pariah states that are in the business of sponsoring international terrorism. The other states on the list are Cuba, Iran, Iraq, Libya, North Korea, and Syria. This list is maintained pursuant to Section 6(j) of the Export Administration Act of 1979. This and related U.S. statutes impose trade sanctions, as well as other restrictions, on countries determined by the U.S. secretary of state to have consistently supported international terrorism. The list is forwarded annually to Congress and is updated anytime during the year as circumstances warrant.

"We are on the terrorist list because the United States is anti-Islamic," proclaimed an angry Turabi. What he did not say was that an Iranian-trained adjunct to the Sudanese military, the quasi-military body known as the Popular Defense Forces (PDF), maintains a series of terrorist camps throughout Sudan (U.S. Department of State, 1994). Turabi claims that these 30-odd terrorist training camps throughout the Sudan countryside are nothing more than a network of militia camps. The Iranians place so much importance on these PDF-run terrorist camps that their ambassador in Khartoum is the infamous Majid Kamal, known for his role in the takeover of the U.S. Embassy in Tehran in 1979 and the development of the Hezbollah terrorist group in Lebanon in the 1980s.

Sudanese terrorist camps serve as convenient transit points, training centers, and safe havens for Iranian-backed terrorist groups such as the Palestine Islamic Jihad (PIJ), Lebanese Hezbollah (Party of God), Islamic Resistance Movement (Hamas), Egypt's al-Gama'at al-Islamiyya (Islamic Group), and Islamic Salvation Front (FIS). According to the U.S. Department of State (1997), "The National

Islamic Front [NIF], which is the dominant influence within the Sudanese Government, also supports opposition and insurgent groups in Uganda, Tunisia, Ethiopia, and Eritrea" (p. 25).

Afghanistan

When the Soviets invaded Afghanistan in 1979 to prop up an embattled communist government, thousands of young warriors of Islam from as far away as Algeria, Egypt, Saudi Arabia, and the store-front mosques of New York and New Jersey answered the call to fight a *jihad,* or holy war, at the side of their Afghan brothers. From around the world, 10,000 or more Muslims, stirred by the stem-winding preaching of incendiary clerics, streamed to Peshawar, Pakistan, for weapons training and indoctrination. The U.S. Central Intelligence Agency (CIA), eager to humble the Soviets in what turned out to be the last superpower tussle, invested billions of dollars in weaponry and training to turn these young warriors of Islam into a cadre of freedom fighters capable of driving out the Soviets. Those who survived the decade-long war helped turn Afghanistan into a veritable boot camp for terrorists. Carrying a Kalashnikov in Afghanistan is as common as wearing a wristwatch in the United States.

In the hills near Kunduz operates one of these boot camps for the grooming of new terrorists. Six more are in the Jalalabad region, and two more are south of the Afghan capital, Kabul. Of the country's nine terror camps, six are run by Gulbuddin Hekmatyar's militant Islamic group, Hezb-i-Islami.

Veterans of these Afghan classrooms have taken their jihad abroad not only to Sudanese terror camps but also to Algeria, Azerbaijan, Bangladesh, Bosnia, Burma, Egypt, India, Morocco, Pakistan, Tajikistan, Tunisia, Uzbekistan, Yemen, and the streets of New York. After all, it was Afghanistan where Mir Aimal Kasi (a.k.a. Mir Aimal Kansi), indicted for the murder of two Americans, fled. It was on January 25, 1993, that Kasi, a Pakistani, killed two and wounded three outside CIA headquarters in Virginia. It was Afghanistan where the men—Mahmud Abouhalima, Ahmad Ajaj, Nidal Ayyad, and Mohammad Salameh—convicted for the bombing of the World Trade Center, learned strategy and tactics and where the "mastermind" of the bombing, Ramzi Ahmed Yousef, fought. It was Afghanistan were Sheik Omar Abdel Rahman—convicted of seditious conspiracy, solicitation to murder Egyptian President Hosni Mubarak, conspiracy to murder President Mubarak, solicitation to attack a U.S. military installation, and conspiracy to conduct bombings—went to visit. Rahman also sent two sons to fight in the Afghan War.[2] And it was also Afghanistan where the American-born Clement Hampton-El, convicted along with Rahman, was wounded while serving as a volunteer medic with Muslim forces fighting the Soviet occupation of that country. In a very real sense, as Israeli Prime Minister Benjamin Netanyahu has suggested, these visitors to Afghanistan are not the inheritors of such groups as the PLO, but the Muslim warriors who battled Christians during the Crusades.

A NEW TERRORISM

"Carlos the Jackal," born Illich Ramírez Sánchez, the product of a Marxist lawyer father and socialite mother, was at one time the world's most wanted terrorist. A Latin American by birth, Carlos was first sent abroad to study at Lumumba University in Moscow and started his terrorist life on behalf of George Habash's Popular Front for the Liberation of Palestine (PFLP). His preferred terrain, however, was Western Europe. In 1974, Carlos was blamed for organizing the Japanese Red Army occupation of the French Embassy in The Hague, the bombing of a drugstore in Paris, and two failed rocket attacks on Israeli airlines at Orly Airport in Paris. After the December 21, 1975, kidnapping for ransom of 11 OPEC oil ministers in Vienna, Carlos became known as "the Jackal." A wanted poster depicting his wide, impassive face in dark glasses over an open-collar shirt became the symbol of defiance for left-wing terrorist groups worldwide. For years after the Vienna ransoming, reports placed Carlos in Syria, in Libya, in Yemen, in terrorist camps in Lebanon, and in Eastern Europe. Although the communist secret police of East Germany, Hungary, and Rumania watched Carlos closely on their soil, they were not concerned with his depredations in other places.

In 1993, Carlos arrived in Sudan without incident. One year later, in August 1994, Carlos was being anesthetized in a Khartoum clinic for liposuction to slim his waistline. He awoke on a French military airplane.[3] The apprehension of others like Carlos would soon follow. In 1995, German authorities extradited Johannes Weinrich, alleged accomplice of Carlos, from Yemen. Weinrich, 48, is accused of carrying out the 1983 bombing of a French cultural center in Berlin that killed 1 person and wounded 22. Also that year, Margot Christa Frohlich, 53, another alleged accomplice of the Jackal, was arrested in Italy for the 1982 terrorist attack on a Paris office of an Arabic newspaper in which two people were killed.

Some would suggest that when the Sudanese government handed over Carlos to the French, it signaled an end to open sanctuary to internationally known terrorists. These observers miss the real point, however: The Sudanese viewed Carlos as a burned-out Marxist-Leninist of no use to anyone, especially the radical Islamic states that sponsor terrorism. Sudan was merely getting rid of someone it considered expendable to try to appear, to untrained observers, that it was abandoning its policy of giving sanctuary to terrorists. Consider that Sudan has long enjoyed the reputation throughout the Islamic world for its hospitality. Any practicing Muslim is allowed to enter the country without a visa, no questions asked. It is also true that many fundamentalist Muslims who fought alongside the Afghan *mujahideen* (freedom fighters) in their war against the Soviet-backed government in Kabul ended up in Sudan. Would the Sudanese give up these terrorists to the French? Of course not. The downfall of Carlos really signaled the changing of the guard, "The old terrorism is dead, long live the new terrorists."

The new terrorists who attend the Afghan and Sudanese terror academies are not privy to the same Soviet training techniques that were once employed by the Jackal. One should not think, however, that they are at any disadvantage. Actually, their militant Islamic instructors have more field experience than the Soviet trainers of the past. They learned bomb-making and other terrorist tactics while fighting alongside the mujahideen in Afghanistan, so these veterans of the Afghan battlefield are experts in guerrilla warfare, antiaircraft weapons, and rocket-propelled grenades (RPGs). They are adept at firing the U.S.-made FIM92A, better known as the Stinger surface-to-air missile, supplied by the hundreds to the Afghans by the CIA in the 1980s. The Stinger, the world's most effective antiaircraft missile, can bring down a commercial airliner.

In 1996, one of these sophisticated CIA-supplied Stingers was confiscated from the home of a former Afghan fighter in Pakistan's Balochistan Province. As a matter of fact, the CIA is reputed to be trying to buy back these Stingers for many millions of dollars more than their initial cost. A General Accounting Office memo reports that a few dozen Stingers out of the more than 6,000 might have found their way onto the terrorist marketplace when they were not returned to the depot after U.S. forces came home from Operation Desert Storm.

Many of these new students of terror come to the training academies directly from a life of poverty and repression. They were not born with silver spoons in their mouths like the Illich Ramírez Sánchezes of the world. They are not from the same Palestinian families whose children went off to study at the university: Yasir Arafat graduated with a civil engineering degree from King Faud University in Egypt; George Habash (PFLP) received a medical degree from the American University of Beirut; and Sadri al-Banna, a.k.a. Abu Nidal, studied engineering for 2 years at the University of Cairo.[4]

The new students of terror enter the Sudanese and Afghan terror camps with a strong belief in Islam as the only way out of their social situation. Their militant fundamentalism is reinforced by trainers who focus on the verses of the Koran and the *hadiths* (the sayings of the Prophet Muhammad) that form the basis of Islamic law and idealize the glory of dying for Allah. They graduate with a religious zeal that makes them more implacable foes than their graying, often flamboyant, Soviet-trained counterparts.

The new students of terror are more difficult to combat as well. Why? They are able to carry out their terror with a wide variety of readily available and less sophisticated devices. The new terrorist is adept in the use of handguns and knives and of splashing lye on the bare legs of mini-skirted female tourists vacationing in the Middle East. Look for what the late FBI Assistant Director in charge of the New York City office during the World Trade Center investigation, James Fox, called a "witches' brew" of nitrate fertilizer and fuel oil in addition to plastic explosives, such as Semtex developed in the former Czechoslovakia.

Less sophisticated also means less organized than their secular predecessors of the 1960s and 1970s and, consequently, more difficult to spot, track, and intercept. In the past, Lumumba University in Moscow and other universities inside the Soviet Bloc were not only centers for recruiting and training terrorists but also places to exchange terrorist rhetoric and to organize terrorist cells. As a consequence, these terrorist groups were visible, and they organized themselves very much like the Mafia or even like a large corporation—that is, pyramidally and linearly, with a discernible descending or ascending power structure.

Knowing the structure of the terrorist group made fighting terrorism easier. Law enforcement and intelligence agencies could contain terrorist organizations such as the PLO by infiltrating them at either the top or the bottom. It is much more difficult for today's law enforcement agencies to infiltrate groups that are fluid and not organized in any systematic way. A leading European terrorist expert put it best when he said, "You can snap a picture of the worldwide Islamic terrorist infrastructure, and shortly thereafter the entire structure will appear radically different."

The new students of terrorism are easily inspired by their spiritual leaders. The involvement of the blind cleric Sheik Omar Abdel Rahman in a terrorist campaign of bombings and assassinations intended to destroy the United Nations Building and other New York landmarks, to kill hundreds, if not thousands, of people, and to force the United States to abandon its support for Israel and Egypt illustrates the power a spiritual leader can have on the actions of his or her followers. So does the story, possibly apocryphal, often attributed to Sheik Rahman, of a young man seeking his spiritual leader's advice on what to do about the opening of a video rental store in Egypt. The cleric, it is said, advised the young man of two courses of action: "Either put an end to it with your own hand or know in your heart that it is evil." The young man asked, "What shall I do?" "The decision must be yours," answered the cleric. The young man blew up the video store. So much for the power of suggestion.

Suicide Bombers

Inspiration may also explain, in part, the spate of suicide bombings that rocked Israel in 1996. In a 9-day span, four separate suicide bombers in Israel killed 59 people, including 2 Americans. These suicide bombers are in no small part inspired to commit the ultimate sacrifice by the prodding of their spiritual handlers. Suicide bombers leave for their missions directly from their mosques, after completing many days of chanting the relevant scriptures aloud with their spiritual handlers. A favorite verse reads: "Think not of those who are slain in Allah's way as dead. No, they live on and find sustenance in the presence of their Lord."

The bombers' frenzied mantras are said to create a strong, as well as pleasurable, belief that they will soon sit with Allah. So strong is their belief that the bombers are able to walk among the enemy without exhibiting the slightest anxiety. On February 25, 1996, Israeli television reported that a suicide bomber dressed in an Israeli army uniform mingled with solders at a bus stop and hitchhiking post in coastal Ashkelon before setting off an explosion, killing two Israeli soldiers and himself. Witnesses to other bombings have told the authorities that they never suspected the bomber on the bus was a suicide terrorist on a mission.

It would be naive to think of these suicide terrorists as merely fanatics. *Fanatic*, like *terrorist*, is a pejorative term that, according to Maxwell Taylor and Helen Ryan (1988), "applie[s] to the state of mind of those who are wholeheartedly committed to a set of beliefs and condemned for it" (p. 92). It would be equally foolish to dismiss the impact of incendiary Islamic clerics, like Sheik Rahman, on the minds of impressionable youngsters, just as it would be to categorize these suicide bombers' actions as just acts of *taqlid*, or blind following, of a spiritual leader. One should be aware, however, of the role inspiration plays in helping precipitate the actions of these new terrorists.

Freelancers

Interspersed within this spate of suicide bombings was another example of how inspiration can lead to a potentially new, more dangerous form of terrorism, *freelance* (or spontaneous) *terrorism*. Freelance terrorism arises whenever an individual or a small group of individuals take it upon themselves to act against a target without the direct support of a traditional-type terrorist organization. These freelancers might have gotten their training, as well as their initial support, from a terrorist organization, but their act of terrorism is largely an outcome of their own rage or stealth. The new terrorism and its organizations are aware of their impact on inspiring these freelancers. They do everything they can to use these freelancers as an extension of their terrorist policies. Unlike the terrorists of a bygone era, freelancers are dangerous in that their allegiance is not to any group, but to their own beliefs. And unlike their graying secular counterparts, these spontaneous actors do not rely on significant financial and ideological support that was necessary to spur the actions of the Palestinians terrorist groups when the PLO and the Soviets were controlling who the targets were.

The specter of the freelancer and his or her threat to the United States is best illustrated by the actions of Ahmed Hamideh, an Arab American, who immigrated to the United States 19 years ago and lived in Los Angeles. In 1995, Hamideh went to the West Bank partly to seek a wife. On February 26, 1995, Hamideh crashed his car into a crowded north Jerusalem bus stop, killing Flora Yechiel, 28, a mother of two, and injuring many more. To some critics, it appeared that Hamideh, who was shot to death at the scene by bystanders, might have lost control of the black Fiat on the wet pavement. A close inspection of the Fiat and the skid marks at the scene showed otherwise. The wheelbase of Hamideh's car did not match the skid marks, and the Fiat's brakes were in perfect working order.

The forensic evidence gathered at the scene of the tragedy in north Jerusalem indicates something other than an accident. Why, then, did Hamideh use his car as a deadly weapon? The answer lies in other facts surrounding the case. A report written by Bill Hutman (1996) appearing in the *Jerusalem Post International Edition* indicated that police found a flyer with propaganda from the Islamic Jihad in the car but that Hamideh, who had recently become fanatically religious, was not a known member of any terrorist group. The same report added that Hamideh told his friends the night before his car plowed into the crowded bus stop to watch for him on television tomorrow. A story in the Hebrew daily *Ha'aretz* reported that his friends thought him to be a Islamic fanatic who showed special interest in the pictures of a bus bombing the Sunday before the incident, and he boasted that he would be seen on television by Monday evening.

Given the forensic evidence, Hamideh's recent behavior, and the timing of the incident—coming between a series of suicide bombs that rocked Israel in March 1996—there is good reason to believe that Hamideh was acting as a freelance terrorist when he drove his car into the bus stop in the French Hill junction in Jerusalem. Actually, terrorists using vehicles as weapons of terror are as commonplace in Israel as suicide bombers. In fact, a March 1993 incident in which one individual killed two Israelis with his car was thought to be an accident until the driver was blown up in an attempted suicide bombing a month later, which further suggested that Hamideh's act was no accident but common practice in the mind of the terrorist.

Police authorities in Israel now classify Hamideh's act as an official act of terrorism. More important, it illustrates the largely uncontrollable act of freelance terrorism and begs the question, Can it happen in the United States? Hamideh was an American citizen residing in Mazra A-Sharkiya, Israel. And it has been suggested by an editorial entitled "The Truth Must Be Told" (1996) in the *Jerusalem Post* that "the identity of the killer [Hamideh] was not what one would expect. He was a Palestinian with an American passport, and possessors of American passports do not fit the profile of suicide killers" (p. 6). Yes, even Israelis can practice denial in the face of the facts. Before answering whether Hamideh's act can happen in the United States, however, it is necessary to look at the terrorist groups and their supporters who have taken up residence in the United States.

THEY'RE HERE: TERRORIST GROUPS AND THEIR ARDENT SUPPORTERS

The Abu Nidal Organization

International terrorists from traditional terrorist groups like the Abu Nidal Organization (ANO) have planted operatives and recruited sympathizers in the United States since the mid-1980s. On July 26, 1994, for example, the U.S. government succeeded in getting Tawfig Musa of Milwaukee, Wisconsin; Saif Nijmeh of St. Louis, Missouri; and his brother Luie Nijmeh, also from St. Louis, to plead guilty to violating one felony count of the Racketeer Influenced and Corrupt Organizations (RICO) Act by conspiring to participate in the ANO and by discussing an attack on the Israeli Embassy in Washington, DC.

Musa and the Nijmeh brothers smuggled, transferred, and transported currency, information, and intelligence to other members of terrorist organizations inside the United States and throughout the world. This same group was also responsible for obtaining fraudulent passports for other ANO member, as well as for supplying weapons, recruiting new members, and collecting information in a clandestine manner. The Nijmeh brothers, Musa, and another ANO member, Zein Isa, had been previously indicted by a federal grand jury in the

Eastern District of Missouri for a substantive violation of the RICO
Statute, Title 18, U.S. Code, Section 1962 (d), on the basis of their
activities in connection with their involvement in the ANO.

On October 21, 1994, the U.S. District Court, Eastern District of
Missouri, sentenced Musa and the Nijmeh brothers to 21 months in a
federal prison. The charges against Isa were dropped because he was
already serving a life sentence in the Missouri Correctional System for
the murder of his daughter, Palestina "Tina" Isa, in 1989. The imprisonment of these ANO operatives culminated an investigation that
took nearly a decade, demonstrating the extent to which these and
other terrorist groups have been operating in the United States.

Isa was also reputed to be the ringleader of a coupon-clipping scam
to raise cash in the United States to fund terrorist activities for the
ANO both here and abroad. The scam involved Palestinian mer-
chants in major cities throughout the United States who would redeem
merchandise coupons for products never purchased. Isa's operation,
based in St. Louis, would obtain coupons by salvaging large quantities
of recyclable newspapers and clipping the unused coupons. Its members would break into printing plants to steal valuable coupons.
Another method involved the forging of coupons through the use of
sophisticated color copiers.

In Brooklyn, New York, a similar phony coupon redemption scam
was allegedly run by Mahmud Abouhalima—now serving 240 years in
prison for his role in the 1993 bombing of the World Trade Center.
Speculation was that Abouhalima and many of his cohorts, some of
whom were involved with Sheik Rahman, used some of the money
obtained from bogus coupons to finance activities related to the World
Trade Center bombing.

A. C. Nielsen, the nation's biggest coupon redemption company,
was reputed to have hired investigators to track the more than $400
million in annual industry losses to fraud when these coupon scams
were uncovered. The investigators supposedly found that operations
run by Isa and Abouhalima funneled approximately $200 million of
the $400 million in annual coupon industry losses to fraud back to the
Middle East to fund terrorist activities. Speculation was that this
coupon money was smuggled out of the United States through travel
agents and banks to offshore Channel Islands financial institutions and
then to the Middle East.

Palestine Islamic Jihad

When its leader and founder Fathi Shikaki was assassinated in front of his hotel on a busy street on the Mediterranean island of Malta on October 26, 1995, the Palestine Islamic Jihad (PIJ) soon named Ramadan Abdullah Shallah as its new leader. Shallah had met Shikaki back in the late 1970s when he attended Zagazig University in Egypt. At that time, Shikaki was the leader of a growing movement to inject orthodox Muslim values into the largely secular Egyptian legal system. During the 1980s, both he and Shikaki became key organizers of the Palestinian uprising in the occupied territories in Israel. In 1991, Shallah moved to Tampa, Florida, and helped establish the World and Islam Studies Enterprise (WISE), an Islamic think tank attached to the University of South Florida (USF) in Tampa.

Soon after the creation of WISE, Shallah applied for an adjunct teaching position at the university and got it. At the same time, he helped bring Basir Nafi to the United States to work for WISE. By 1992, WISE and the Middle Eastern Committee at USF agreed to cosponsor programs around the Middle East, to train graduate students, and to share libraries. In April 1995, Shallah left the university and turned up 6 months later in Syria, where he was elected head of the infamous terrorist organization PIJ following the assassination of its leader and founder, Shikaki.

When Shallah emerged as the head of the PIJ, the U.S. Department of the Treasury froze WISE assets under a presidential executive order prohibiting fund-raising for 12 international terrorist groups. It found an enormous stockpile of intelligence material that indicated WISE and its leaders were involved in Islamic Jihad operations in the United States. In other words, Shallah; Nafi, who was deported in July 1996; and Professor Sami Al-Arian, who helped create WISE, raised millions of dollars, obtained visas for terrorists to come to the United States, and helped direct terrorist operations of Islamic Jihad's terrorist operations back in the Middle East.

The selection of Shallah was not in itself significant. What was significant was that a radical terrorist group, like Islamic Jihad, that devotes much of its energy to suicide attacks against Israelis inside Israel would reach out to someone with close ties to organizations right here within the United States.[5] This is not to say that a foreign entity cannot have supporters in the United States, but rather it emphasizes just how events in the volatile Middle East have relevance to events here at home. It certainly raises questions about how a major American university can have ties to a terrorist front organization for nearly 5 years without it raising the eyebrows of university officials, not to mention law enforcement.[6]

Hamas

On July 28, 1995, Musa Mohammed Abu Marzook was detained by Immigration and Naturalization Service (INS) agents at John F. Kennedy International Airport in New York. Abu Marzook's name came up on a "watch list" of suspected terrorists while attempting to reenter the United States from a trip to the United Arab Emirates. For almost 14 years prior to his arrest, Abu Marzook, the self-proclaimed chief of the Political Bureau of Hamas, lived with his family in Falls Church, Virginia, and more recently in Brooklyn, New York. Abu Marzook traveled freely between Damascus, Iran, Jordan, Sudan, Europe, and the United States. During that time, he helped establish a large, clandestine financial network, including an international network of front groups and death squads that experts reason was indirectly responsible for the murder and wounding of more than 1,600 Israelis and 5,000 suspected Palestinian collaborators.

Abu Marzook was born in 1951 in Rafiah, the Gaza Strip. In 1975, he graduated with an engineering degree from an Egyptian university and soon after moved to the United States to pursue his doctorate. By the early 1980s, experts say, Abu Marzook became increasingly involved with militant Muslims in the United States and elsewhere who were tied to the 1979 Iranian revolution, the 1981 assassination of Anwar Sadat, and the holy war against Soviet occupation of Afghanistan. With several associates, Abu Marzook created an umbrella organization called the Islamic Association for Palestine (IAP) and soon was chosen to head its governing council.

Several years before the formal creation of Hamas in 1987, the IAP had already established offices in Arizona, Indiana, and California and published the virulent anti-Semitic magazine *Ila Falistin*. Internal Hamas documents seemingly indicate that the Hamas charter was first penned by members of the IAP in the United States. The IAP is now headquartered in Richardson, Texas.

In 1987, as Hamas began its terrorist operations inside Israel and the occupied territories, the campaign was being controlled and funded from inside the United States. Information from several captured Hamas operatives inside Israel indicates that Abu Marzook had engineered terrorist attacks in Israel by helping select and dispatch military commanders to Israel, with specific instructions on selected targets.

While Abu Marzook was nurturing the growing military wing of Hamas from inside the United States, he was also busy establishing Hamas as a religious and research organization. Evidence from federal documents reveals that, in 1989, Abu Marzook became the founding president of the United Association of Studies and Research (UASR), a "think tank" that, according to intelligence sources, is a covert branch of Hamas disseminating propaganda and providing a center for strategic and political planning.

On July 31, 1995, the Israeli government formally notified the United States that it would seek Abu Marzook's extradition to face criminal charges of terrorism and conspiracy to commit murder. Shortly thereafter, on August 8, 1995, FBI agents acting on a warrant from an Israeli court arrested Abu Marzook pending a formal extradition hearing. U.S. officials said that most of the evidence gathered against Abu Marzook by the Israeli court had come from Muhammad al-Hamid Khalil Salah, a Palestinian used-car dealer from Chicago who Israeli officials say visited Israel to deliver money from Abu Marzook to Hamas leaders. Back in January 1993, Israeli authorities had arrested Salah as he entered Israel. During his military trial, Salah was reported to have confessed to supplying money for arms. At the time of Abu Marzook's detention in the United States, Salah was serving a 5-year prison term. Salah also told Israeli authorities that Abu Marzook knew of terrorist raids inside Israel and had participated in the recruiting of terrorists and the purchasing of weapons for Hamas. Israeli authorities have long alleged that Abu Marzook was responsible, as chief of the Political Bureau of Hamas, for attacks that killed, maimed, or wounded scores of Israeli citizens, as well as foreigners. Israel had never contended, however, that Abu Marzook participated in these acts.

On May 8, 1996, U.S. District Judge Kevin Thomas Duffy ruled that Abu Marzook was eligible for extradition to Israel. Hamas and the PIJ immediately reiterated their veiled threats to retaliate inside the United States if Abu Marzook was extradited to stand trial in Israel.

After more than 18 months at the Metropolitan Correctional Center in New York, Abu Marzook shocked everyone by withdrawing his extradition case from the Second U.S. Circuit Court of Appeals in Manhattan. Abu Marzook said "he would rather 'suffer martyrdom' in Israel than fight extradition through an unjust U.S. court system." Abu Marzook's surprise action and impending extradition to Israel by the United States caused an immediate threat from Mahmoud Zahar, the top Hamas official in Gaza. Zahar was quoted as saying, "Israel will gain nothing from taking Marzook in custody, and the United States will gain nothing by gaining a new enemy–Hamas."

On April 3, 1997–citing fears of terrorist reprisals reminiscent of those that rocked the Jewish state in 1996 after the assassination of master bomb maker of Hamas, Yehiya Ayyash, who engineered suicide bomb attacks that killed more than 50 Israelis and wounded several hundred more since 1994–Israel withdrew its request for extradition. This not unexpected action put the Abu Marzook case back in the domain of the INS. On May 6, 1997, after weeks of behind-the-scenes negotiations among Israel, Jordan, and the United States, Abu Marzook was deported to Jordan.[7]

Networking From Coast to Coast

Particularly disturbing is the fact that many foreign terrorists and the organizations they represent are networking with each other right here in the United States. Steven Emerson, in his award-winning documentary *Jihad in America* (1994), captured on videotape some of the world's most notorious Islamic radicals meeting throughout the heartland in the late 1980s and early 1990s. Many of these meetings took place well before the bombing of the World Trade Center in February 1993.

In June 1991, according to Emerson, the Virginia-based Islamic think-tank UASR sponsored the largest gathering of radical Islamic leaders ever assembled inside the United States. Shockingly, U.S. intelligence authorities, says Emerson, were unaware of the meeting on the outskirts of Washington, DC, until after it took place. The conference, which addressed U.S. involvement in Iraq, entertained high-ranking representatives of almost every militant fundamentalist organization, including such notorious terrorist groups as Palestine Islamic Jihad and Hezbollah.

The United States has played host to other such conferences. Audio- and videotapes obtained by Emerson demonstrate how Hamas helped plan its terrorist activities. In 1991, Emerson related how a video of a conference in Kansas City Convention Center, attended by 3,000, captured no other than Musa Mohammed Abu Marzook and 10 other radical leaders addressing the conference while extolling the merits of waging holy war. At one panel called "The Blessed Uprising (Intifada)," Abu Marzook appeared with Mohammed Abu Faris, a radical member of the Jordanian Islamic Front. To the tumultuous shouts of "Allahu Akbar" (Allah is great), Abu Faris swore allegiance to the Hamas goals of driving Israelis into the sea and of killing all who participated in the Camp David Agreement.

These terror conferences frequently result in the sharing of information and expertise. With a common enemy in the United States, these often divergent organizations may be contemplating cooperative efforts against the United States. Steven Emerson (1998) sums up the threat best when he relates a statement made by a well-known American Islamic leader. The leader, speaking to a gathering at an annual Islamic conference in the United States, " told his audience that if they were outside the United States, they could all pray, 'May Allah destroy America'; if they were in the United States, they had to refrain from violence because Islam on its own would take over the United States." Emerson goes on to say that for "one Middle Eastern visitor to the IAP [Islamic Association for Palestine] convention, it was 'like attending a radical Islamic conference in Gaza. The only difference was that some of the sessions were in English'" (p. 53).

The fact that top terrorist leaders of the PIJ and Hamas, as well as operatives within the ANO, were found to have been living in the United States indicates that these groups are using the country to further their activities. Often these groups have more freedom to operate here than in the very countries that gave them life. In the case of Hamas and the PIJ, these terror groups not only have raised considerable amounts of money in the United States but also have set up operational headquarters in the United States to direct terrorist attacks and military strategies abroad. The ANO, the PIJ, and Hamas have succeeded, in large measure, in establishing their support infrastructure because these groups have networked together with other militant groups throughout the United States.

Good News, Bad News

What's the good news about the state sponsorship of these conferences and activities that have taken place within the United States? At
the end of the 20th century, only a handful of states still support international terrorism. This is not to say, however, that other pariah states
are not in the business of dealing with terrorism as an extension of
their foreign policy; rather, these states have begun to distance themselves from their role as sponsors of terrorism ever since the Persian
Gulf War. Take, for example, Syrian President Hafez al-Assad, who in
the past favored the use of terror. For the most part, he relied on sporadic secret attacks to avoid detection. He did not wish to make himself a target for retribution as Libya's Colonel Moammar Gadhafi did
in 1985, when he directed a terrorist act against Americans in West
Germany. Assad favored oscillation between sponsor and intervener
as he did in the Lebanese hostage situation. In the wake of the Persian
Gulf War, Assad began to distance himself from terrorism to improve
his relations with the West. He distorted his links with various Middle
Eastern groups engaging in terrorism. The Oslo Accord saw Syria further distance itself from its role as provider of terrorist training camps
near Damascus and throughout Syria. Cleverly, he moved his trained
terrorists to Lebanon's Bekaa Valley, which Syria controls.

In short, terrorism experts within and outside the government generally agree that the role of states in promoting terrorism will continue to decline. Data from Britain's Center for the Study of Terrorism
and Political Violence appear to support this. From the mid-1980s
through the mid-1990s, these data indicate a sixfold drop in the number of state-sponsored terrorist attacks worldwide.

What's the bad news? Terrorists, often a rather innovative lot, can
find needed funds, weapons, and technology from other sources.
Additionally, the British data indicate that terrorism increasingly is
attributable to the new terrorists. In other words, the diminishing
ranks of state-sponsored terrorists will be replaced with "freelance"
extremist   groups   supported   outside   national   boundaries.
Furthermore, the so-called state sponsors of terrorism still have their
hands in encouraging the new breed while on the surface they protest
any hint of complicity with terrorist organizations. For example, Iraqi
leader Saddam Hussein, who once supported secular terrorist groups
like the Abu Nidal Organization, has been hosting militant Muslim

fundamentalists from all over the world since his defeat in the second Persian Gulf War. Rumor has it that he is currently giving shelter in Baghdad to the last known fugitive of the World Trade Center bombing, Abdul Rahman Yasin.

THEY'RE HERE TOO: THE FREELANCERS

Terrorists, such as Ramzi Ahmed Yousef of World Trade Center bombing fame, walk the streets of New York one day and of Islamabad, Pakistan, the next. Members of Sheik Rahman's group, al-Gama´at al-Islamiyya, congregate in the suburbs of Cairo and train in the terrorist camps in Jalalabad, Afghanistan. And freelancers, like Ahmad Hamideh, travel to Israel from the United States to perform their spontaneous acts of terror in the streets of Jerusalem.

These new students of terror have a global reach thanks to cheap airfares and easily accessible high-tech communications. Their travels take them to wherever Muslims gather, as well as to the outer limits of the Western world. The World Trade Center bombing and the aborted plot to bomb other landmarks in New York City tell us that the Ramzi Yousefs of the world and the followers of Sheik Rahman are also here, with their well-documented penchant for taking care of business. More troublesome is that freelance terrorism, like that practiced by Ahmed Hamideh in Jerusalem, might have already reached the United States. The consequences are chilling.

Mir Aimal Kasi

On the morning of January 25, 1993, Mir Aimal Kasi, a 29-year-old Pakistani, using an AK-47 automatic rifle, shot five individuals as they sat in a rush-hour traffic jam outside the gates of CIA headquarters in Langley, Virginia. All but one worked for the CIA. Two CIA employees—Lansing Bennett, 66, a physician; and Frank Darling, 28, a communications engineer—died. Kasi worked for a Virginia courier company that serviced the CIA. And Kasi's hometown, Quetta, Pakistan, was a CIA command post during the Afghan War. Rumor had it that Kasi was a CIA informant during the war and was under the protection of followers of the rabidly anti-Western Gulbuddin Hekmatyar.

Kasi bought a one-way ticket to his native Pakistan hours after the shooting and left the next day. Then, on June 15, 1997, Kasi was asleep in the Shalimar Hotel, a seedy establishment in Dera Ghazi Khan, a city in central Pakistan, when he heard a knock at the door. He went to open the door, thinking he was being aroused for morning prayers. Like most observant Muslims, Kasi prays five times a day, beginning about 4:30 A.M. He was not alarmed until he saw the five-agent FBI team.

In June 1997, almost 41/2 years after the murders and with a $2 million reward on his head, Mir Aimal Kasi was handed over by "Afghan individuals" to a joint task force of CIA and FBI agents. Kasi went on trial in November 1997 for the murder of the two CIA employees. Actually, he was only charged with the capital murder of Frank Darling, in part, because of evidence that Kasi first wounded Darling and then returned to blow off his head with the assault rifle while Daring's wife cowered beside him in the car. On Monday, November 10, 1997, Kasi was found guilty. Only 4 days later, the jury, deliberating under heavy security, decided that the Pakistani man should get the death penalty.

The source of Kasi's rage was still unknown. Or was it? In the Fairfax court where Kasi stood trial, the prosecutors said he had been motivated by anger at U.S. policies that he believed created suffering among Palestinians, Bosnian Muslims, and others. Chief Prosecutor Robert Horan said that Kasi deliberately chose the CIA as "a symbol of American power and murdered its employees to protest this country's policies." Others attributed Kasi's rage to a belief that the United States was responsible for "meddling in Muslim countries" and bombing innocents in Iraq during the Persian Gulf War. Still others said that his rage might be related to the death of his father or his uncle or a friend who fought in Afghanistan. If Kasi, a member of the Pathan tribe, which flourishes on both sides of the Khyber Pass linking Pakistan and Afghanistan, had not behaved like an impetuous freelancer, his act would have violated the old Pathian saying: "One hundred years is too short a time to wait for revenge."

As justice would have it, 2 days before the fifth anniversary of the attack, January 23, 1998, Fairfax Circuit Judge J. Howe Brown sentenced Kasi to death. In his first public statement since being arrested, Kasi said he was not proud of what he had done but that his motives were political. "This is the result of a wrong policy toward

Muslim countries," he said in heavily accented English. Who said the source of Kasi's rage was unknown?

Rashid Baz

On March 1, 1994, Rashid Baz spray-fired a Cobray M-11/9 assault pistol at a van carrying Hasidic students across the Brooklyn Bridge in New York. Four young men were wounded in the attack, and one of them, Aaron Halberstam, 16 years old, lay in a coma for 4 days before dying. Israeli-born Nachum Sosonkin, also wounded in the attack, survived and testified at Baz's trial with a 9-mm bullet still lodged in his head. The students were 4 of about 100 who traveled in separate vehicles to a New York hospital in support of their spiritual leader, Rabbi Menachem Schneerson, grand rebbe of the Lubavitcher Hasidic sect, who underwent cataract surgery.

Was Baz's actions on the bridge related to post-traumatic stress disorder? Nuha Abudabbeh, who examined Baz on behalf of his lawyer, Eric Sears, thought so. According to Abudabbeh, Baz was exposed to so much bloodshed and cruelty during the Lebanese civil war that he suffered from post-traumatic stress disorder and numerous bouts of paranoia. Abudabbeh testified that she would not have been surprised if Baz saw something on the bridge the day of the shooting that was not there and that he thought the students were shooting at him so he reacted in self-defense.[8] Using Abudabbeh's testimony, Sears went on to argue that Baz should not be held responsible for killing Aaron Halberstam and wounding three other teens because his years in the Lebanese militia left him with diminished capacity to comprehend fully the consequences of his actions.

Or was Baz's actions related to the earlier massacre of 29 Palestinian worshippers by an ultra-Orthodox Jewish terrorist, Baruch Goldstein, in a mosque in the Cave of the Patriarchs shrine in the occupied West Bank city of Hebron?[9] A statement made by codefendant Jordanian-born Bassam Reyati, 26, owner of the Brooklyn taxi service that employed Baz, sure makes it look that way. Reyati told police after the arrest that Ray (Baz's nickname) was very angry and mad after the Hebron massacre and that he wanted to kill all the Jews who did it. During the trial, defense experts admitted that Baz was easily agitated when things happened in the Middle East and that possibly the murder of Muslims in the Hebron mosque by a Jewish settler

5 days before the bridge shooting triggered the incident.

On December 1, 1994, a Manhattan Supreme Court jury, rejecting the testimony of defense experts, found the 28-year-old Lebanese immigrant cab driver guilty of second-degree murder and 14 counts of attempted murder. Baz, who showed no emotion in court as the verdicts were read, was also convicted on weapons possession charges. The late State Supreme Court Judge Harold J. Rothwax, on January 18, 1995, sentenced Rashid Baz to life in prison.

Ali Hassan Abu Kamal

Sixty-nine-year-old Palestinian Ali Hassan Abu Kamal arrived at John F. Kennedy International Airport in New York on Christmas Eve of 1996. On January 11, 1997, the elderly schoolteacher from the West Bank left for Florida to purchase a semiautomatic .380 Beretta handgun. How does someone like Abu Kamal know about setting up residency in Florida in order to purchase a handgun? The answer is he wouldn't, at least without help. In any event, he later returned to New York, where he reputedly went on binges of buying lottery tickets and walked the city streets in search of food that would remind him of home. On Saturday, February 22, 1997, he visited the Empire State Building for the first time. He told a high school friend from the Middle East, Taysir H. Badanoro, whom he had not seen in more than three decades, that he was going to take a walk to see the Empire State Building.

On Sunday afternoon, February 23, 1997, Abu Kamal returned to the Empire State Building, carrying his semiautomatic handgun under his coat. Witnesses said he muttered something about Egypt seconds before he drew his gun and began firing at about 5:00 P.M. onto the panoramic outdoor deck that surrounds a large, windowed room on the 86th floor. When the rampage was over, two were dead, including Abu Kamal, who had shot himself, and six others were injured. The other dead man was 27-year-old Danish musician Chris Burmmeister. In critical condition were the dead man's American friend, Matthew Gross, 27, of Montclair, New Jersey; a 52-year-old Argentinean man; and a 30-year-old Swiss man. The others were less seriously wounded.

Two versions of a handwritten letter, a suicide note—one in English, the other in Arabic—were found tucked into the pouch that Abu Kamal wore around his neck. After reading the words of this visitor from the West Bank, consider the possibility of Abu Kamal's link with terrorism:

> *The First Enemy*: Americans–Britons–French (though the French now seem friendly after Chirac's visit to Palestine) and the Zionists. These 3 Big Powers are the first enemy to the Palestinians ever since their three-partite Declaration in the early fifties, and they are responsible for turning our people, the Palestinians, homeless. The Zionists are the paw that carries out their savage aggression. My restless aspiration is to murder as many of them as possible, and I have decided to strike at their own den in New York, and at the very Empire State Building in particular. The Zionists have usurped my father's land at 'Abbassiya near Lydda Airport and which is now worth ten million US dollars at least. ("The Letter," 1997, p. B3)

Gazi Ibrahim Abu Maizer and Lafi Khalil

On July 31, 1997, two suicide bombers with Middle Eastern connections were arrested in an explosive-laden Brooklyn, New York, apartment before they could carry out an attack on the subway. The responding police officers were acting on a tip from a man who arrived at the 88th Precinct accompanied by two Long Island Railroad police officers. The informant told police: "My friend is going to kill people on the subway."

As tactically trained Emergency Service Unit A-Team officers from the New York City Police Department burst into the apartment a block from the Gowanus Canal at 4:30 A.M., one suspect flicked one of four toggles on a detonator and was shot. Moments later, his companion was shot after he lunged for an officer's weapon. One bomb in the apartment was a 9-inch pipe packed with gunpowder, nails, and 9-mm bullets. The other, which the suspect had tried to detonate, was made of four lengths of ordinary pipe clumped together, covered with construction-grade nails, and taped into a bundle. The bigger bomb was attached to a body harness for a suicide bomber and was designed to explode when all four switches on the command box were hit. New York City Police Commissioner Howard Safir told reporters that computer analysis indicated the four-pipe monstrosity the suspect tried to detonate was capable of killing everyone within 25 feet if detonated in an enclosed area like a subway car and would injure within 100 feet in an open area.

As the men–Gazi Ibrahim Abu Maizer and Lafi Khalil–were carried off to a hospital, one was reputed to have told the officers that he wanted to join "the hero martyrs in Jerusalem." The reference was to two suicide bomb attacks that rocked Israel on July 30, 1997, killing 15 and wounding 150.

At the hearing at U.S. District Court in Brooklyn the night of the arrest, prosecutors charged in a complaint that one suspect, Abu Maizer, a 23-year-old West Bank Palestinian, acknowledged that the bombs in his apartment were meant for detonation on the subway. Investigators searching Abu Maizer's apartment found a completed immigration asylum application in which Abu Maizer indicated he had been previously arrested in Israel and accused of being a member of Hamas. Apparently, Abu Maizer entered the United States illegally from Canada in January 1997 and was held by the INS for approximately 1 month, after which he was released on $5,000 bond. This was not the first time Abu Maizer had tried to sneak across the boarder. In June 1996, he was caught twice trying to enter the United States from British Columbia but was sent back. In April 1997, free on bond in the United States, Abu Maizer applied for asylum. Although he withdrew his application in June, Abu Maizer was not immediately deported but simply was instructed to leave the country by August 23, 1997. At this time, apparently neither the INS nor any other federal agency bothered to keep track of him even though details about his background should have come up on some type of U.S. "watch list."

The other suspect, the 22-year-old Palestinian Lafi Khalil, had in his address book the name of a known terrorist organization, according to the complaint, which charged the two with a bombing conspiracy.

Wanna-bes, Freelancers, or What?

To this day, there is no hard evidence of a direct connection between Mir Aimal Kasi, Rashid Baz, Ali Hassan Abu Kamal, Gazi Ibrahim Abu Maizer, and Lafi Khalil and events in Israel or with a particular terrorist group. This much is certain, however: These individuals are, at the very least, sympathetic to events that occur halfway around the world and are willing to spew rhetoric that makes their actions appear to be related to some other event. Consider the fact that, in the Empire State Building shooting case and the averted subway suicide bombing in Brooklyn, suicide notes were found. Both notes discussed hatred for the United States and its allies. And remember that one of the captured suicide bombers expressed his desire to join other suicide bombers who were successful in blowing themselves up in Israel. Sources said the note was to be carried with the bomber in a container designed to survive the blast. Police found the note during a 17-hour search of the apartment. Also found in the apartment of the Brooklyn suicide bombers were hundreds of pages of Hamas propaganda and a portrait of Sheik Rahman. And in the earlier shootings outside CIA headquarters and on the Brooklyn Bridge, both shooters, it is safe to say, were not fans of U.S. policy throughout the Muslim world and especially in the Middle East.

One law enforcement official summed it up best when talking about the actions of Abu Maizer: "This guy is crazy. He might be a wanna-be, but that doesn't solve the problem—because even wanna-bes can kill." And that is just the point. Simply stated, freelancers are just as dangerous as card-carrying members of any traditional terrorist group with a predictable record of carrying out terrorist attacks.

WHAT IT ALL MEANS

Freelancers and loosely affiliated groups of terrorists are difficult to identify and do not easily conform to the rigid categorizations used by Western law enforcement organizations. Members of these groups may not consider themselves citizens of any particular country, but instead seek common political, social, or personal objectives that transcend nation-state boundaries. The FBI Terrorist Research and Analytical Center (1994) labels these freelancers and these loosely affiliated groups of terrorists and their criminal or terrorist actions as international radical terrorism (IRT).

The World Trade Center bombing and the plot to destroy other New York City landmarks are prime examples of IRT. Persons indicted or identified with these events include Egyptians, Iraqis, Jordanians, Palestinians, Sudanese, a Puerto Rican, and other U.S. citizens, naturalized and otherwise. But their actions best typify those of a loosely knit group coming together to hatch a plan. Here is how this loosely knit group of terrorists planned and executed their act of international radical terrorism:

On September 1, 1992, Ahmad Ajaj and Ramzi Yousef arrive at

John F. Kennedy International Airport in New York from Pakistan, using phony passports. Ajaj has with him manuals and material for constructing bombs. In October 1992, Mohammad Salameh and Nidal Ayyad open a joint bank account with a cash deposit of $8,567. Together they withdraw $8,560 in cash from the account, and Salameh deposits $8,570 into an account in his own name. The next month, Salameh cashes a $3,000 check drawn on his account. Using the name Kamal Ibraham, he rents a storage locker in Jersey City, New Jersey. Yousef, using the same alias used by Salameh, orders chemicals, including urea and nitric acid, for delivery to the storage locker in Jersey City. He pays $3,615 in cash.

In the first 2 months of the next year, Salameh, Yousef, and Yasin mix chemicals to make the bomb in an apartment in Jersey City. On February 2, 1993, Ayyad orders additional chemicals from the same supplier used by Yousef. Early in the morning 7 days later, Yousef calls Eyad Ismoil at a grocery store in Dallas from a pay phone in Jersey City. A few hours later, Ismoil buys a plane ticket to New York. Ismoil arrives at John F. Kennedy International Airport on February 21, 1993.

On February 23, 1993, Salameh rents a Ryder van in Jersey City. The next day, Ayyad calls a compressed-gas supplier from his office and exchanges telephone calls with Salameh at the storage locker. Soon thereafter, Salameh gets a delivery of three tanks of hydrogen gas at the storage locker, allegedly to boost the power of the bomb, and loads them into the rented Ryder van. He then reports the van stolen to the police.

On February 26, 1993, Salameh and Yousef drive the van to a Jersey City service station for gasoline. Mahmud Abouhalima arrives at the service station and pays for the gas, as well as for gas for his own car. Ismoil, with Yousef as a passenger, drives the now infamous yellow Ryder van to New York and parks it in the B-2 level garage below the World Trade Center. At 12:18 p.m., 1,200 pounds of explosives kill six and injure hundreds more.

Although an international radical terrorist act like the World Trade Center bombing is a rare occurrence, terrorist groups remain reluctant to strike here, and their contingency plans for a possible action continue to progress. Just 2 years after the World Trade Center bombing, the FBI reports that

terrorist supporters in the United States continued a trend toward improving their ability to collect information, raise money, and issue rhetoric. Advanced technology allows some extremists to communicate efficiently and securely. Supporters of terrorist groups also continued to send and receive information from like-minded zealots overseas. (FBI, 1996, p. 14)

Unfortunately, support infrastructures for these terrorists are constantly upgraded, and group members are receiving training in terrorist boot camps throughout Sudan and Afghanistan. The World Trade Center bombing shattered the illusion that the United States is immune from the hands of the new terrorists. The actions of possible freelancers such as Mir Aimal Kasi, Rashid Baz, Ali Hassan Abu Kamal, Gazi Ibrahim Abu Maizer, and Lafi Khalil will only embolden and inspire other freelancers and groups who also hold a deep-seated hatred for the United States. Additionally, the FBI (1996) warns that terrorists may also learn from their deeds: "Studying the attack [of the World Trade Center]—including the resulting damage, media coverage, and investigative techniques used to apprehend suspects—could prompt future terrorists to plan their attacks with greater care" (p. 14).

The swift punishment of these terrorists does little to deter the problem. Consider, for example, the conviction, as well as the forthcoming execution by lethal injection, of Mir Aimal Kasi. Kasi's conviction was immediately followed by the murder of four American oil company auditors—Ephraim Egbu, senior auditor; Joel Enlow, manager of audit projects; Larry Jennings, audit manager; and Tracy Richie, senior audit supervisor—who worked for Houston-based Union Texas Petroleum and their Pakistani driver in Karachi, a port city of 7 million that has become noted in Pakistan for waves of violence that have seen at least 5,000 people killed from 1993 to 1997. In 1995, after the capture of Ramzi Yousef by U.S. and Pakistani agents, similar violence was directed at Americans when two employees of the U.S. Consulate were slain in a drive-by shooting.

Although federal counterterrorism experts had no hard evidence to link the killing of the four Americans from the biggest international oil company in Pakistan to the Kasi conviction 36 hours earlier, the FBI dispatched a team of agents to Karachi to gather evidence. Senior police officials in Pakistan said the murders were most likely the result of Kasi's conviction.

Kasi's conviction was a leading item in Pakistani radio and television reports on the night after the conviction and in newspaper headlines the day of the shootings. In fact, the U.S. Department of State was so concerned about the Kasi conviction that it issued a formal advisory in Washington, warning Americans in Pakistan to be especially alert because of the risks of retaliation by Kasi's sympathizers and to avoid Baluchistan and other areas in Pakistan. Militants in Kasi's native province, Baluchistan, vowed to revenge Kasi's removal from Pakistan in 1996 via a U.S. military airplane without any extradition or other court hearing in Pakistan.[10] It was reported that while in the Fairfax County, Virginia, jail, Kasi told a family member that "Islamic militants would take revenge for his prosecution" and that "'his people' would not spare 'the Americans' and whoever had disclosed his whereabouts." One shudders to think of the consequences after Kasi is executed.

In the meantime, the presence of Kasi and other high-profile terrorists such as Ramzi Yousef and Sheik Rahman and his followers in prisons throughout the United States can only spell trouble for the authorities. Calls for retaliation for their imprisonment will no doubt echo wherever their supporters gather to spew their venomous rhetoric against Americans both here and abroad. In the case of Rahman, the threat is even more serious than with Kasi.

Immediately after the January 1996 sentencing of the blind sheik and his followers to long terms in federal prison for their acts of terrorism, U.S. forces in Bosnia were put on high alert following intelligence reports suggesting that militant Muslim groups intended to retaliate. In January 1997, such retaliation might have begun. Three letter bombs were intercepted before reaching parole officers at Leavenworth Federal Prison, where Mohammed Saleh and Victor Alvarez, both convicted with Rahman, are serving time for the plot to blow up the United Nations headquarters and other buildings in New York. Like the bombs that were sent later in the month to the Arab newspaper *Al-Hayat* offices in Washington, DC, the United Nations, and London, these parcels bore the postmark of Alexandria, Egypt.[11]

Outside the United States on November 17, 1997, Rahman's al-Gama'at al-Islamiyya claimed responsibility for a killing spree outside an ancient Pharonic temple in Luxor, Egypt. When the carnage was over, 58 foreign tourists and 4 Egyptians were dead. Four Americans survived by hiding among Luxor's antiquities. The six terrorists wielding assault rifles called themselves the Battalion of Havoc and Destruction, and one of their stated aims was to seize hostages and demand that America free the jailed, blind fundamentalist cleric.[12] Witnesses reported that some of the terrorists took out their daggers and maimed and mutilated the bodies of the tourists. In passing, it is worth noting that this horrendous attack at the popular tourist attraction of the 3,400-year-old Hatsheput Temple in the Valley of the Kings on the Nile River came days after the November 12, 1997, conviction of Ramzi Yousef, an associate of Rahman.[13]

Speculation aside, vigilance is appropriate, given the new terrorism the United States faces in the 21st century. Suffice it to say that, in the case of conspiracies like the one involving the blind cleric and his cohorts, action is a calculation that considers the extent of the group's rage against the real danger of retaliation. In cases where their anger becomes uncontrollable, they throw caution to the wind and strike out against the United States. Consider the words of Yousef after hearing his sentence for the World Trade Center bombing:

> This case is not about so-called terrorists who planted a bomb for no reason but just to kill innocent people for the fun of it. What this case is about is about the outcome of terrorism . . . You have been supporting Israel throughout all the years in killing and torturing peoples, innocent peoples . . . You enjoy seeking people having war together. You enjoy sucking blood and shedding blood . . . You are the first one who introduced this type of terrorism to the history of mankind when you dropped an atomic bomb . . . And since this is the way you invented . . . It was necessary to use the same means against you because this is the only language you understand. ("Strong Language," 1998, p. A3)

Freelancers, however, have no formula or calculus other than their raw emotions. Adding to the problem is the fact that both categories of the new Islamic terrorists call on an interpretation of their religion to justify their aberrant actions. But their interpretation of religion is just that—an interpretation, one that calls on a narrow and twisted version of Islam far removed from the one practiced by the world's Islamic community. Whatever the case, the future is dangerous for the United States.

ENDNOTES

1. Those interested in pursuing an understanding of Shiites and Shiism are referred to the Dilip Hiro's *Iran Under the Ayatollahs* (1987) or Thomas Lippman's excellent little paperback *Understanding Islam* (1990) or Matti Moosa's *Extremist Shiites* (1988).

2. Sheik Omar Abdul Rahman, an Egyptian, arrived in the United States in 1990 after brief stays in Sudan and Pakistan. As the spiritual leader of al-Gama'at al-Islamiyya, who has long sought to overthrow the Egyptian government, Rahman was acquitted in Egypt of any involvement with the 1981 assassination of President Anwar Sadat and in two seditious rioting cases. He was, however, convicted in absentia in a 1994 retrial of one of the riot cases and was sentenced to 7 years in prison. Before his arrest, the blind Muslim cleric resided in Jersey City, New Jersey, and often preached in mosques in Jersey City and Brooklyn, New York.

3. On December 12, 1997, Carlos went on trial in Paris for the June 27, 1975, killing in a Latin Quarter apartment of two French security officials–Jean Donatini and Raymond Dous–and a Lebanese informant. The latter, Michel Moukharbal, was being investigated by police for his role in the attacks against the Israeli airline El Al at Orly Airport in Paris. On December 23, 1997, Carlos was convicted and sentenced to life in prison. On hearing the sentence, Carlos defiantly raised his left hand, shook his fist, and shouted, "Vive la revolución!"

4. Abu Nidal's father, Khalil, was one of the wealthiest men in Palestine before the al-Banna land was taken over by the Israeli government in 1948.

5. After the Shallah takeover, the Iranians reportedly cut off funding to the PIJ because they feared the group's new leader was a Western intelligence mole. Western intelligence vehemently denied any ties but noted that Iran was indeed unhappy with the Shallah selection, as well as with his relatively moderate image.

6. Steven Emerson (1998) has conducted interviews with senior university officials and professors at USF and reports that the activities of Shallah and his associates were not unknown to them. Emerson states, "In 1991 and 1992, the university ignored a series of caveats from professors on campus who specifically warned that foreign but unidentified money was being poured into a university offshoot [WISE] with radical Islamic connections" (p. 54).

7. The *Jerusalem Post International Edition* reported that FBI Director Louis Freeh visited Israel in February 1997 to cut a secret deal that would avoid extraditing Abu Marzook from the United States to Israel. The U.S. Embassy in Tel Aviv rejected the *Jerusalem Post* story ("U.S. Denies," 1997, p. 6).

8. Under cross-examination by Prosecutor Armand Durastanti, Abudabbeh, a Palestinian who was raised in Turkey and Jordan, admitted that she had done little research in the field of post-traumatic stress disorder. She nevertheless insisted that Baz's experiences were clouded by his experiences, including witnessing his boyhood friend burned to death.

9. In 1981, Goldstein wrote to the *New York Times*, warning that Israel would soon face the same fate as Northern Ireland if it did not remove all Arabs from within its borders. Goldstein emigrated from Brooklyn to Israel in 1983.

10. The U.S. Department of State has, from time to time, issued warnings cautioning Americans about terrorist risks abroad. In addition to the worldwide warnings that followed the convictions of Mir Aimal Kasi on November 10, 1997, and Ramzi Yousef on November 12, 1997, the department had issued worldwide cautions in 1991 during the Persian Gulf War and in 1993 after the World Trade Center bombing, after the arrest of eight terrorism suspects in New York City, and after a military strike against Iraq.

11.   *Al-Hayat*, which means "life" in Arabic, was founded in Beirut in 1946. When the Lebanese civil war made publishing the paper impossible, it relocated its main office to London. With a circulation of nearly 200,000, it is read by presidents, kings, and other heads of state. Over the years, it has been extremely critical of Islamic fundamentalist movements throughout the Arab world, especially in Algeria and Egypt. The lone exception is its coverage of Saudi Arabia. Its position on Egypt and the fact that Saudi Prince Khalid Ibn Sultan owns the paper might have been the precipitants for the recent spat of letter bombs.

12.   Lynne Stewart, lawyer and spokesperson for Sheik Rahman, denied that the fundamentalist cleric had incited followers to attack tourists at the Egyptian temple.

13.   On January 8, 1998, Judge Kevin Duffy sentenced Ramzi Yousef to spend life plus 240 years in prison. Judge Duffy urged that Yousef spend his sentence in solitary confinement in the nation's most secure prison, the new federal "supermax" prison in Florence, Colorado. On hearing the sentence in court, Yousef defiantly proclaimed: "I am a terrorist and I am proud of it." The sentences levied by Judge Duffy applied to two separate cases. The first, the World Trade Center bombing, predated the 1994 federal law that allowed the death penalty. The other case involved a conspiracy he called "Project Bojinka" (chaos in the sky), hatched in Manila and never carried out, concerning a plan to bomb a series of U.S. airlines in the Far East. Federal prosecutors did not seek the death penalty in that plot. As with the Yousef conviction, the U.S. Department of State issued a warning to Americans traveling abroad to be aware of the possibility of reprisals for Yousef's sentencing.

Chapter 3

DOMESTIC TERRORISM

THE THREAT FROM WITHIN

On Wednesday, April 19, 1995, at 9:02 a.m., just over 2 years after the World Trade Center bombing, a yellow rental van exploded in front of the Alfred P. Murrah Federal Building in Oklahoma City, killing 168 people and injuring 850 others. A short time later, 75 minutes to be exact, Timothy James McVeigh was pulled over on Interstate 35 by Oklahoma Highway Patrol Officer Charlie Hangar for driving without a car tag. When Hangar noticed that the crew-cut McVeigh was carrying a pistol in a shoulder holster beneath his jacket, he arrested him on a concealed weapons charge. Also in McVeigh's possession at the time of his arrest was an envelope stuffed with antigovernment clippings. Handwritten underneath a quotation from the American Patriot Samuel Adams were the words McVeigh had penned: "Maybe now there will be liberty." The whole world would soon learn that "John Doe No. 1," the subject of the greatest manhunt in U.S. history, was not a foreign-born terrorist, but one of the homegrown variety.

Was the anger that precipitated the greatest act of terrorism on U.S. soil also impossible to predict? Probably not. Just listen to the rhetoric that was about just before the Oklahoma City bombing: *Guns & Ammo*, for instance, a popular magazine among antigovernment and militia types and on newsstands the day of the bombing, had the following sentiments published in a popular write-in column: "I dread the weighty taxes, grinding inconveniences and petty indignities of the leviathan state more than I dread violent confrontation with its enforcers" and "Speaking for myself, there is only one government on earth I don't feel safe from—and it isn't Russia's" (Cooper, 1995, p. 105).

But the same terrorism textbook authors who did not think that foreign terrorism would reach the United States also underestimated the evil within. For example, in *Perspectives on Terrorism* (1991), Vetter and Perlstein reason it is highly unlikely that the United States would ever again experience the widespread terrorism that scourged the rural South during the 1950s and 1960s. In *Terrorism: An Introduction* (1991), White, too, writes about a downward trend in the incidents of domestic terrorism and cites a report by John Harris (1987) in *FBI Law Enforcement Bulletin* to support the decline. Additionally, Brent Smith, in his *Terrorism in America: Pipe Bombs and Pipe Dreams* (1994), while acknowledging the possibility of an increase in right-wing and environmental terrorism before the close of the 20th century, makes no real mention of the antigovernment movement that could have given rise to the Oklahoma bombing.

Yet, many observers of a fast-growing antigovernment movement presented a clear and present danger to specific federal targets, as well as to U.S. society itself. The most vocal of the lot were the advocacy organizations that monitor hate and extremism. The Anti-Defamation League (ADL), for example, which has been tracking the activities of hate groups in the United States for nearly a century, documented back in the early 1980s the proliferation of paramilitary training camps run by racist groups in clandestine training centers across the country.[1] In October 1994, the ADL released a fact-finding report, *Armed and Dangerous: Militias Take Aim at the Federal Government*, alerting the public, as well as law enforcement, to the danger posed by militia activity in 13 states. Also that month, the Southern Poverty Law Center (SPLC), famous for its aggressive stance against extremist groups, announced that it was forming a Militia Task Force to monitor systematically any developments in the antigovernment militia movement. Then on November 1, 1994, Morris Dees, the founder of SPLC, sent a letter to U.S. Attorney General Janet Reno, warning her about the potential for violence by heavily armed militias that harbored right-wing extremist views.

On April 10, 1995, just 9 days before the bombing of the Murrah Federal Building, Kenneth Stern (1995), of the American Jewish Committee, issued a report that warned of the impending danger of militia violence. In the preface to *Militias: A Growing Danger*, Stern states that he is issuing his background report on the militia movement now, in early April 1995, with a sense of urgency.[2] Stern, like the ADL, the SPLC, and a host of other human rights groups, knew of the symbolic significance of April 19. The date, which marks the anniversary of the Battle of Lexington in 1775, is favored by "false" patriots—who profess a commonality with the patriots of the revolutionary war era—as a day to oppose the tyranny of the federal government. In fact, the Militia of Montana (called "MOM"), formed by white supremacist and anti-Semite John Trochmann in February 1994, devoted its 1995 newsletter, *Taking Aim,* to the importance of the date to the Patriot movement, as well as to the upcoming April 19 execution of Richard Wayne Snell, a white supremacist who murdered a black Arkansas state trooper during a routine traffic stop. Trochmann instructed his readers not to forget that it was also April 19 when the federal government ended its 51-day siege of the Branch Davidian compound in Waco, Texas, leaving more than 80 dead, including 21 children.

Before Waco, however, came Ruby Ridge. As an episode in antigovernment paranoia, the 1992 shoot-out and siege, which began on April 19, of white separatist Randall Weaver ranks second only to the inferno of the Branch Davidians in the following year. Federal agents rallying in body armor and black ninja uniforms, armored cars rumbling up hillsides, even fabled black helicopters rotoring overhead—Ruby Ridge had all the elements of a paranoid fantasy, with the difference that it really happened. In the 10-day standoff, Weaver's wife, Vicki, was shot dead as she held her daughter Elisheba, age 11 months, in her arms. A day earlier, Weaver's 85-pound son, 14-year-old Sammy, and U.S. Marshall William Degan had been killed. Eventually, Weaver was talked off the mountain by Green Beret Vietnam War veteran and right-wing celebrity Colonel James "Bo" Gritz and Jack McLamb, a retired Phoenix, Arizona, police officer with ties to antigovernment extremists.[3]

With Waco, agents of the Bureau of Alcohol, Tobacco, and Firearms (ATF) mounted the biggest raid in their bureau's history to seize what they believed was a cache of illegal weapons at the Davidian compound, named Mount Carmel. Lax bureau security allowed David Koresh and his followers to be forewarned of the impending raid. In a subsequent shoot-out, four ATF agents and six Davidians were killed. The Clinton administration then ordered the FBI's elite Hostage Rescue Team to replace the ATF, setting up a tense, 51-day standoff with armed cult members in the compound. On April 19, the FBI moved in with tanks to force the cultists to give up. After three attempts to inject tear gas into the buildings, a ferocious fire burned Mount Carmel to the ground.

The government's handling of Waco and Ruby Ridge, as well as the passage of the Brady Bill (handgun control) and the assault weapons ban, convinced antigovernment extremists that they needed to defend themselves against an overly aggressive federal government. Some formed militias and began to train actively for violence against the federal government.[4] Others, like Linda Thompson, an Indianapolis-based attorney and militia advocate, became obsessed with getting the so-called truth out about America. She produced two videotapes—*Waco: The Big Lie* and *Waco II: The Big Lie Continues*—that charged the 1993 raid on the Davidian compound was a calculated plan by the federal government to murder David Koresh and his followers. McVeigh and cohort Terry Lynn Nichols and unnamed others, with revenge in their hearts, went on the offensive and took matters into their own hands.

What beliefs do these antigovernment extremists share that make them so full of hate, fear, and revenge that only murder on a grand scale could satisfy? Who are these people? Before identifying them or explaining their beliefs and practices, it is important to mention that extremism is not necessarily terrorism. The Constitution grants citizens the right to maintain and foster unpopular political beliefs. For many people, this right was reaffirmed in 1988 when a jury in Fort Smith, Arkansas, ruled in the trial of white supremacists indicted for sedition that their extremist pronouncements were rhetorical and not necessarily a call for a holy war.

CHRISTIAN IDENTITY: THE BELIEF THAT BINDS

Christian Identity—used interchangeably with *Identity, Kingdom Identity*, and *Christian Israel*—provides the spiritual link that ties together today's antigovernment extremist groups in the United States. Introduced by the Englishman Richard Brothers, the Identity movement has its origins in "Anglo-Israelism," an oddity of mid-Victorian England that held that the people of Great Britain were the true descendants of the 10 lost tribes of Israel. White Anglo-Saxons, not Jews, are the true Israel in which biblical promises to the "chosen people" are to be fulfilled. Some Identity adherents even believe that the word *British* really means "man of the covenant" from the Hebrew *beritish,* further demonstrating Christ's Aryan ancestry.

The Identity movement was brought to the United States by the unabashedly anti-Semitic Gerald L. K. Smith, publisher of the anti-Semitic periodical *The Cross and the Flag* and Henry Ford's diatribe on the international Jewish conspiracy, *The International Jew.* The latter was an outgrowth of a series of articles that first appeared in a Ford Motor Company periodical, *The Dearborn Independent.*[5] Smith inherited his venomous anti-Semitic beliefs from membership in the U.S. analogue to the Sturmabteilung, or Brownshirts of Adolf Hitler, the Silver Legion (or more commonly, the "Silver Shirts").[6]

Smith's good friend, the Methodist minister Wesley Swift, popularized Identity theology during the 1940s and 1950s. It teaches that, for Christ to return and set up his kingdom, God's law on the earth must first be established through an apocalyptic battle between the forces of good and evil, Armageddon. It declares the United States to be the New Jerusalem and holds that the Articles of Confederation, the original Constitution, and the Bill of Rights are valid, God-given law. For Identity believers, only white Christian men are true sovereign citizens. Blacks and other people of color are the "beasts of the field" or "mud people" on the same spiritual level as soulless animals. They are not true citizens, but "Fourteenth Amendment citizens," the creation of an illegitimate federal government. In other words, because the Fourteenth Amendment grants citizenship to all persons born or naturalized in the United States, including blacks, Identity believers view anyone winning citizenship through the amendment as a citizen of the state, not as a true citizen. Also in keeping with Anglo-Israelism, the Jews are portrayed as the spawn of Satan, the descendants of an unholy union between Eve and the serpent, and the killers of Christ.

By the time of his death in 1970, Swift managed to attract a sizable following to his congregation of Identity followers in Lancaster, California. In 1973, Silver Shirt alumnus Richard Grint Butler—who was introduced to Swift by Pastor William Potter Gale, a retired U.S. Army colonel, of another Identity church located in California and the organizer of the paramilitary group called the California Rangers—moved Swift's church to its current location in Hayden Lake, Idaho. Once in Hayden Lake, Butler constructed the Church of Jesus Christ Christian as the direct successor to Swift's church, which Butler had attended. Shortly thereafter, Butler formed the paramilitary hate group Aryan Nations around his Identity church.

In his church, Butler continued to preach that the Aryan race was the "chosen seed" of Israel and that the Jews conspired to eradicate "God's chosen people." Anyone, according to Butler, who dares to marry a Jew will be put to death. Using violence against Jews is appropriate, reasons Butler, because in his mind they are, by definition, Antichrists.

In the early 1980s, Butler was also active in the Aryan Nations prison ministry, corresponding regularly with prison inmates through the newsletter *Calling Our Nations*. Butler hoped that his anti-Semitic and racist literature would find converts in newly released inmates. In any event, it was used expeditiously by the Aryan Brotherhood, a substantial prison gang with particular presence in the West and Southwest, to recruit adherents for its racist agenda. Today, the Aryan Brotherhood gang of racist thugs faces off Black Muslim and Hispanic gangs with its own racist agendas in jails and prisons across the country. Who said that one can judge society by its prisons? Or is it that a society is a microcosm of its prisons and vice versa?

In 1987, Butler's Aryan Nations began to provide administrative and financial support for another prison outreach newsletter, *The Way*. The editor of this newsletter was a prisoner, David Lane, who was also affiliated with the Order. The latter, one of the most violent and notorious domestic terrorist groups of the early 1980s, was responsible for armed robberies, murders, and counterfeiting operations. The Order's earliest counterfeiting operations were reportedly carried out in the print shop of the Aryan Nations. In February 1987, Aryan Nations members Edward and Olive Hawley were sentenced to 4 years in prison and 4 years' probation, respectively. The chief of security for the Aryan Nations, David Dorr, was sentenced to 6 years for his role in the counterfeiting scheme.

Again in 1987, Edward Hawley and David Dorr were in court, this time pleading not guilty to charges that they were involved in a series of bombings in Coeur d'Alene, Idaho, in the fall of the previous year. In a hearing in September 1987, former Order member and government witness Robert Pires pleaded guilty to the bombings. In April 1997, Butler was indicted along with several others on charges of seditious conspiracy. Shortly thereafter, Butler underwent heart bypass surgery. On April 7, 1988, Butler and the other defendants were acquitted of all charges.

In the years following Butler's acquittal in Fort Smith, Arkansas, the Aryan Nations was besieged by arrests for bomb conspiracies, infiltrated by an FBI informant, and faced with the loss of key members over internal squabbles with Butler. Butler's leadership problems became even more evident at the July 1995 Aryan Nations World Congress in Hayden Lake when Butler drew a noticeably small crowd at his annual speech. Later that year, Butler's wife, Betty, died of cancer, further compounding his frail health. Nevertheless, Butler's "World Congress," held annually in Hayden Lake to coincide with the anniversary of Hitler's birthday, April 20, continues to be a forum, as well as a training ground, for U.S. right-wing extremists. In recent years, World Congresses have attracted significant numbers of skinheads to network with older, more articulate race haters and baiters. Butler never disguised reaching out to these bigoted youngsters as a way to replenish attrition in his ranks and to create support for his leadership. Nevertheless, Butler's leadership remains in doubt, as well as who will replace him as head of the Aryan Nations.

For Richard Grint Butler, like a goodly number of other apocalyptic Identity preachers, the battle between the forces of good—the white Israelites—and evil—the armies of Satan, represented by the Jewish-controlled federal government—is inevitable. These preachers counsel their followers that the efforts to combat the Jewish domination of the U.S. government pleases God. Butler, however, ever since his bout with sedition in 1987, has toned down his references to being at "war" with the federal government. Nevertheless, Identity followers and other right-wing, antigovernment extremists refer to the U.S. government as the Zionist occupation government (ZOG) and await Armageddon.

In preparation for the "final battle," some Identity followers have retreated into heavily armed and fortified compounds such as Elohim City, located on a 400-acre tract of land along the Oklahoma-Arkansas border in Adair County, Oklahoma. Elohim City was founded in 1973 by Robert G. Millar, a U.S. resident alien from Canada with ties to the Covenant, the Sword and the Arm of the Lord (CSA), a paramilitary survivalist group that operated an Identity settlement, "Zarephaph-Horeb" after the biblical purging place, near the Arkansas-Missouri border. About 100 residents make Elohim City their home. These Identity followers wholeheartedly believe that a messiah will soon be resurrected from the dead to lead a white revolution against ZOG.[7]

Others, like the prominent Identity leader "Pastor" Peter J. "Pete"

Peters, run active Identity churches. Peters, whose hairstyle and mustache are reminiscent of Hitler's, has modeled his Church of Christ, in La Porte, Colorado, on the militant Identity beliefs of the late Arizona-based anti-Semite preacher Sheldon Emry. Peters and his followers reached national attention in 1985 when it was reported that several members of a terrorist group had attended his church during the height of the Order's terrorist activities. Peters is a popular speaker on the "hate-speech" circuit, and his invectives against Jews and other minorities can be read in his newsletter *Scriptures for America* or heard on his radio and television broadcasts. He also conducts an annual Rocky Mountain Bible Retreat featuring Identity speakers. Additionally, Peters convened an October 1992 meeting in Estes Park, Colorado, to protest the government's siege of the Weaver family cabin and to condemn the killings of Vicki Weaver and her son Samuel by federal agents. The more than 150 attendees included Aryan Nations leader Richard Butler, Aryan Nations "Ambassador at Large" Louis Beam, and Kirk Lyons, an attorney with ties to both Butler and Beam.

James K. Warner is yet another long-time anti-Jewish propagandist whose Identity activities help spread a message of hate and extremism. Warner's New Christian Crusade Church, in Metairie, Louisiana, publishes the anti-Jewish and racist monthly tabloid *Christian Vanguard.* Warner also runs the Christian Defense League (CDL), of Arabi, Louisiana, whose stated mission is to organize the white Christian majority to force the Antichrist from churches and to remove Antichrist Jews from any political positions they may hold. Through its publication *The CDL Report,* the CDL is dedicated to exposing ZOG.

Whether Identity followers come together in armed communities, seek support through the activities of Identity churches, or pursue their apocalyptic beliefs separately, they remain the significant binding force behind today's antigovernment movement. Their ranks have slowly increased since Anglo-Israelism was introduced to the United States by Smith in the mid-1940s. In recent years, they have made successful alliances with other extreme right religious followers, such as the Christian Reconstructionists, as well as converts among militia members, Klan members, Freemen, skinheads, survivalists, Populists, gun enthusiasts, militant antiabortionists, secessionists, tax protesters, neo-Nazis, millennialists, white supremacists, home schoolers, and common law court adherents. Identity group watchers, such as the ADL and the SPLC, put their current numbers at around 35,000. Friends, sympathizers, and allies swell the number to thousands more.

THEORY INTO PRACTICE: POSSE COMITATUS

Whereas the Identity movement established a spiritual link for a variety of antigovernment extremist groups by its distorted interpretation of the Bible and its scapegoating of blacks, Jews, gays, and other minorities, the Posse Comitatus movement was the first to link Identity teachings with practice. The Posse Comitatus movement was founded by Henry Lamont Beach while living in Portland, Oregon, in 1969. Beach, once active in the Silver Legion, developed many of his ideas in his infamous "Blue Book" that became the foundation for the contemporary antigovernment ideas, including common law courts. But credit for inspiring the original concept of the Posse movement really belongs to Pastor William Potter Gale, an early leader in the Identity movement.

Posse Comitatus, or "power to the county," is a Latin term that dates back to medieval England, where the local sheriff enlisted residents to enforce laws against criminals and critics of the crown. In the United States, posses were used by sheriffs in the Old West to apprehend criminals. Because Posse Comitatus members believe that the federal government is controlled by "enemies," which usually means the Jews, they reject the U.S. monetary system, the federal reserve system, the income tax, all amendments except the Bill of Rights, as well as state and federal authority over local control. Posse members believe, for example, that the Federal Reserve Bank is a creation of the "international Jewish banking conspiracy" that seeks to bankrupt and enslave the United States. Because the Sixteenth Amendment was never ratified, the Internal Revenue Service is illegal and has no authority to collect taxes, a belief widely held outside the Posse movement as well. Posse members recognize the county sheriff as the highest officer of the law under their interpretation of the U.S. Constitution; hence, they are often referred to as Sheriff's Posse Comitatus.

During the 1970s and 1980s, membership in the Posse's decentralized semiautonomous units spread quickly throughout 13 states, particularly in the Midwest, plains states, and West. But during the farm crisis of the 1980s, argue Devin Burghart and Robert Crawford in their *Guns and Gavels* (1996), the Posse achieved its greatest successes. With the demise of more than a quarter of the owner-operated family farms throughout the Midwest, Posse leaders offered phony loan schemes, bigoted conspiracy theories, and when all else failed, armed confrontation as a solution to the family-farm problem. Posse members in the early 1980s engaged in a variety of illegal activities, such as counterfeiting and arms dealing. In 1983, for instance, three members of the Colorado Posse were convicted of manufacturing explosives. Posse members also began an active campaign of issuing threatening edicts against government officials. Such was the case when a man identifying himself as a Posse member threatened to bomb a Kansas school unless both the sheriff and the undersheriff turned themselves over for execution. And more than 100 county sheriffs in Kansas received letters demanding the arrest of judges for ordering seizures of private property.

Also in the mid-1980s, the Posse formed autonomous sovereign communities throughout the Midwest and West, such as the Township of Good Faith in southeastern Washington. The most notorious, however, was a tract of land, donated by Donald Minniecheske, near the Embarrass River in Wisconsin known as "Tigerton Dells." James P. Wickstrom, an associate of Gale and Richard Butler and the Identity pastor of the Life Science Church in Wisconsin, declared himself the municipal judge of the newly created "common law township." Wickstrom's Constitution Township of Tigerton Dells, like the Township of Good Faith in Walla Walla County, then began to elect its own public officials, from foreign ambassadors to judges, and to flood the local courts, notwithstanding it own courts, with harassment suits.

Local residents in nearby Tigerton complained of having to awake to the rattle of gunfire from camouflage-wearing men who were darting from tree to tree. The 600-acre encampment—with a sign that read "Federal Agents Keep Out. Survivors will be prosecuted."—was a paramilitary base for Posse adherents. In 1985, law enforcement authorities, after surveying the encampment with light aircraft, swept down and confiscated property and removed trailers that violated local zoning laws. Wickstrom, who served 13 months during 1984 and 1985 for impersonating a public official, was sentenced in 1990 to 38 months in prison for conspiracy to counterfeit money and to pass bad checks to fund an underground guerrilla army. The empty Posse paramilitary encampment in Tigerton Dells stands in testimony to events in the Republic of Texas and to the experience of the Montana Freemen in "Justice Township" that occurred more than a decade later. The Posse movement set the stage.

Another of Gale's somewhat dubious accomplishments, in addition to his friendship with Wickstrom, was his tenacious sponsorship of paramilitary training camps and guerrilla warfare training for Posse members expecting a war with the government. His book on guerrilla warfare, *The Road Back*, outlined a strategy for sabotage because a militarily superior enemy will win any effort at direct confrontation. Gale calls for acts of sabotage that will destroy the enemy's greatest weapon: apathy. Once the people of the United States see that acts of sabotage snowball into victories, they will create the means to encourage more people to take up the fight against the government.

Gale was convicted in 1987 for plotting to kill a Nevada state judge and IRS officials. In January 1988, Gale and four other members of the Committee of the States, a now defunct right-wing extremist protest group formed by Gale, were sentenced to a year and a day in jail for their threats. The legacy of Gale's Committee of States lives on, however, in common law court movements of the 1990s. The Committee of States "Compact," which was drawn up on July 4, 1984, and signed by, among others, Richard Butler of Aryan Nations fame, declared that, under the Articles of Confederation, it was taking over as the governing body of the United States. This declaration paved the way for others in the organization, such as Arthur Stigall, another signer of the compact, to articulate how the new government was to operate. In fact, Stigall's guide to establishing a common law grand jury appears in one form or another in the common law courts of today.

In April 1988, at age 71, William Potter Gale, retired U.S. Army colonel and Identity adherent, died peacefully in jail. Yet, his hateful legacy grows every time someone files a bogus lien in a common law court. His memory lives on, too, whenever some new militia member picks up Gale's guerrilla warfare manual, which was reissued in 1994 by Robert Plummer, formerly with the Florida State Militia.

Another Posse member who achieved national notoriety was the World War II tail gunner and father of six, Gordon Wendall Kahl. Back in 1974, Kahl, a member of the Identity-affiliated Gospel Doctrine Church of Jesus Christ in Texas and active Posse Comitatus adherent, refused to pay his federal income tax and to renew his driver's license. Many Posse members refuse to obtain driver's licenses because obtaining them would acknowledge the legitimacy of the government. In fact, many Posse members, as well as common law court adherents such as the Freemen, try to revoke all contracts with government, including driver's licenses and automobile registrations, thereby gaining "quiet title," a common law procedure that supposedly frees a person from state and federal jurisdiction and regulations.[8] In any event, Kahl was subsequently arrested and convicted of income tax evasion 1977. After serving time and then being released with a 5-year commitment to probation, Kahl returned home to North Dakota but failed to report to his probation officer, just as he ignored paying taxes.

On the evening of February 13, 1983, the 63-year-old Kahl drove north on Route 30 in Medina, North Dakota, after a meeting at Dr. Clarence Martin's clinic, where a dozen or so locals had met to discuss what was wrong with their country. Also with Kahl were his son Yorie, 23, and his friend Scott Faul, 29. Although the authorities had ignored him for a while for his probation violation, they were determined this evening to enforce the law. Atop a small hill, Kahl came upon a roadblock. Kahl, his son, and the friend leaped out of the car, their guns drawn. The silence of the tense Western-style standoff that ensued was soon shattered when someone fired. Yorie Kahl was the first to fall. Kahl immediately opened fire, killing U.S. Marshall Robert Cheshire, with his Ruger mini-14 rifle. Within minutes, Kahl killed another law officer, Kenneth Muir, and wounded two others. As Kahl calmly walked over to gather up his son to take him for medical treatment, someone allegedly asked him, "Was it worth it?" Kahl reportedly responded, "To me it was." Kahl then drove his wounded son back to Martin's clinic, where the doctor was already tending a wounded deputy. For the next 4 months, Kahl was hidden by Identity adherents and others such as former Posse leader Leonard Ginter, who later served a 5-year sentence for harboring Kahl. While hiding from the authorities, Kahl wrote that the United States is a conquered country and occupied by the Jews.

Several months after the incident in Medina, Kahl was killed in a firefight with state and federal law officers in rural northern Arkansas. The firepower used by the authorities left Kahl's body charred almost beyond recognition and the Arkansas house in cinders. Kahl's fiery death in the Ozarks ended a 6-year struggle that had been foreshadowed in his 1977 trial, when he proudly wore a hangman's noose button in his lapel, the symbol of the Posse movement, to the courtroom. Almost immediately after his death, Kahl became a folk hero and martyr for both the antigovernment and Posse movements.

Over the years, the Posse Comitatus movement has brought together under its ideology neo-Nazis, Klan members, and other anti-Semites. Among the most ardent Posse supporters were ex-neo-Nazi and Klan member David Duke of Louisiana; the Western Front of Los Angeles, run by collaborators of the late anti-Semite Gerald L. K. Smith; and Council of the Committee to Restore the Constitution (CRC) founder Archibald "Arch" E. Roberts, a retired U.S. Army lieutenant colonel , who was one of the most energetic proponents of the extreme right. Elements of the Posse's virulent ideology, most notably its unwavering hatred of the federal government, are echoed by today's antigovernment extremists. And the how-tos of Henry Beach's Blue Book provide the syllabus for the United Sovereigns of America in Del City, Oklahoma, the leading national proponent of common law courts, linked with court efforts in at least 13 states.

THE GURU OF THE EXTREME RIGHT: WILLIAM PIERCE

Significant numbers of antigovernment extremists are drawn to the hateful teachings of the Identity movement and the extreme practices of Posse Comitatus. Although some groups may not have adhered to all the precepts of these extremist movements, the antigovernment extremists of today have become known to each other through the efforts of an outspoken, notwithstanding articulate, Identity adherent, William Pierce.

Pierce, a native of Atlanta, Georgia, received a doctorate in physics from the University of Colorado in 1962 and immediately joined the faculty of Oregon State University (OSU) as an assistant professor of physics. At OSU, Pierce joined the John Birch Society. In 1965, he left OSU to take a job in private industry as a laboratory researcher. This career change was short-lived because, in 1966, he linked up with the American Nazi Party in Arlington, Virginia, founded and led by the notorious bigot George Lincoln Rockwell.

After Rockwell's assassination in 1967, Pierce became a leader in the American Nazi Party, subsequently renamed the National Socialist White People's Party (NSWPP). He later left the NSWPP to become affiliated with the National Youth Alliance, a group spouting Nazi rhetoric and later renamed the National Alliance. Today, Pierce runs the National Alliance out of his Cosmotheist Church in Hillsboro, West Virginia, which he no doubt expanded with the membership lists he obtained from Rockwell's organization.

In addition to his work with the National Alliance, Pierce publishes a bimonthly magazine, the *National Vanguard* (formerly called *Attack!*), and an internal party periodical, *National Alliance Bulletin* (formerly titled *Action*), as well as hosts a radio show, *American Dissident Voices*. Pierce is most well known, however, as the author (under the pseudonym Andrew Macdonald) of *The Turner Diaries* (1978). The book chronicles in shockingly graphic detail the violent overthrow of the federal government by a group of white revolutionaries. *Diaries* is looked upon as a "bible" by many white supremacists espousing violent antigovernment sentiments.

A decade later, Pierce, again under the same pen name of Andrew Macdonald, publishes *Hunter* (1989) as a sequel to *The Turner Diaries*. *Hunter* tells the story of a drive-by killer who assassinates interracial couples and Jews in order to save white America. Pierce dedicates the book to Joseph Paul Franklin, the convicted killer of at least two black men. Both books are favorites of the extremist community. They are made available through various antigovernment mail-order distributors and have sold upwards of 250,000 copies, according to sources near Pierce.

Pierce also has a hand in the production of a series of racist comic books aimed at white teenagers. In *New World Order Comix No. 1*, subtitled *The Saga of White Will*, Will confronts blacks and Jews at his school. Will's father tells him that minorities want whites to become *wiggers*, or white niggers, devoid of white pride and a sense of identity. These insidious writings are made available to various extremist organizations to help with their recruitment activities. Needless to say, they are favorites with white supremacists of all ages.

At a September 1983 National Alliance convention in Arlington, Virginia, Robert Jay Mathews, the fair-haired boy of Pierce and leading contender for the leadership role in the Christian Identity movement, informed the crowd of the need to prepare for the impending race war—the so-called "War in '84." Shortly thereafter, Mathews took a page from *The Turner Diaries* and formed a white supremacist underground movement. In a ritualistic ceremony, inductees into the Order—which was also the name of the white supremacist resistance movement in Pierce's novel—are sworn to combat the "evil, Jewish anti-Christ's" who seek to eradicate the "true seed of Christ."

After a Seattle bank robbery in 1983, Mathews told an acquaintance that he was the robber and that the American Nazi revolution depicted in *The Turner Diaries* had now begun. In April 1984, Mathews sent word through a former Klan leader that he wanted to meet with Frazier Glenn Miller, the leader of Carolina Knights of the Ku Klux Klan (later renamed the White Patriot Party), to contribute to the good work of his organization. Although the meeting never took place, the Order members went to North Carolina to deliver $1,000. Then, in July 1984, the Order netted $3.8 million in the robbery of an armored truck in Ukiah, California. Within a week of the robbery, Mathews began sharing the money with other extremist leaders, reportedly giving $300,000 to the charismatic Miller.

Mathews was on a roll until two events spelled the end for him and his Order. The first event occurred when the gun used in the Ukiah robbery was traced to an Order member. The second event was the arrest of an Order member and active National Alliance member who decided to turn informant. Working with the FBI, the informant arranged a meeting with Mathews in Portland, Oregon, in late November 1984. When FBI agents raided the motel where the men were meeting, Mathews escaped but was wounded in the process. Seeking refuge in a series of safe houses throughout Washington state, Mathews wound up on Whidbey Island, a small island in Puget Sound, Washington. On December 8, 1984, Mathews died in a firestorm as a result of a shoot-out with FBI agents on the island. Soon thereafter, other Order leaders were convicted and sentenced to long prison terms for their crimes, which included counterfeiting, armored car and bank robberies, and murder.[9]

After Mathews was killed on Whidbey Island, Miller, armed with a war chest provided by Mathews, took over where the Order left off. He obtained the services of military personnel to assist with the paramilitary training of his renamed White Patriot Party (WPP). This alarmed Morris Dees, the outspoken critic of the extreme right and the chief trial counsel of the Southern Poverty Law Center (SPLC) in Montgomery, Alabama. Dees filled a lawsuit demanding an investigation of the military's links with WPP paramilitary training. After a federal judge issued a court order enjoining Miller from conducting paramilitary training, Miller wanted Dees dead. Shortly after Dees's intervention, Miller and his cohorts were in and out of court while they bungled robberies and tried to get the "revolution" off the ground. By the end of the 1980s, Miller pled guilty to possessing illegal hand grenades and to having mailed a declaration of war and death threats against Morris Dees. A part of the plea agreement, Miller agreed to testify in an ongoing federal trial in Fort Smith, Arkansas, involving white supremacists charged with sedition. The WPP disbanded soon thereafter, with some members joining another white supremacy group in Maryland, the National Democratic Front.

The disbanding of the WPP and the fiery death of the real-life Aryan warrior Mathews did not diminish Pierce's enthusiasm for the cause. His publication *National Vanguard* praised the Order for having "set its sights on a full-scale, armed revolution, ending with the purification of the U.S. population and the institution of a race-based authoritarian government." Pierce's editorial asked, "How will the Jews cope with the man who does not fear them and is willing, even glad, to give his life in order to hurt them? What will they do when a hundred good men rise to take Robert Mathews' place?"

Nearly a decade later, on April 19, 1995, Pierce might have thought that his wish for "good men" rising up had come true. The destruction of the Murrah Federal Building in Oklahoma City with a 2-ton ammonium nitrate and fuel oil bomb at 9:02 in the morning took a page directly from *The Turner Diaries*. In the Pierce novel, which Timothy McVeigh sold at gun shows, a small underground cell of patriots uses a similar bomb to destroy FBI national headquarters at 9:15 in the morning to begin a race war. Those who knew McVeigh in the military tell of how he frequently carried Pierce's book around with him and mailed copies to friends to read. He was carrying it when he was picked up after the explosion. In fact, Pierce was so sure that his wish had come true that he was seen on national television a little more than a week after the blast, speculating that the blast would lead to more terrorism on a scale the world has never seen before.

TACTICAL TRAINING FOR ARMAGEDDON: LOUIS BEAM

Whereas William Pierce provided today's antigovernment extremists with their ideological underpinnings though his writings, Louis R. Beam gave today's antigovernment extremist the wherewithal for Armageddon. In 1968, Beam joined Robert Shelton's Alabama-based United Klans of America and later switched, in 1976, to David Duke's Texas Knights of the Ku Klux Klan, where he eventually became elevated to Grand Dragon.[10] Beam's chief responsibility in both Klan groups was to instruct members in the finer points of guerrilla warfare.

In 1981, Beam became "ambassador at large" for Butler's Aryan Nations in Hayden Lake, Idaho. While in his new post, he created a "point" system for the assassination of federal officials and minority members, as well as the first white supremacist computer bulletin board network–the "Aryan Nations Liberty Net." Participants in Beam's point system game vied for the title Aryan Warrior by amassing the most points that were based on the importance of the government official or minority member they would kill.

In April 1987, Beam, along with several other extremists, was indicted in Fort Smith, Arkansas, on charges involving conspiracy to overthrow the U.S. government. Before the indictment could be returned, however, Beam fled to Mexico and made the FBI's Ten Most Wanted list. A short time after, he was arrested and returned to stand trial. An all-white jury later acquitted him, along with his codefendants, on all charges, which included conspiracy to conduct firebombings, bank robberies, railroad sabotage, water supply poisonings, and assassinations.

At a spontaneous rally staged only moments after his 1988 acquittal, Beam proclaimed his victory over ZOG, stating, "to hell with the federal government." Shortly thereafter, he began publishing a journal, whose title, *The Seditionist*, was intended to poke fun at the government for its failure to convict him of sedition. In the journal, Beam announced that he was forming a new extremist movement, the New Right, that would ally itself with other races that have conducted successful campaigns of liberation against the Jews, as did Yasir Arafat and his Palestine Liberation Organization. To better ally the New Right, Beam totally embraced the tenets of Christian Identity, with all its rhetoric against Jews, blacks, gays, and other minorities.

In January 1992, the former Klansman, making his first public appearance since his acquittal, was the keynote speaker at a Klan rally appropriately held in the city where the hooded secret society was born—Pulaski, Tennessee. Hundreds of Klan members, neo-Nazis, skinheads, and other antigovernment extremists turned out to hear him. They were not disappointed. In classic Beam fashion, he railed against the federal government, telling his adoring audience to go take back America. He ended his incendiary speak by shouting the racist code words "white victory."

In February 1992, writing for *The Seditionist,* Beam called on "underground" groups to reconsider their leadership-based organizational structures in favor of nonorganizational "leaderless resistance." The latter term, Beam tells us, is being adapted from the concept of leaderless resistance first used by Colonel Ulius Louis Amoss in 1962. Amoss, a tireless opponent of communism, proposed that antigovernment militants break up into tiny "phantom cells" to instigate actions against the government without having to coordinate plans with a central leadership. In a pyramid-type organization, Beam says, an infiltrator can easily destroy anything beneath, or even above, the level of infiltration. Infiltration at the top surely guarantees the destruction of the organization. In a cell-type structure, however, all individuals and groups operate independently of each other without reporting to a central leader, as it is with a typical pyramid organization.

At first blush, Beam suggests, leaderless resistance appears to have no organization. But leaderless resistance through phantom cells or individual action requires that all participants know what they are doing and how to do it. In this way, it becomes the responsibility of the individuals to acquire the requisite skills through organs of information such as newspapers, leaflets, and computers. Orders will not be necessary as long as those committed to the cause either take their cues from those who preceded them or act when they think the time is ripe.

A well-implemented strategy of leaderless resistance leads to very small or even one-person cells of resistance. According to Beam, the smallness and rigor of the cell structure will weed out the weekend warriors and wanna-bes who want membership in a white supremacist organization without paying the price of commitment to the cause. The structure will also create an impossible situation for law enforcers in their ability to infiltrate a movement without a centralized hierarchy of leadership.

Later in 1992, Beam attended a meeting at Estes Park, Colorado, called by Pete Peters to discuss the government's handling of Ruby Ridge. After those present—including Butler of the Aryan Nations and 100,000-member Gun Owners of America (GOA) head Larry Pratt[11]— endorsed militias and tagged April 19 as "Militia Day," they endorsed Beam's call for leaderless resistance. Peters later republished Beam's call to terror in his report of the conference, and it became widely circulated throughout antigovernment circles.

Beam's call for leaderless resistance at the 3-day conference at Estes Park is at the forefront of the time line of events that will incite war with the federal government. This call, along with his rabble-rousing speeches at a Pulaski Klan rally and Aryan Nations World Congress in 1992 and 1995, respectively, moves him to the front of a short list of replacements for the ailing and beleaguered head of the Aryan Nations, Richard Butler.

CYBERSPACE: THE ANTIGOVERNMENT EXTREMIST'S ROAD TO HIGH-TECH COMMUNICATIONS

The Internet

Louis Beam's "Aryan Nations Liberty Net," which was first set up to advertise a point system for killing government officials and minorities, was also meant to allow proponents of the extreme right to communicate with each other through their computers. The idea was a bit ahead of its time, however. Actually, the technology was ready, but the extremists were not. Maintaining a computer network in the 1980s was technically difficult and much too expensive for the average extremist. Calling a private computer bulletin board often meant making expensive long-distance calls. The extremists themselves did not own enough computers to make the system work. The network quickly faded into obscurity.

The Internet, ironically a tool first designed by the federal government in the 1960s to secure a communications link in the event of nuclear attack, has made available to antigovernment extremists of today what Beam envisioned years ago. The "Net," as it is called by many, makes it easy and inexpensive to reach a large, widely separated audience with information that is almost instantly available to anyone at anytime. It is a worldwide network of computers with access to a rapidly growing audience of tens of millions. Open around the clock 365 days a year, it offers a wealth of information on demand. The information is available on *Net servers*, or computers that are both multitasking and multiuser. This means each computer can do many tasks while serving many users simultaneously. Users need not contend with busy signals, as they do with telephones, and it is impossible to miss a broadcast. Anyone on the network can get information from networked computers anywhere in the world at any time. All a user needs, besides the obvious computer, is a MOdulator-DEModulator (or *modem*), which allows a computer to communicate with other computers over telephone lines.

The Net is also *interactive*, which means user-controlled. Users can select what they want or need and ignore the rest. An information provider cannot dictate the pace and sequence of user viewing. It is relatively inexpensive to use, easy to learn, and is for the most part devoid of regulations.

The Net gives antigovernment extremists spread out across the country, often in isolated areas, a way of effectively communicating with each other. More important, however, they can sell their beliefs, spread their conspiracies, and recruit new members while keeping their anonymity. The technologically astute antigovernment extremists and their racist organizations are exploiting various aspects of the Net, especially, the Usenet.

The Usenet

The *Usenet* is a collection of public discussion lists (listservers), electronic bulletin board systems (BBSes), and news groups. *Listservers* make use of the Net's process known as *electronic mail* (or simply e-mail). E-mail allows the direct written communication between two people on the computer. The process is fast, inexpensive, and open to anyone having a modem. Usually, a moderator operates a "site" where members of the "list" send e-mail messages to one another. All subscribers to the list receive the e-mail message and can respond to it if they so desire. In news groups such as *misc.activism.militia* and *alt.revolution.american.second*, antigovernment extremists post messages to servers. With few limitations, anyone who has access to the news group can read the message, although software is now available to make it easier to protect communication between subscribers to a news group.

As of the late 1990s, a network of more than 250 antigovernment and related computer bulletin boards, as well as at least 50 Net news groups, were making use of the Net to spew their information and tactics through at least 40 states, Canada, and Europe. A substantial number of the same were run by neo-Nazis, skinheads, Identity adherents, and others of the same ilk.

The World Wide Web

The Net and the related Usenet require knowledge of several software programs in order to perform the most ordinary of tasks, such as sharing files or sending e-mail. Compatibility problems emerged because of the diversity of programs used to share information. Introduction of the World Wide Web (WWW), the newest and fastest growing of the Net technologies, solved this problem through the use of hypertext markup language (html). *Hypertext* is a system that allows different parts of a document stored in different computers to be brought up with the click of a mouse button. The user need not proceed sequentially. If, for example, this book were in hypertext, the user could go from this sentence to another part of the book if the book was designed to allow for such jumps between text segments. This ability of a user to choose his or her own path makes the Web interactive—that is, permits user choice. Additionally, the link between other computers is also simplified because the hypertext language can be read by all computers.

The Web was made even more user-friendly with the introduction of *browsers* that allow computers to interact with each other through a graphical interface. With popular browsers like Microsoft Explorer and Netscape, users are able to obtain pictures and text created by other users on their servers. Sound and video are also added to home pages. (A *home page* is a Web document that appears when a particular Net location is accessed.) Add to the equation the dramatic decrease in the cost of computers, increase in access onto the Net through companies such as America Online and Compuserve, and increase in modem speed, and activity on the Web has increased substantially. The 1990s have seen a veritable explosion in the number of home pages, with millions more pages projected by the end of the century.

Finding a home page on the Web is easy and even easier after the user "bookmarks" the page on her or his computer for future reference. Companies such as Yahoo and Alta Vista even offer *search engines* that serve as databases with the addresses of hundreds of thousands of home pages. These search engines allow the user to key in search words or phases that make searches broader or more precise. Typical searches last anywhere from a few seconds to about 1 minute. Clicking on one of the "links" provided by the search sends the user directly to the page in question. (In Web documents, *links* are usually underlined and appear in a different color.)

Once on the home page, the user is able to click on buttons, icons, and highlighted text to go to other areas of the site or to related sites. A typical extremist home page is replete with information about the group, as well as information about other sites espousing similar ideology. Performing this process, as well as the search process described above, the interested user "surfs the Web" for easily accessible extremist rhetoric.

So, what Beam imagined years ago when he set up his "Aryan Nations Liberty Net" is readily available to antigovernment extremists today. Identity believers, Christian Reconstructionists, militia members, Klan members, Freemen, skinheads, survivalists, Populists, gun enthusiasts, militant antiabortionists, secessionists, tax protesters, neo-Nazis, millennialists, white supremacists, home schoolers, and common law court adherents can all meet on the Net and share their thoughts quickly, cheaply—and in private. The latter is particularly disturbing to law enforcement authorities.

The clandestine groups that characterize the concept of leaderless resistance have a cyberspace version of the midnight ride of Paul Revere to pass the word along. Instantaneous communications can take place between extremists across the county or, for that matter, the world. Distance is not a problem, nor is the cost of communicating terrorist thoughts. Any extremist group's home page can be made quite attractive and official looking so as to compete with a version of the same information by a legitimate enterprise. More important, any group's home page looks just as valid as the next group's. Information on one site that is well researched and documented is read with the same intensity as an extremist's site with its extremist opinions and misinformation. Old news, so to speak, is integrated with current events. The medium makes it difficult for the novice to determine what is current and valid and what is not. For example, a Web surfer might come across sound sites that offer messages from dead extremists such as Robert Mathews, Gordon Kahl, and George Lincoln Rockwell. Forgeries or not, these sound bites are dramatic and help deliver the extremist rhetoric to often uninformed and impressionable individuals.

In 1981, Stephen Donald "Don" Black and nine other neo-Nazis and Klansmen in Slidell, Louisiana, were arrested and charged with plotting to invade the Caribbean island of Dominica and overthrow its government. While serving 3 years in federal prison from 1982 to 1985, Black learned to use computers. During the next decade, he became so proficient at their use that he was able to adapt the World Wide Web quickly to advance his own virulent racist views. In March 1995, Black went on-line with the first Web site to unite white supremacists. "Stormfront," the site Black runs from his West Palm Beach, Florida, home, is located at *http://www2.stormfront.org.*

Black's computerized hate service links the visitor with many white supremacist groups, such as William Pierce's National Alliance. Clicking on the National Alliance button transfers the visitor immediately to the Web page of this neo-Nazi organization, *http:\\www.natvan.com.* Once there, the visitor can click on any of a number of buttons to bring up information, for example, on the book or radio broadcasts of the National Alliance.

"Stormfront" also provides visitors with a plethora of literature, including Louis Beam's often-quoted "leaderless resistance," Pierce's racist writings, former Klansman David Duke's thoughts, and abstractions from assorted other extremists. In addition, "Stormfront" provides the e-mail addresses of Net mailing lists of white supremacist organizations. News groups of interest to white supremacists are listed as well. So, too, are the numbers for dial-in BBSes. Actually, "Stormfront" first started as a private electronic bulletin board with three users in 1990 and graduated to a publicly accessible one in 1994.

Although the traditional communications tools of antigovernment extremists—meetings, newsletters, book, magazines, videotapes, fax networks, shortwave radio, and the telephone—are still much used to spread their message, the Net, especially the World Wide Web, will continue to grow in importance to them. It gives access to an audience many times larger than Beam ever hoped for, providing a national, even global, platform for a movement that in the past had much more success organizing into local units than creating a national coalition.

ANTIGOVERNMENT EXTREMISTS IDENTIFIED

Antigovernment extremists come from all regions of the country and from all walks of life. Their ranks are made up of police officers, accountants, plumbers, teachers, auto mechanics, preachers, and carpenters. They also include Identity believers, Christian Reconstructionists, militia members, Klan members, Freemen, skinheads, survivalists, Populists, gun enthusiasts, militant antiabortionists, secessionists, tax protesters, neo-Nazis, millennialists, white supremacists, home schoolers, and common law court adherents, to name a few. All are somewhat different, but they nevertheless share a few characteristics. They are predominately white, usually Christian, and overwhelmingly male. Some are midwestern teenagers with skinhead affiliations; others are aging Identity preachers from the deep South. Most are "30-something" like the domestic terrorists of the mid-1980s. All, however, are united in their mistrust and hatred for the federal government and are dismayed by what they think the United States has become.

They express their dissatisfaction with U.S. society in a variety of ways. They might study the Constitution, read the Bible, school their children at home, amass weapons, practice survival skills, trade conspiracy theories at gun shows, and refuse to pay their taxes. They subscribe to a variety of mail-order catalogs that offer military equipment, and they use the Net to communicate with each other about how to make explosive devices or to extend the latest conspiracy theory. They read *Guns & Ammo* and *Soldier of Fortune* and write letters to the editor about black helicopters flying low over their property and jack-booted federal agents misusing their authority.

Many consider themselves ordinary citizens fed up with the federal government interfering in their everyday lives. They see the North American Free Trade Agreement (NAFTA) as interfering with their ability to earn livings. They believe that all the jobs that Americans once had are leaving the country. They are of the opinion that the Internal Revenue Service is without the mandate of the people and is illegally levying taxes. They are fed up with a federal government that is systematically taking away their right to bear arms. Their distorted interpretation of the Second Amendment tells them that the Brady Bill and the assault weapons ban are unconstitutional.

Many of these antigovernment extremists are filled with nostalgia for the early days of the Republic. They believe that the government immediately after the American Revolution was responsive to its citizens. The Constitution and the Bill of Rights were the concern of every government bureaucrat. Town meetings were called to air problems and to develop ways of dealing with them. Citizens, not the government, were involved in making decisions. They say that today's federal government has abandoned the ideas and practices our forebears had established. Some call these antigovernment extremists Patriots.

The antigovernment extremist movement makes a diversified group of disappointed individuals welcome. For failures, it offers a mission, as well as camaraderie with other fellow failures to band together with a new sense of mission. For survivalists and gun collectors, it offers the companionship of others who enjoy hunting, shooting, and plinking. On weekends, the rifle ranges at the local gun shops are replete with individuals, dressed in camouflage, shooting their weapons with a sense of pride reserved only for the obsessed.

For those who view themselves as victims of a particular injustice, the antigovernment movement is a warm place to garner sympathy. They sit around the campfire, so to speak, trading stories about how the civil rights movement and affirmative action legislation took away their jobs. They say that blacks and women now have their jobs. They believe that Jews and the federal government have engineered their current status in life. Knowing that others believe as they do adds to their resolve, especially so for those who are meek. The victimized can now act like the "hunter" in the Pierce novel of the same name.

A timid individual may first approach the antigovernment movement with caution, attending a public meeting on local land rights, for example, or browsing a survivalist expo, or monitoring a Net news group discussion on Second Amendment rights. As soon as the individual enters the movement, any grievances brought with him or her are quickly multiplied. The individual finds that thousands of others share the same concerns and discovers a whole litany of other, seemingly related, grievances that point to a much greater conspiracy than he or she had ever imagined.

Hungry for explanations and evidence, antigovernment neophytes subscribe to extremist publications, tune to shortwave radio broadcasts, or order videotapes and books from right-wing extremist catalogs. This misguided search for knowledge introduces them to even more complex and terrifying tales of the dangers Americans face at the hands of their own government. And when these conspiracies are explained to them by the venerable elders of a movement, they believe the authenticity. How can impressionable beginners dispute arcane interpretations of the Magna Carta, the Articles of Confederation, or the New Testament itself? They can't. And they soon find themselves mouthing some abstruse laws as if they were speaking in tongues.

Finding their fears justified, individuals caught up in the antigovernment extremist movement soon discover that only among others who are equally paranoid do they obtain comfort. The movement tells them that their paranoia is acceptable and a reasonable reaction to a federal government that has become repressive to its own people, usually white Christian males. The extremist movement becomes home to these individuals and provides an island of safety in a treacherous world. The infamous words of Louis Beam can be heard resonating in their ears: "We are viewed by the government as the same—enemies of the state. When they come for you, the federal government will not ask if you are a Baptist, Church of Christ, Christian Identity, Covenant believer, Klansman, or home schooler . . . you are enemies of the state."

THE NEW DOMESTIC TERRORIST

Today's domestic terrorist belongs not to a large group or even to a moderate-sized one, but to a movement that includes Identity believers, Christian Reconstructionists, militia members, Klan members, Freemen, skinheads, survivalists, Populists, gun enthusiasts, militant antiabortionists, secessionists, tax protesters, neo-Nazis, millennialists, white supremacists, home schoolers, common law court adherents, and other extremists. The popularity of structured groups like the Ku Klux Klan—whose membership once soared to more than five million members in the mid-1920s—is long over. In fact, Klan membership is at its lowest since it was first founded at the end of the Civil War. This decline promises to continue as Klan members either seek the comfort of smaller Klaverns or the confines of other groups that do not require the traditional garb associated with the robed-and-hooded society.

Today's domestic terrorists—with the exception of neo-Nazis and skinheads, with their distinct dress and physical appearances—dress in styles of the day. Even neo-Nazis and skinheads are shedding their identifying clothing, with an eye toward blending in to the rest of the population. In this way, they can nurture their hideous beliefs without their uniforms turning some people off before they have a chance to win the people over.

Today's domestic terrorists are bound together by a few beliefs that transcend the peculiarities of their individual needs and beliefs. The most obvious is their mistrust and hatred for the federal government. They all hold the federal government responsible for their positions in life. They hate what they think the United States of America has become.

Because an overwhelming number of these extremists are men who are Christian, they follow a religion that honors their plight. They revel in the words of Identity preachers who put them at the top of the food chain. They are given the right to persecute anyone—especially Jews, blacks, gays, and other minorities—who prescribed their station in life. Identity philosophy teaches that this is all right because Jews, blacks, gays, and other minorities are subhumans who need to be destroyed. Foolish as that may sound, antigovernment extremists have bought into Identity teachings in a big way. It is the belief that binds.

Expect a significant number of those in the antigovernment movement to act on their beliefs much in the same way as the international terrorists did who came here to destroy the World Trade Center. The bombing of the Murrah Federal Building in Oklahoma City says they already have. Expect more acts of domestic radical terrorism. Expect the freelancers to raise their ugly heads as well. Look for them to target federal buildings, abortion clinics, law enforcement officers, synagogues, gay establishments, and civil rights activists. Those with military experience who continue to train as weekend warriors in illegal paramilitary training camps throughout the United States are particularly dangerous. Their killing skills are as developed as those of any graduate of the Afghan terror academies.

The leaderless resistance they practice makes them just as difficult to track as their militant Islamic fundamentalist counterparts who hang together in loosely configured structures capable of chameleon-like changes. Domestic terrorists may even be in a better position to communicate between their phantom cells because of their ability to adapt to computer technology. The World Wide Web allows them to communicate secretly among themselves the call to holy war. Suffice it to say that domestic freelancers are as potent as any that arrive in the United States to undertake a jihad. Moreover, domestic terrorists have a greater advantage of blending in to the very fabric of American society. They are truly the evil within.

ENDNOTES

1. In 1886, the U.S. Supreme Court upheld the right of the states to ban unauthorized military organizing and paramilitary training (*Presser v. Illinois*, 1886). Today, more than 110 years later, in addition to a federal ban on paramilitary training, 41 states have laws banning private armies or paramilitary training.

2. In the preface to his report, Stern states that he is "issue[ing] this background report on the militia movement now, in early April, 1995, with a sense of urgency. While this movement is not a clear and present danger to American society, it is quickly spreading and has all the ingredients to lead to disaster. . . . Some people connected with this movement advocate killing government officials. They may attempt such an act."

3. In 1993, Weaver and family friend Kevin Harris went on trial for Degan's murder, among a host of other charges. But an Idaho jury acquitted both men of murder and conspiracy, and Weaver ultimately began serving 4 months in prison for missing his court appearance on the original weapons charge. The Weaver family then brought suit against the government for the wrongful deaths of Vicki and Sammy Weaver. In what many believed was an effort to dampen repercussions from the 1992 Idaho siege, the government, admitting no wrongdoing, agreed on August 15, 1995, to pay $3.1 million to Weaver and his three surviving children.

4. The SPLC (1996, p. 20) reports that the militia phenomenon grew most rapidly during 1994 and 1995. Its Militia Task Force reports that, by the end of 1995, 441 active militias were in all 50 states.

5. Henry Ford was introduced to the "Jewish conspiracy" after reading *The Protocols of the Learned Elders of Zion.* The *Protocols* is a forgery purported to be a document outlining the plans of an international Jewish group for world domination. Ford repudiated anti-Semitism in 1942 when he stopped publishing *The Dearborn Independent.* He also wrote an apologetic letter to the Anti-Defamation League in which he said he hoped that, after the war ended, so too would anti-Semitism and other hatreds of racial and religious groups.

6. William Dudley Pelley traveled throughout Russia, where he developed a

hatred for Jews after buying into the thesis set forth in T*he Protocols of the Learned Elders of Zion*. When Hitler came to power in Germany on January 30, 1933, Pelley was dumbfounded. The very next day, Pelley founded the Silver Legion to obtain political power and someday replace the U.S. government with a racist state based on the fundamentals of *Mein Kampf*. Silver Legion members wore caps identical to those of Hitler's storm troopers, blue corduroy trousers, leggings, ties, and silver shirts with a red *L* over the heart. By 1936, Pelley was a nationally known figure. Silver Shirts training units flourished throughout the United States. With no central headquarters, the Chief, as Pelley was called by his followers, ran the Legion from his Ford motorcar.

Pelley wanted to run for president in 1940, and he made it on the Washington State ballot thanks to a door-to-door campaign. Reportedly, the likes of Charles A. Lindbergh, Jr., and Walt Disney attended his public rallies. As the 1940 election neared, membership in the Silver Shirts grew to an estimated 100,000 nationwide. With the advent of World War II, Pelley was convicted of sedition and was sentenced to 15 years' confinement at a maximum security federal prison. The Silver Shirts were disbanded. Frail, yet maintaining a strong hatred for Jews, blacks, and other minorities, Pelley died on July 1, 1965, at the age of 75 in Noblesville, Indiana.

7. On the day of the Oklahoma City bombing, the *New York Times* reported that Reverend Millar visited Richard Wayne Snell, witnessed his execution, and arranged for Snell's body to be buried in Elohim City. Millar served as a spiritual advisor to Snell, a CSA member, who was sentenced to life in prison for the 1984 assassination of a black Arkansas state trooper and then sentenced to die in 1985 for the 1983 murder of a pawn shop owner in Texarkana, Arkansas, who he mistakenly thought was Jewish. Some say that Millar left Snell's casket open for a few days just in case his friend rose from the dead as the messiah that would lead white Israelites in battle.

8. Antigovernment extremists also subscribe to the Nullification Doctrine, a political concept that dates back to 1798. The doctrine incorrectly contends that states can void repugnant federal laws within their jurisdiction. Today's antigovernment extremists believe that this "right" of nullification extends beyond the states to individual "sovereign" citizens as well. For example, Norm Olson, former leader of the Michigan Militia, contends that "[n]o man-made law can abolish the citizen militia since such a law would be in fact an unlawful act designed to dissolve the power vested in the people" (1997, p. 13).

9. The most famous of these crimes was the assassination of the Jewish host of a radio talk show, Alan Berg. A longtime critic of the Aryan Nations and Tom Metzger's White Aryan Resistance, Alan Berg took Identity beliefs to task on his call-in radio program. On June 18, 1984, Bruce Carroll Pierce and two other members of the Order machine-gunned Berg to death outside his home in Denver, Colorado.

10. The Ku Klux Klan (KKK) was founded in 1865 in Pulaski, Tennessee, near the Alabama border, by six Confederate veterans, including General Nathan Bedford Forrest. From the beginning, it waged a violent campaign against newly freed black slaves and their supporters until it was officially disbanded in 1869. The robed-and-hooded order's second incarnation came in 1915, when it broadened its activity to include bigotry against Catholics, Jews, and newly arrived immigrants. By the mid-1920s, Klan membership soared to more than five million throughout the United

States. But after 1925, internal scandals led to a rapid decline in membership until the civil rights movement in 1960s. Today, the Klan continues to shrink, owing to intense internal factionalism and a tendency to divide into small splinter groups.

11. The GOA is the radical alternative of the broad-based National Rifle Association (NRA). Its leader, Larry Pratt, has mingled throughout the years with an assortment of militia members, common law court advocates, and white supremacists. Pratt's links with the racist antigovernment movement drew national attention when it became public that he was a cochairman of the presidential campaign of conservative talk show host Patrick Buchanan. In 1995, Pratt wrote the book *Safeguarding Liberty: The Constitution and Citizens Militia* in which he speculated that had the federal government feared a militia, it might not have massacred the Branch Davidians in Waco.

Chapter 4

THE TIMES THEY ARE A-CHANGIN'

ONCE UPON A TIME

In Chapter 1, I suggested that any definition of terrorism used to explain terrorism in America today should not exclude from it terrorist acts committed by individuals. The definition offered there does not: "Terrorism is the use of force (or violence) committed by individuals or groups against governments or civilian populations to create fear in order to bring about political (or social) change." Definitions that do not make room for the acts of individuals are wedded to a conception of terrorism fashioned from the actions of, for example, Palestinian terrorist groups of the late 1960s and 1970s, with their well-defined organizational structures.

Earlier definitions of terrorism that excluded individuals and focused instead on Soviet-trained groups withstood criticism because they readily explained any act of terrorism directed against the United States. As long as the behavior of these groups remained constant and their support structures remained intact, both scholars and law enforcement analysts alike understood their behavior and fashioned analyses and definitions to explain it to others.

With the subsequent breakup of the Soviet Union and the creation of support structures, such as the Iranian revolution and the Afghan experience, for militant Islamic fundamentalism came the decline of the tightly organized and centrally directed state-sponsored terrorists networks and the development of a new type of terrorist group. Today's terrorist groups are small, dispersed, and not as well organized as their graying secular counterparts of a bygone era. The best way to describe them is to liken their structures to the changing constellations in the night sky. Recall from Chapter 2 the leading European terrorist expert's excellent description, "You can snap a picture of the worldwide Islamic terrorist infrastructure, and shortly thereafter the entire

86

structure will appear radically different." The new, ephemeral type of terrorist structure vitiates the old model of terrorism used by scholars and law enforcement officials to judge the threat of terrorism to the United States.

Today, international terrorists likely to target the United States are individuals who may not consider themselves citizens of any particular country, but instead are sworn to common political, social, or personal objectives that transcend nation-state boundaries. The criminal or terrorist actions of these individuals, operating in loosely affiliated groups, dubbed international radical terrorism (IRT) by the FBI, pose a real threat to the United States. In fact, all the significant acts of terrorism committed on U.S. soil in recent years have been attributable either to terrorists committing IRT, such as the actors responsible for the World Trade Center bombing, or to the work of freelancers not tied to any particular group, such as Timothy McVeigh and Terry Nichols's bombing of the Murrah Federal Building; Mir Aimal Kasi's actions outside CIA headquarters; Rashid Baz's attack on religious students on the Brooklyn Bridge; Ali Hassan Abu Kamal's rampage on the observation deck of the Empire State Building; and Gazi Ibrahim Abu Maizer and Lafi Khalil's intended suicide bombing of the New York subway system.

Terrorist groups like Hamas, which receive aid from diverse sources such as rogue states like Iran and contributors inside the United States, have altered their behavior as well. Instead of keeping a tight lid on who commits their terrorist acts, these groups encourage others, members or otherwise, through their incendiary rhetoric to strike out against the same individuals and groups they themselves have targeted. In so doing, they have increasingly come to rely on the work of freelancers. Actually, this is the best way to operate because the hands of the terrorist organization remain clean while the terrorist act of the freelancer calls attention to its grievances. As long as the groups can keep law enforcement authorities, albeit public opinion, from their door, they can reap the benefits of being a "free rider" without expending their money and manpower.

TERRORIST GROUPS OF THE FUTURE

International terrorists–specifically, militant Islamic fundamentalists, who may not consider themselves citizens of any particular country, but instead are sworn to common political, social, or personal
objectives that transcend nation-state boundaries–pose a serious threat
to the United States. These terrorists, who commit acts of international radical terrorism, all share in a hatred for the United States, its
allies, and the nations it supports. First, they view the West, in general, and the United States, in particular, as an enemy of Islam. The
"they" is a diverse group of individuals made up of Muslims from all
regions of the world. Consider, for example, the makeup of those
involved in the World Trade Center bombing and the plot to blow up
other New York City landmarks. These Muslims came from Sudan,
Egypt, Jordan, and even Puerto Rico and the United States. The
youngest was a 22-year-old computer specialist from Jordan, Eyad
Ismoil, who drove the bomb-laden truck to the subterranean garage of
the World Trade Center; the oldest was a 55-year-old American black
hospital technician from Brooklyn, Clement Hampton-El, convicted
for seditious conspiracy, bombing conspiracy, and attempted bombing
of New York City landmarks. Representing a variety of ethnic back-
grounds, occupations, and ages, militant Islamic fundamentalists come
from a myriad of countries, including those just mentioned and others
such as Afghanistan, Algeria, Iran, Pakistan, Libya, Syria, and Tunisia,
to name a few.

Central to the view of all militant Islamic fundamentalists is that
the Islamic body of law known as *Sharia* is the immutable source of
law concerning family life, the law, money, worship, hygiene, diet, and
dress. Militant Islamic fundamentalists also believe that Islam is
inspired by God and so is superior to Western governments. With its
separation of church and state, the West, particularly the United States,
is seen as the enemy because its ways are counter to the true spirit of
Islam. Islamic terrorists in the habit of blowing up buildings find support for their terrorist actions within interpretations of the *sunna* (the
example and teaching as expressed in the deeds and words of Prophet
Muhammad) and recorded in the *hadiths* (the sayings of Prophet
Muhammad). All Muslims, fundamentalist or otherwise, accept the
authority of these hadiths in principle, but not all Muslims accept the
same hadith as authentic. Count on the militant Islamic fundamental-

ists to seek the truth of their internal reality in the tenets of the words and sayings of the prophet that support their position.

Second, these militant Islamic fundamentalists are vehemently opposed to U.S. support for Israel. Revisit the chilling words of Ramzi Yousef, the mastermind of the World Trade Center bombing, after being sentenced to life plus 240 years by Judge Kevin Duffy:

> This case is not about so-called terrorists who planted a bomb for no reason but just to kill innocent people for the fun of it. What this case is about is about the outcome of terrorism. . . . You have been supporting Israel throughout all the years in killing and torturing peoples, innocent peoples. . . . You enjoy seeking people having war together. You enjoy sucking blood and shedding blood . . . you are the first one who introduced this type of terrorism to the history of mankind when you dropped an atomic bomb. . . . And since this is the way you invented . . . [i]t was necessary to use the same means against you because this is the only language you understand. ("Strong Language," 1998, p. A3)

U.S. support for Saudi Arabia and Egypt has also angered militant Islamic fundamentalists fighting to liberate these two rather different societies. In Saudi Arabia, fundamentalists have been accused of deadly bombings, such as those in Riyadh and Dihahran, against U.S. service personnel stationed in the desert kingdom. America's strong support for the Hosni Mubarak regime in Egypt is also not without its detractors, particularly the followers of Sheik Omar Abdel Rahman. The blind cleric and his associates have a long history of trying to topple the secular government of Egypt. Egyptian fundamentalists over the years have assassinated President Anwar Sadat, persecuted Coptic Christians, and murdered foreign tourists visiting the antiquities in Luxor. These same terrorists have threatened on more than one occasion to unleash their wrath if the United States did not cut aid to the Mubarak regime and free the ailing sheik from prison.

In the United States, domestic terrorists, like their foreign counterparts, also come together to commit criminal and terrorist acts–domestic radical terrorism (DRT)–because of common political and social objectives that transcend their allegiance to any particular terrorist or extremist organization. Take, for example, the actions of Timothy McVeigh and Terry Nichols and their role in the Oklahoma City bombing. Like the group that came together to blow up the World Trade Center, these two army buddies, and possibly others unnamed in the conspiracy, had much in common. Both were from broken homes; McVeigh was 16 when his parents separated, and

Nichols was 2 years older. McVeigh's father was an auto worker; Nichols's father was a farmer who moonlighted on the auto assembly lines of Flint, Michigan. Before enlisting in the Army, McVeigh stockpiled barrels of water in the basement of his father's Lockport, New York, home, with the intent of constructing a bomb shelter; before Nichols signed on, he buried himself in survivalist magazines that counseled the stockpiling of food in the event of a nuclear war, and he kept his savings confined to silver and gold coins. On May 24, 1988, both men enlisted in the U.S. Army. They both left the service with a profound mistrust of their government.

Interviews with Nicholas at the time of his trial indicate that McVeigh's anger with the federal government dates back to the Ruby Ridge incident that occurred 1 year before the 51-day siege of the Branch Davidian compound in 1993. In any event, McVeigh's anger with the overzealous actions of the government at Waco is well-known; likewise, his interest in *The Turner Diaries* (Macdonald, 1978), the fictional account of a worldwide white revolution that became the model for right-wing terrorist groups during the 1980s. Clearly, McVeigh's actions on April 19, 1995, closely parallel those of a small cell of white racist warriors in *The Turner Diaries* that blow up a federal building in Washington at 9:15 in the morning.

Like the World Trade Center bombing conspirators, McVeigh and Nichols were joined together in their hatred for the federal government that transcended any affiliations they might have had with a particular group. Actually, the only link these two had to a group was their military service and unsubstantiated reports that they attended militia meetings. Theirs is a description of other domestic terrorists who would come together to commit criminal and terrorist acts, or DRT, because of common objectives that transcend their allegiance to any particular terrorist or extremist organization.

In the cases of the World Trade Center and of the Murrah Federal Building bombings, individuals came together to make a statement more likely of revenge than to effect political or social change. Nevertheless, they made a statement. It is frightening that, in both cases, the individuals felt an uncontrollable need to punish the U.S. government for its past actions and policies. It is even more frightening that the difference in their behavior is negligible, a commonality that is sure to spell trouble in the future.

Another similarity between the two threats is that the various terrorist groups representing the threats use similar recruiting techniques. Both foreign and domestic terrorist groups use the Internet to get their message across and to recruit new members, sometimes from the ranks of those just "surfing the Web." The latter occurs when someone visits a Web site only to become intrigued with the cyberspace information being advanced by groups professing to be something else. Consider the Web site for the Islamic Association for Palestine (IAP) (*http:llwww.iap.org*), which is the principal support group for Hamas. Currently located in a strip shopping mall in Richardson, Texas, the IAP has affiliate branches on several college campuses and elsewhere throughout the United States. The IAP has set up an elaborate publications network and video operation (Aqsa Vision) to promote Hamas activities both here and abroad. Its *Muslim World Monitor*, and its sister publication put out by Hamas, *Al-Zaitanouh*, are the largest indigenously published Muslim newspapers in the United States. Some unsuspecting Web surfer coming upon the IAP information might take it as gospel.

On the domestic side, Don Black's Web site, "Stormfront," acts like a recruiting office for anyone wishing to become a white supremacist. The visitor to the Web site can choose among a variety of news groups, chat rooms, and bulletin boards. The site is also home to a massive amount of racist humor and extremist rhetoric. Visitors can peruse, and even download, a copy of Louis Beam's 1992 edition of *The Seditionist* in which he laid out the strategy for leaderless resistance. One domestic animal terrorist group, the Animal Liberation Front (ALF), invites all who visit its Web site and read it to consider themselves members of the group if they agree with its philosophy. The same invitation is extended by other domestic and foreign terrorist groups who welcome supporters and give them counsel in the form of shelter, training, and encouragement. The hope is that one day these new members, as well as anyone who targets their enemy, might go out on their own espousing the violent behavior of the terrorist group. In this way, the group gains the benefit from an egregious act committed by a freelancer without risking its own assets. Most Middle Eastern terrorist groups are quick to go on record condemning the act in order to sway or win public support for their position. Such was the case when Hamas strongly condemned those responsible for the Oklahoma City bombing.

Still another similarity between these threats can be found in their ephemeral structures. Foreign groups, particularly the militant Islamic fundamentalist ones, have a loosely-knit structure of small independent cells that behave very much like the changing constellations in the night sky. These ever-changing configurations of loosely-knit cells make it almost impossible for law enforcement and intelligence gathering agencies to amass the necessary information to make infiltration possible. The U.S. version of these changing constellations is the strategy proposed by Louis Beam: leaderless resistance. Recall that this former Klansman-turned-tactical-strategist for the right-wing extremist movement called on members of all "underground" extremist groups to reconsider their leadership-based organizational structures in favor of nonorganizational "leaderless resistance." The new strategy called for antigovernment militants to break up into tiny "phantom cells" capable of instigating actions against the government without having to coordinate plans through a central leadership. The idea was to weed out the weekend warriors and wanna-bes who wanted membership in white supremacist organizations without paying the price of commitment to the cause and, at the same time, to create an impossible situation for law enforcement in their ability to infiltrate a movement without a centralized hierarchy of leadership.

THE DAY OF THE FREELANCER

The greatest threat to the security of the United States in the next millennium will come from the hands of the freelancer. Freelancers arise whenever individuals or small group of individuals, foreign or domestic, take it upon themselves to act against a target without the direct support of a terrorist organization. Their actions are largely the outcome of their own rage or stealth, despite the encouragement, subliminally or otherwise, from others harboring similar hatreds.

The day of the freelancer is best illustrated by the past actions of Mir Aimal Kasi, Rashid Baz, Ali Hassan Abu Kamal, Gazi Ibrahim Abu Maizer, and Lafi Khalil, who were willing to spill the blood of Americans. Listen to the words of Kasi after his conviction:

> I wanted to punish those who do wrong things against Muslim countries like Iraq. . . . I wanted to shoot James Woolsey [at the time of the shootings, the newly appointed Director of Central Intelligence] . . . but was not able to find him. . . . If I had found Gates [former Director Robert M. Gates] I

would have attacked him, as these people who make up policies for C.I.A. or U.S. Government. . . . I am sad the people who came under attack were not powerful people. . . . I am not against the U.S.A. or the American people. I am against the policies of the U.S. Government toward Islamic countries or towards Muslims. (Weiner, 1998, p. A11)

Now compare Kasi's words with those of the handwritten letter in English that police said was in the pocket of Abu Kamal when he shot seven tourists, one fatally, on the observation deck of the Empire State Building:

> *The First Enemy:* Americans–Britons–French (though the French now seem friendly after Chirak's visit to Palestine) and the Zionists. These 3 Big Powers are the first enemy to the Palestinians ever since their three-partite Declaration in the early fifties, and they are responsible for turning our people, the Palestinians, homeless. The Zionists are the paw that carries out their savage aggression. My restless aspiration is to murder as many of them as possible, and I have decided to strike at their own den in New York, and at the very Empire State Building in particular. The Zionist have usurped my father's land at 'Abbassiya near Lydda Airport and which is now worth ten million US dollars at least. ("The Letter," 1997, p. B3)

Consider the statement made by codefendant Bassam Reyati, owner of the taxi service that employed Baz, to police after his arrest in connection with the Brooklyn Bridge shootings: "When Jerusalem happened, Ray [Baz's nickname] was very angry and mad. He said we should kill all Jews who did this." Abu Maizer and Khalil were also fixated on events in Israel. As the men were carried off to the hospital after being shot by police, one was said to have told the officers that he wanted to join "the hero martyrs in Jerusalem." The reference was to two suicide bomb attacks that had recently rocked Israel, killing many people and wounding many more. In addition, the pair's Brooklyn apartment contained what was described as a terrorist manifesto expressing hatred for the United States and Israel.

Now once again return to Ramzi Yousef's words, after he was sentenced to spend the rest of his life behind bars, and contrast them with Kasi's and Abu Kamal's:

> This case is not about so-called terrorists who planted a bomb for no reason but just to kill innocent people for the fun of it. What this case is about is about the outcome of terrorism. . . . You have been supporting Israel throughout all the years in killing and torturing peoples, innocent peoples. . . . You enjoy seeking people having war together. You enjoy sucking blood and shedding blood . . . you are the first one who introduced this type of terrorism to the history of mankind when you dropped an atomic bomb. . . .

> And since this is the way you invented . . . it was necessary to use the same
> means against you because this is the only language you understand.
> ("Strong Language," 1998, p. A3)

These freelancers might express themselves differently, their
intended targets might vary, but their intent remains the same. Kasi
and Abu Kamal express unequivocal disdain for the United States and
its perceived treatment of Muslims. Baz, Abu Maizer, and Khalil
direct their rage toward Israel but are willing to attack targets inside
the United States. Obviously, the young men, dressed in the distinctive black garb worn by the ultra-Orthodox Lubavitcher Jews, return-
ing from a visit to the Manhattan hospital where their sect's leader was
being treated, were too much for Rashid Baz to resist. All the freelancers involved in these acts of terrorism were willing to spill
America blood on American soil without giving it a second thought.
Had they, they would not have been acting like freelancers.

The actions of these freelancers will embolden and inspire other
freelancers and groups that hold a hatred for the United States. Others
inclined to blow themselves up to achieve a seat on the fast track to
heaven will learn from the mistakes of these freelancers. Studying the
attacks on the World Trade Center and the Murrah Federal Building–
including the resulting damage, media coverage, and investigative
techniques used in apprehending suspects–could prompt future terrorists to plan their attacks with more precision.

WHAT'S A LAW ENFORCEMENT AGENCY TO DO?

In the case of conspiracies like the one involving Sheik Rahman
and his cohorts, action is a calculation that weighs the extent of the
group's anger against the real danger of apprehension and retaliation.
When anger turns into rage, however, terrorists like those involved in
the plots to bomb the World Trade Center and other landmarks in
New York City will defy the danger and strike out against their targets.
Consider for a last time, but please remember, the measured words of
Ramzi Yousef:

> This case is not about so-called terrorists who planted a bomb for no reason
> but just to kill innocent people for the fun of it. What this case is about is
> about the outcome of terrorism. . . . You have been supporting Israel
> throughout all the years in killing and torturing peoples, innocent peoples.

. . . You enjoy seeking people having war together. You enjoy sucking blood and shedding blood . . . you are the first one who introduced this type of terrorism to the history of mankind when you dropped an atomic bomb. . . . And since this is the way you invented . . . it was necessary to use the same means against you because this is the only language you understand. ("Strong Language," 1998, p. A3)

Freelancers never have a formula or calculus other than their unbridled raw emotions. Almost by definition, freelancers are not tied to any traditional terrorist group—or any other group, for that matter. They take solitary action with only their sometimes conscience to guide them. The advice or counsel of others, even those sympathetic to the cause, is for the most part absent. A concerned, tentative, or even frightened comrade, however, can often stop a suicide action from taking place. This may have been the case when a possible acquaintance of the suicide bombers Abu Maizer and Khalil approached officers of the 88th Precinct in the Fort Greene section of Brooklyn and said, "My friend is going to kill people in the subway." Even today, it is not clear whether the tipster was one of the men, Abdul Shakur, police had questioned in the case. As of this writing, only Abu Maizer and Khalil have been charged.

A lesson learned from this aborted suicide attempt is that more than one freelancer makes for a group of freelancers in which someone else's actions, impulsive or not, might compromise the mission of the group. An adage attributed to organized crime members applies here: "Two can keep a secret if one is dead." Two, three, or more freelancers acting in concert are, in theory, less dangerous than one solitary freelancer acting alone. But freelancers most likely will not be acting together, thus making it more difficult for the authorities to uncover them.

Using the behavior of one freelancer to help predict or explain the actions of another freelancer will prove difficult, if not impossible, given the differences between individuals. Take, for example, the actions of Theodore John Kaczynski, the Unabomber. Knowing the Unabomber's behavior would prove helpful only if other serial bombers were also to build 10 x 12-ft cabins without electricity or running water on the edge of the continental divide. They don't, however. Future serial bombers or freelancers might what to live the life of a hermit and decry the evils of modern technology; then again, they may not. They will have their own peculiarities and grievances, and that's why profiling is an art, rather than a science. And that's why freelancers pose such a problem.

What, then, should a law enforcement agency do? Before doing anything else, it should identify the problem. Only then can security protocols be developed to deal with it. At this time, however, it appears that authorities are not aware of any problem with international and domestic radical terrorism, as well as freelance terrorism. At least, that is the impression one gets from reading what is reported in the newspapers.

In both the shootings that took place on the Brooklyn Bridge and on the observation deck of the Empire State Building, the gunmen were portrayed as just that—gunmen. No link to terrorism was offered. In fact, New York Mayor Rudolph Giuliani and Police Commissioner William Bratton and his successor Howard Safir went out of their way to downplay the danger of these acts to the community at large. They did acknowledge the significance to the Jewish community, however. But it is difficult to tell whether their intentions were to calm the fears of the Jewish community, to curry favor with the same, or to keep New Yorkers from pointing an accusatory finger at Arab Americans for being terrorists. The point is that all of New York was the target. In any event, consider the reactions of the mayor and the others after these events and ask yourself whether the freelancer terrorist problem is being recognized.

After, for example, the Brooklyn Bridge shooting by Baz, Mayor Giuliani and Commissioner Bratton said the police department was already on "high alert" because of the anniversary of the World Trade Center bombing, the trial of the four men accused in the bombing, and the massacre of 29 Palestinians in a Hebron mosque by Baruch Goldstein. The implication was that the attack on the Brooklyn Bridge falls somewhere outside these events because if Baz were a real terrorist, he would have attacked a target they had alerted. Instead, he was some kind of crazed gunman who happened to come upon an unmistakable Jewish target, such as young Jewish men with their traditional dress and hairstyles. Ironically, this describes the actions of a freelancer. But that is not what the mayor and the police commissioner had in mind.

The mayor and his new police commissioner, Howard Safir, were also quick to dismiss the Empire State Building rampage as an act of terrorism aimed at the general population. The shooter, Ali Hassan Abu Kamal, a 69-year-old Palestinian schoolteacher from the West

Bank, did not fit the profile of a terrorist, they said. But while the mayor was announcing to the public that Abu Kamal acted the way he did because he had been swindled out of his life savings, mayoral aides were busy confiding to two major Jewish organizations that the Palestinian gunman had anti-Israel motives. As with the Baz case, the Giuliani administration was treating these attacks as if they were a Jewish problem with little risk (or significance) to the entire community. But the killings on the 86th-floor observation deck of the Empire State Building were aimed at everyone, not just at a van full of easily identified Jewish targets. Whom did Kasi and McVeigh have in mind when they committed their acts of terrorism? Clearly, their acts of freelance terrorism were not aimed only at Jews.

The apprehension of two suicide bombers in Brooklyn—Gazi Ibrahim Abu Maizer and Lafi Khalil—was also greeted with many questions about their legitimacy. Bomb plot investigators even attempted to paint the two Palestinians as more aimless than ardent. The so-called feckless behavior of the two suspects—so different from the discipline characteristic of Islamic suicide bombers operating in Israel—puzzled the authorities. The investigators even went so far as to describe in some detail the sexual preference of Abu Maizer and Khalil, thus indicating that devout Muslims would not be interested in women in that way. These same investigators must have been aware of the promise of 75 virgins to any male suicide bomber in Israel who blew himself up in the name of the Almighty. Such a promise would have little meaning if it did not please the suicide bomber. Not only were the bomb investigators working with a mistaken conception of what makes a suicide bomber tick, but they were also clueless about the reality of the freelancer. But don't be too harsh on them; the Israelis themselves had a difficult time admitting that Ahmed Hamideh, the American citizen who drove his car into a crowed bus stop in 1996, was a freelance terrorist. Bear in mind that it was an editorial in an Israeli newspaper that indicated Hamideh did not fit the profile of a terrorist because he had a U.S. passport. Like the authorities in New York, the usually astute Israelis, especially when it comes to identifying terrorists, also can practice denial in face of the facts.

In a strange way, denying the existence of the freelance terrorist is reminiscent of the public's surprise at the World Trade Center bomber who went back to the van rental agency to report the now infamous yellow van stolen in order to retrieve his deposit. This seemingly stupid act led not only to his arrest but also to the arrest of others involved in the bombing. What the public, as well as law enforcement, needs to remember is that terrorists committing acts of either international or domestic radical terrorism do things that other people do. Their flawed actions do not diminish the presence or danger of the terrorist threat to the United States. Knowing this is the first step to addressing the evil within.

Chapter 5

TERRORIST AND EXTREMIST GROUPS IN THE UNITED STATES

TAKING INVENTORY

The history of terrorism in the United States is as old as the Republic itself. Discussions of the past would not prove fruitful, however, for several reasons. First, until recently, many scholars were reluctant to classify past political violence in America as "terrorism." Their reluctance has not been without controversy. A fairer statement would be that the debate rages on. Second, to revisit the past might resurrect both the problem in defining the concept of terrorism and the rather bothersome freedom fighter/terrorist controversy. The latter appears every time it is suggested that George Washington's actions could be construed as terroristic. Third, and the best reason for not dwelling on the past, the nature of terrorism itself has changed so significantly that it renders most historical analyses somewhat unnecessary in helping to judge future events. This is not to say that discussions of past events will not take place. They will whenever it is necessary to explain how the current state of affairs has developed. The goal, however, is to give the reader enough information to understand why things happen the way they do.

The analysis here concentrates only on those domestic and foreign terrorist and extremist organizations either currently active or in a position to make an immediate comeback. Under each group heading is a brief analysis of the group's capacity for committing terrorism. Following each analysis is a list of organizations, along with their location(s) or area(s) of operations.

DOMESTIC GROUPS

Animal Rights and Environmental Groups

Radical animal rights and environmental groups have two major concerns: (a) the use of animals to further human needs and (b) the destruction of the environment. Their crimes range from small-time vandalism (spray-painting "McMurder" inside a Michigan McDonald's restaurant) to large-scale destruction (destroying power lines that lead to uranium mines near the Grand Canyon). Animal-rights extremists, for example, have been blamed for at least 85 attacks on research laboratories since the late 1980s.

Law enforcement authorities suspect that most members of these groups are college-age activists with ties to legitimate animal rights and environmental groups. Consider, for example, the support for Rod Coronado, the 31-year-old Native American founder of the Animal Liberation Front (ALF), who is serving a 5-year prison term for his role in the destruction of a research laboratory at Michigan State University in 1992. People for the Ethical Treatment for Animals (PETA), the nation's largest animal rights-group, dutifully defends ALF, even paying Coronado's substantial legal fees. Coronado at one time worked for PETA and documented allegations of abuse on fur farms in America for another animal rights-group, Friends of Animals.

Radical animal rights and environmental groups tend to have no traditional structure. Their members work in tiny secretive cells and receive guidance from underground publications and the Internet. ALF's Web page even goes so far as to proclaim that anyone who takes up its call is welcome to call him- or herself part of the group. The invitation that ALF makes might be taken up by fleeing Justice Department activists thought to have crossed over into the United States from Canada. This violent Canadian animal-rights group has claimed responsibility for sending envelopes rigged with poison-covered razor blades to hunting groups. The merger of ALF and the Justice Department can only spell trouble for law enforcement.

Animal Liberation Front (ALF)
Arizona

Earth First
Tucson, Arizona

Earth Night Action Group
California

Evan Mecham Eco-Terrorist International Conspiracy (EMETIC)
Arizona

Justice Department
Canada, United States

Common Law Courts

Using pseudolegal theories based on selective, albeit bizarre, inter-pretations of the Bible, the Magna Carta, and the Bill of Rights, par-ticipants in common law courts (and illegal townships and jural soci-eties) use phony liens, money orders, and other documents in an attempt to defy the authority of actual courts. Common law courts render rulings on a wide variety of cases involving such matters as foreclosures, taxes, motor vehicle registrations, and custody disputes. They issue multimillion-dollar liens and phony summonses, using offi-cial-looking documents to deceive the police and the courts. Retailers have lost thousands of dollars after honoring their bogus checks and money orders. In extreme cases, these courts have charged govern-ment officials with treason or other high crimes, as well as issued war-rants for their arrest. In a particularly disturbing example, Clerk/Recorder Karen Mathews of Stanislaus County, California, was beaten severely in the garage of her home in 1994 when she refused to record liens against the property of IRS agents and other govern-ment officials filed by a group calling themselves the Juris Christian Assembly.

Proponents of common law courts perpetuate the movement by holding seminars in how to produce their bogus writings, which some have labeled "paper terrorism." Elizabeth Broderick of Palmdale, California, dubbed the "Lien Queen" by herself, one of the more than 800 people who took classes on antigovernment tactics offered by the Freemen of "Justice Township" near Jordan, Montana, started teaching a variation on what she learned in Montana. Hundreds of Californians attended her seminars during the 6 months she offered them. Many started producing their own bogus liens, checks, and other documents and, in many cases, trying to record them in the California secretary of state's office.

In some parts of the country, paper terrorism has reached epidemic proportions. In Texas, for example, members of the group Republic of Texas, which argues that the 1845 annexation of Texas was unconstitutional, filed thousands of bogus liens in courthouses across the state, clogging small-town courts and creating financial and legal headaches for businesses and some state officials, including the chief judge of Texas. In response to this insidious threat to the normal operations of the courts, the U.S. Department of Justice undertook in 1998 to draft model legislation to stem the tide of paper terrorism by these antigovernment extremists. The legislation would outlaw the filing of bogus liens and criminal indictments against public officials and employees and would also outlaw frivolous lawsuits filed in federal courts to harass public employees. Until this legislation becomes law, expect more of the same from extremists involved in common law courts.

ALASKA

Common Law Court, Anchorage

ARIZONA

Common Law Court, Graham County
Common Law Court, Maricopa County
Common Law Court, Mohave County
Common Law Court, Payson
Pima County Grand Jury, Tucson

ARKANSAS

We the People, Yellville

CALIFORNIA

Butte County Jural Society, Butte County
Common Law Court, Butte County
Jural Society, Canoga Park
Sovereign Patriot Group, Chico
Common Law Court, El Dorado County
Common Law Court, Garden Grove
Common Law Court, Kern County
Common Law Court, Los Angeles County
Juris Christian Assembly, Modesto

Rancho Simi Jural Society, Rancho Simi
Northern California House of Common Law, San Rafael
Common Law Court, Solano County
Common Law Court, Stanislaus County
Tamalpais Jural Society, Tamalpais

COLORADO

Common Law Court, Arapahoe County
Common Law Court, Baca County
Common Law Liberty, Denver
Common Law Court, Denver
Common Law Court, El Paso County
Common Law Court, Jefferson County
Common Law Court, Larimer County
Common Law Court, Montrose County

FLORIDA

Christian Jural Court, Brevard County
Common Law Court, Orange County
Restoration Township Jural Society, Palm Bay
Constitutional Court of We the People, Tampa
Common Law Court, Volusia County

GEORGIA

Common Law Court, Cobb County

HAWAII

Common Law Court, Honolulu

IDAHO

Common Law Court, Ada County
Idaho Sovereignty Association, Boise Common Law Court, Boundary
County
Common Law Court, Kootenai County
Common Law Court, Lewis County

ILLINOIS

Common Law Court, Clark County

Common Law Court, Madison County

INDIANA

Christian Common Law Foundation, Boonville
Common Law Court, Delaware County
Common Law Court, Marion County
Common Law Court, Warrick County

IOWA

Common Law Court, Delaware County
Common Law Court, Floyd County
Common Law Court, Jackson County

KANSAS

Christian Court, Abilene
Common Law Court, Butler County
Common Law Court, Rice County
Common Law Court, Sedgwick County
Common Law Court, Stafford County
Common Law Court, St. Mary's
Christian Court, Topeka

LOUISIANA

Common Law Defense Fund, Lafayette
Common Law Court, Lafayette Parish

MICHIGAN

Common Law Court, Jenison
Common Law Court, Manistee County
Common Law Court, Ottawa County
Michigan Common Law Venue Supreme Court, Ottawa County
Common Law Court, Sanilac County

MINNESOTA

Common Law Court, Hennepin County
Common Law Court, St. Paul

MISSISSIPPI

Common Law Court, unspecified location

MISSOURI

Common Law Court, Clay County
Common Law Court, Dade County
George Gordon's School of Common Law, Isabelle County
Common Law Court, Jefferson County
Common Law Court, McDonald County
Common Law Court, Texas County

MONTANA

Common Law Court, Billings
Bozeman Freemen, Bozeman
Common Law Court, Cascade County
Common Law Court, Garfield County
Montana Freeman/Justus Township, Jordan Common Law Court, Musselshell County
Common Law Court, Ravalli County

NEBRASKA

Common Law Court, Hamilton County

NEVADA

Common Law Court, Clark County

NEW HAMPSHIRE

Common Law Court, Sullivan County

NEW MEXICO

Common Law Court, Albuquerque
Common Law Court, San Juan County
House of Common Law School for Responsible Sovereignty, Santa Fe

NEW YORK

Truth Fellowship Order of Protection, Schenectady

NORTH CAROLINA

Common Law Court, Franklin
Common Law Court, Kinston
Common Law Court, Otto

NORTH DAKOTA

Common Law Court, Douglas

OHIO

Common Law Court, Central Ohio
Common Law Court, Columbus
Common Law Court, Southwestern Ohio

OKLAHOMA

Common Law Court, Alfalfa County
Common Law Court, Bryan County
Common Law Court, Cherokee
Common Law Court, Garfield County
Common Law Court, Grant County
Common Law Court, Kay County
Common Law Court, Kingfisher County
Common Law Court, McCurtain County

OREGON

Common Law Court, Lane County
Common Law Court, Multnomah County
Common Law Court, Prineville
Jural Society, Portland
Common Law Court, Stayton

PENNSYLVANIA

Common Law Court, Montgomery County
Common Law Court, Potter County

SOUTH DAKOTA

Common Law Court, Lawrence County
Common Law Court, Pennington County

TEXAS

Austin Jural Society, Austin
Common Law Court, Bexar County
Republic of Texas Movement, Fort Davis
Common Law Court, Kendall County
Common Law Court, Orange County

WASHINGTON

Common Law Court, Amboy
Common Law Court, Chelan
Common Law Court, Ellensburg
Common Law Court, Grant County
Common Law Court, Moses Lake
Common Law Court, Seattle
Common Law Court, Snohomish County
Common Law Court, Wenatchee
Common Law Court, Whatcom County

WISCONSIN

Common Law Court, Columbia County
Common Law Court, Crawford County
Common Law Court, Grant County
Common Law Court, Juneau County
Common Law Court, LaCrosse County
Common Law Court, Manitowoc County
Common Law Court, Milwaukee
Common Law Court, Portage County
Common Law Court, Shawano County
Common Law Court, Taylor County
Common Law Court, Trempleau County
Common Law Court, Waupaca County

WYOMING

Common Law Court, Laramie County

Criminal Gangs

The El Rukn street gang began as the Blackstone Rangers in 1963 and immediately began to vie for control of the turf surrounding Blackstone Street on the south side of Chicago. In 1969, Jeff Fort, the gang's leader, brought together 21 black gangs to form the Black P. Stone Nation. Arrested for making false statements to obtain federal money, Fort was sentenced to the federal penitentiary, where he converted to Islam.

In 1976, Fort changed his gang's name to El Rukn, a name borrowed from the cornerstone of an Islamic shrine in Mecca, Saudi Arabia, the Kaaba. Rearrested, convicted, and sentenced to federal prison, he was able to confound prison authorities by maintaining control of El Rukn and organizing its activities, which included arranging for his fellow gang members to attend a conference in Libya held by Moammar Gadhafi. Because the gang members told Gadhafi they could carry out terrorist activities in the United States, Gadhafi sent them back with the promise of $2.5 million in exchange for their services. In September 1986, a 55-count indictment was returned against Fort and other El Rukn members for their pact with the Libyan strongman. Fort was latter sentenced to 80 years, in addition to a $255,000 fine for his terrorism-for-hire scheme.

El Rukn's name resurfaced in the mid-1990s during a book-signing tour in Chicago by Salman Rushdie. Jerome Glazebrook, charged with protecting Rushdie when he is in the United States, was tipped off by federal law enforcement authorities that El Rukns might try to assassinate the British author while he was on tour in Chicago (J. Glazebrook, personal communication, January 1998). A multimillion dollar reward is still supposedly waiting for anyone taking Rushdie's life. This death sentence, or *fatwa*, was issued back in 1989 by Ayatollah Khomeini, who found Rushdie's book *The Satanic Verses* blasphemous against Islam. Regardless of whether El Rukn could muster enough support to carry out a contract killing of this magnitude or whether someone would even deliver the multimillion dollar reward, both law enforcement authorities and Glazebrook took the threat seriously.

El Rukn
Chicago, IL

Jewish Groups

The premier Jewish terrorist group in the United States today is the Jewish Defense League (JDL). The JDL, formed in 1968 in New York by Rabbi Meir Kahane, was responsible for almost all the terrorist acts committed by Jewish groups between 1978 to 1986. During that period, JDL members targeting the Soviets for their treatment of Jews set off bombs outside the Washington office of the Soviet airline Aeroflot, shattering windows; unleashed a tear gas attack at the Metropolitan Opera House in New York, forcing patrons to flee a performance of a Soviet dance troupe; and laid down a smoke bomb in the Carnegie Hall Cinema in New York, disrupting the showing of a Soviet film.

The intense federal investigations that followed Jewish terrorist bombings of the late 1970s to the mid-1980s led to the arrest in 1987 of four key JDL members. All four pled guilty, but one committed suicide prior to being sentenced. The remaining members, two males and one female, received sentences ranging from home detention to 10 years in prison. In the years following these arrests, FBI records were devoid of incidents attributable to Jewish terrorist elements.

Today, the JDL uses the Internet to get its message across. It asks visitors to its Web page (*http://www.jdl.org*) to help them "advertise by telling your friends and posting our URL [address] to newsgroups, chatrooms, and other appropriate places." It even tells visitors, "We'd be honored if you nominated us for inclusion in hot lists and cool sites," and that they have already won awards for their Web site. Behind the new cyberspace image rests the same JDL that seeks confrontations, verbal or otherwise, with anyone or anything it deems an enemy to the Jewish people. The list includes Nazi war criminals, Holocaust deniers, black and white anti-Semites, and even Arab Americans who support or who detest the Middle East peace talks.

In the future, the JDL can be counted on to face its perceived enemies whenever and wherever it sees fit. The hope is that it will not return to the violent behavior it exhibited almost two decades ago. Betting that it will not may prove wrong.

Jewish Armed Resistance (JAR)
New York

Jewish Defense League (JDL)
New York

Jewish Defense Organization (JDO)
New York

United Jewish Underground (UJU)
New York

Klans

The Ku Klux Klan (KKK) was founded in 1865 in Pulaski, Tennessee, by six Confederate veterans, including General Nathan Bedford Forrest. From the beginning, it waged a violent campaign against newly freed black slaves and their supporters until it was officially disbanded in 1869. The second incarnation of the robed-and-hooded order came in 1915, when William Simmons, a Georgia preacher, broadened its activity to include bigotry against Catholics, Jews, and newly arrived immigrants. By the mid-1920s, Klan membership had soared to more than five million members throughout the United States. In 1925, at the height of its popularity, 40,000 robed-and-hooded Klan members marched down Washington's Pennsylvania Avenue to the Washington Monument to make a political statement.

After 1925, internal scandals led to a rapid decline in membership until the civil rights movement in the 1960s. Today, with an estimated membership of about 3,000, the Ku Klux Klan is the weakest and most fragmented since its founding. The Knights of the Ku Klux Klan based in Harrison, Arkansas, and led by Thom Robb is the largest and most active Klan faction operating in the United States today, with a hard-core membership of about 500.

Much of the decline in Klan membership is attributable to civil lawsuits brought by civil rights organizations such as the Southern Poverty Law Center (SPLC) in Montgomery, Alabama. The most famous is the suit filed by Beulah Mae Donald in 1987 against what was then the largest and strongest Klan faction, the United Klans of America. Morris Dees, cofounder of the SPLC, arguing for the plaintiff contended that the Klan was responsible for the murder of Michael Donald because its members were carrying out an organizational policy set by the Klan. The jury agreed with Dees's "theory of agency" and awarded Mrs. Donald $7 million. Soon thereafter, the Klan turned over to Mrs. Donald the deed to its only significant asset, the national headquarters building in Tuscaloosa, which later was sold for $55,000.

The passage by numerous states of ADL-formulated hate crime legislation and paramilitary training statues also has contributed to the decline in Klan membership. Intense internal factionalism and the tendency to subdivide into smaller autonomous units further accounted for the Klan's decline. That's the good news. The bad news is that Klan members are still active in small-town law enforcement, says Jerome Glazebrook (personal communication, January 1998), security expert. In making security arrangements for the visit of a nationally recognized civil rights activist to a small midwestern town, Glazebrook was informed by federal authorities that the local police, made up of 10 sworn police officers, was controlled by the Klan and that 6 of the officers were active Klansmen. Needless to say, other arrangements were made to guarantee the safety of Glazebrook's high-profile client.

Another piece of bad news is that Klan members have also gravitated to other white supremacist and antigovernment groups—particularly those with Christian Identity and neo-Nazi roots—taking over leadership roles, as well as swelling their ranks. The most notable of the crossovers were Louis Beam, former Grand Dragon of the Texas Knights of the Ku Klux Klan, and Frazier Glenn Miller, leader of the Carolina Knights of the Ku Klux Klan. Despite the overall reduction in the Klan's numbers, however, individual Klan cells remain active on a local level, and Klan recruitment and propagandizing continue. So, too, do Klan members' proclivities to involve themselves in terrorist acts against blacks, Jews, gays, and other minorities.

ALABAMA

Federation of Klans Knights of the Ku Klux Klan
American Invisible Empire Knights of the Ku Klux Klan, Hartselle
Militant Knights of the Ku Klux Klan, Higdon
JWS Militant Knights, Valley Head

ARIZONA

International Keystone Knights of the Ku Klux Klan, Mesa

ARKANSAS

Knights of the Ku Klux Klan, Harrison

CALIFORNIA

American Knights of the Ku Klux Klan, Modesto

COLORADO

Knights of the Ku Klux Klan, Parker
Knights of the Ku Klux Klan, Watkins
Knights of the Ku Klux Klan, Yoder

CONNECTICUT

International Keystone Knights of the Ku Klux Klan, Meridan

FLORIDA

Suwannee River Knights of the Ku Klux Klan, Chiefland
Commonwealth Knights, Christmas
International Keystone Knights of the Ku Klux Klan, Davie
Rangers of the Cross, Deland
Royal Knights of the Ku Klux Klan, Deltona
Bedford Forest Brigade, Gainesville
Klay Kounty Klavern, Grandin
Confederate Independent Klansmen, Holder
United Klans of the Confederacy, Interlachen
Knights of the Ku Klux Klan (An Invisible Empire), Kathleen
Florida Knights of the Ku Klux Klan, Lake City
Fraternal White Knights of the Ku Klux Klan, Lantana
Bayou Knights, McDavid
Florida Black Knights of the Ku Klux Klan, Micanopy
Southern Knights of the Ku Klux Klan, Monticello
Knights of the Ku Klux Klan, New Port Richie
Knights of the Forest Ku Klux Klan, Ocala
Knights of the Ku Klux Klan, Orlando
Templar Knights of the Ku Klux Klan, Port St. Lucie
Knights of the Apocalypse, Valrico

GEORGIA

International Keystone Knights of the Ku Klux Klan, Auburn
American Invisible Empire Knights of the Ku Klux Klan, Rome
JWS Militant Knights, Rydal
U.S. Klans Knights of the Ku Klux Klan, Stockbridge

IDAHO

Idaho Knights, New Plymouth

ILLINOIS

Federation of Klans Knights of the Ku Klux Klan, Chicago
Order of the Ku Klux Klan, Rockville
Illinois Knights of the Ku Klux Klan, Smithboro
Knights of the Ku Klux Klan, Wood River

KENTUCKY

Federation of Klans Knights of the Ku Klux Klan, Central City
Confederate Knights of the Ku Klux Klan, Lexington
International Keystone Knights of the Ku Klux Klan, London
Templar Knights of the Ku Klux Klan, Owensboro

LOUISIANA

Bayou Patriots Knights of the Ku Klux Klan, Choudrant
Knights of the White Kamellia, Lafeyette

MARYLAND

Eastern Shore White Patriots, Childs
Invincible Empire Knights of the Ku Klux Klan, Rocky Ridge

MICHIGAN

Knights of the Ku Klux Klan, Waters

MISSOURI

Ku Klux Klan New Order Knights, Overland

NEW JERSEY

International Keystone Knights of the Ku Klux Klan, Vineland

NEW YORK

International Keystone Knights of the Ku Klux Klan, Salamanca

NORTH CAROLINA

Aryan Christian Knights of the Ku Klux Klan, Browns Summit
Confederate Knights of the Ku Klux Klan, Henderson
White Shield Knights of the Ku Klux Klan, Hickory
Christian Knights of the Ku Klux Klan, Mount Holly

OHIO

International Keystone Knights of the Ku Klux Klan, Sandusky

PENNSYLVANIA

Knights of the Ku Klux Klan, Altoona
International Keystone Knights of the Ku Klux Klan, Johnstown
Cavalier Club, Philadelphia

SOUTH CAROLINA

Christian Knights of the Ku Klux Klan, Beaufort
International Keystone Knights of the Ku Klux Klan, Laurens

TENNESSEE

Southern National Party, Memphis

TEXAS

True Knights of the Ku Klux Klan, Boyd
Knights of the Ku Klux Klan, Waco

VIRGINIA

Confederate Knights of the Ku Klux Klan, Sandston

WEST VIRGINIA

International Keystone Knights of the Ku Klux Klan, Fairmont
White Shield Knights of the Ku Klux Klan, Parkersburg

Left-Wing Extremist Groups

A rather large number of student radicals of the 1960s received
support from Fidel Castro's Marxist government in Havana. It is
almost legendary how members of the now defunct Students for a

Democratic Society (SDS) shuffled back and forth from Cuba as part of the Vinceremos Brigades. Cuba was also a safe haven for left-wing extremists like William Morales and JoAnne Chesimard. With Cuba's increasing economic woes stemming from the U.S. boycott, however, and made worse by the breakup of the Soviet Union, Castro's generous support of America's left-wing extremists is all but over. Today, Havana is home to several nonterrorist U.S. fugitives.

Actually, left-wing extremist groups began declining long before Cuba's current troubles. The end of the Vietnam conflict in the early 1970s removed a major irritant and catalyst for much left-wing recruitment on college campuses. Graying baby boomers abandoning their leftist ideals in favor of careers and opportunities on Wall Street also depleted the ranks of numerous left-wing extremist groups, particularly those involving causes related to the civil unrest of the 1960s.

Despite the occasional discovery of a few aging leftist radicals holed up in some urban setting, the left-wing movement at the end of the 20th century is all but over. Animal rights and environmental groups that once allied themselves with left-wing extremists because they felt an ideological kinship have taken to fighting their own wars. Those that remained united have, for all intents and purposes, also directed their efforts to animals rights and environmental issues, all but deserting the leftist rhetoric of the 1960s. As a consequence, look not for the leftist acts of terrorism that plagued the United States during the late 1960s through the mid-1980s, but rather for animal rights and environmental terrorists in the next millennium.

Animal Liberation Front (ALF)
Arizona

Earth First
Tucson, Arizona

Earth Night Action Group
California

Evan Mecham Eco-Terrorist International Conspiracy (EMETIC)
Arizona

Justice Department
Canada, United States

Militias

Following the tragedies at Ruby Ridge and Waco, bands of armed right-wing militants calling themselves "militias" began to appear in several states across the United States. Today, the radar screens of many extremist monitoring groups track a few hundred militia units operating in at least 40 states, with membership reaching some 15,000.

Militia members are united in their obsession with protecting Americans' constitutional rights and preventing infringement of these rights by the federal government. Beyond this commonality, it is difficult to categorize the movement because it is made up of individuals and groups as diverse as those who believe conspiracy theories about the federal government, who use the Internet to espouse racist theories, who are involved in home schooling, and who in camouflage suits partake in paramilitary training. Guns and government, however, are the main concerns of the movement. Among other conspiratorial beliefs, they believe that the federal government, through such actions as the Brady Bill and restrictions on assault weapons, is conspiring to disarm and control the American people.

The Oklahoma City bombing and the intense coverage it brought concerning McVeigh's and Nichols's alleged visits to militia meetings in Michigan caused some militia members to rethink their positions. Some militia members viewed the bombing of the Murrah Federal Building and the death of so many innocent children as such an egregious act that they wanted nothing to do with the militias they had joined. A few militias even closed down. Today, however, the movement, some say, is stronger than ever, thanks to the shakeout.

Militia members have been involved in dozens of confrontations with law enforcement authorities, most commonly in connection with firearms. Other criminal activities include planned bombings, attacks on law enforcement officials, and armed robberies. It is safe to say that some within the movement harbor intense feelings against the federal government and might well strike out to revenge a perceived affront or to announce a complaint. The most dangerous are those with military training obtained either during the Vietnam or Persian Gulf wars. These wars no doubt provided the same learning opportunities for Americans as did the war in Afghanistan for militant Islamic fundamentalists. Let's hope these veterans do not use their killing skills to register their complaints.

ALABAMA

Gladsden Minutemen, Attalla
U.S. Free Militia, Darmanville
Jefferson County Militia, Leeds
Alabama Constitutional Militia, Millbrook
America Constitutional Militia Network, Millbrook
Sons of Liberty, Mobile
Eastern Diamondbacks Militia, Roanoke
Alabama Unorganized Militia, Wilmer

ARIZONA

Arizona Constitutional Militia, Cornville
Constitutional Militia of 1791, Cornville
Arizona Patriots, Kingman
Yavapai County Militia, Mayer
Militia of Arizona, Payson
Arizona Unified Militia, Phoenix
First Mounted Ranger, Phoenix
Fourth Battalion, Phoenix
Second Continental Army of the Republic, Phoenix
Unorganized Militia of Arizona, Phoenix
Viper Team, Phoenix
Unites States Constitutional Rangers, Tempe
Tucson Militia, Tucson

ARKANSAS

Unorganized Militia Affiliate, Alpena
Washington County Militia, El Dorado
United States Constitutional Rangers, Fort Smith
Marion County Militia
Citizen Militia, Osage
Red River Militia, Ozarks

CALIFORNIA

Kern County Militia, Bakersfield
Conditional Militia of Southern California, Brea
Unorganized Militia of California, Fort Bragg Unit, Fort Bragg
San Joaquin County Militia, Manteca

Alameda County Free Militia, Oakland
Ojai Jural Society Militia, Oakview
El Dorado Militia, Placerville
Placer County Militia, Roseville
San Diego Militia, San Diego
Santa Clara County Militia, Santa Clara County
National Alliance of Christian Militias, Shingletown
Shingletown Militia, Shingletown
Tehama County Militia, Tehama County
Morongo Militia, Yucca Valley

COLORADO

Boulder County Militia, Boulder

CONNECTICUT

Nonmarching Militia, Wallingford

DELAWARE

Delaware Regional Citizens Militia, Smyrna

FLORIDA

Union County Militia, Alachu
Florida State Militia, Avon Park
Florida State Militia 7th Regiment, Avon Park
Marion County Citizens Militia, Belleview
Manatee Minutemen Citizens Militia, Bradenton
Constitutional Militia of Florida, Brevard County
U.S. Field Forces National Militia, Camp Bradley
NAAWP Militia, Eagle Lake
Florida State Militia, 1st Florida Regiment, Englewood
Constitutional Militia of Florida, Fort Pierce
Florida State Militia, Fort Pierce
Okaloosa County Militia, Fort Walton Beach
North Florida Militia, Jacksonville
Spartan Militia, Jacksonville
Martin County Militia, Jensen Beach
1st Regiment Florida State Militia/United States Militia, Key Largo
Lee County Militia, Lee County

19th Regiment, Melbourne
Middleburg Militia, Middleburg
108th Regiment, Orlando
Florida Unorganized Militia, Orlando
Santa Rosa County Militia, Pace
Santa Rose Militia, Pace
Brevard County Militia, 19th Regiment, Palm Bay
Constitutional Militia of Florida, Palm Bay
Escambia County Militia, Pensacola
Hillsboro County Militia, Plant City
48th Regiment, St. Petersburg
77th Regiment of Pinellas County, St. Petersburg
2nd Regiment Ocala, Silver Springs
Constitutional Common Law Militia, Tampa
55th Regiment, Tampa
82nd Regiment, Tampa
Constitutional Militia of Florida, West Palm Beach
3rd Regiment, West Palm Beach
Central Florida Militia Association, Winter Haven
Northwest Florida Militia, Youngstown

GEORGIA

Georgia Militia, Bolingbroke
Georgia Civilian Militia, Columbia County
111th North Georgia Militia, Dublin

HAWAII

Hawaii Unorganized Militia, Honolulu
Honolulu Unorganized Militia, Mililani

IDAHO

United States Militia Association, Blackfoot
Unorganized Militia of Idaho, Hayden Lake

ILLINOIS

Northern Illinois Minutemen, Arlington Heights
Northern Illinois Minutemen, Elburn
Morgan County Minutemen, Jacksonville

Illinois Minutemen, Lombard
Western Illinois Militia, Monmouth
Northern Illinois Minutemen, Romeoville

INDIANA

North American Militia, Boonville
Indiana Citizens Volunteer Militia, Harrison County
Black Panther Militia, Indianapolis
Marion County Militia of Indiana, Indianapolis
Sovereign Patriots, Indianapolis
Unorganized Militia of the United States, Indianapolis
Indiana Citizens Militia, Kokomo
Tippecanoe County Militia, Lafayette
Indiana Citizens Volunteer Militia, Morgan County
Delaware County Patriots, Muncie
Patriots of Liberty, Rochester
Greene County Militia, Worthington

IOWA

Iowa Militia, Cedar Rapids

KANSAS

Kansas Citizens Militia, Lyndon
Kansas Second Amendment Militia, Spring Hill
1st Mechanized Infantry Militia, Towanda
American Constitutional Militia Network, Wichita
Kansas City Militia, Wichita

KENTUCKY

Defenders of Liberty, Boone County
Kentucky Riflemen Militia, Brooks

LOUISIANA

Norwela Common Militia, Bossier City
Red River Militia, Bossier City
Louisiana Unorganized Militia, Lafayette
Kitchen Militia, Starks

MAINE

Maine Militia, Belfast
Maine Militia, Biddeford
2nd Maine Militia, Parsonfield

MASSACHUSETTS

Massachusetts Militia, Springfield

MICHIGAN

Michigan Militia Corps, Alanson
Northern Michigan Regional Militia, Alanson
Southern Michigan Regional Militia, Battle Creek
Central East Michigan Regional Militia, Bay City
Southern Michigan Regional Militia, Burton
Michigan Militia St. Clair County, Capac
Michigan Militia, Decker
Detroit Constitutional Militia, Detroit
Michigan Militia At Large, Dexter
Central East Regional Militia, Flint
Southern Michigan Regional Militia, Frankfort
Central West Michigan Regional Militia, Grand Rapids
Superior Michigan Regional Militia, Gwinn
National Coalition of Militias, Harbor Springs
National Confederation of Citizens Militias, Harbor Springs
Straits Area Constitutional Militia, Harbor Springs
Southern Michigan Regional Militia, Hillsdale County
United States Militia At Large, Hillsdale County
Michigan Militia, Isabella County
Superior Michigan Regional Militia, Ishpeming
Michigan Militia Wolverine Corp, Kalamazoo
Central West Michigan Regional Militia, Lakeview
Superior Regional Militia, L'Anse
Central East Regional Militia, Mount Pleasant
Northern Michigan Regional Militia, Pellston
Southern Michigan Regional Militia, St. Clair
Central West Michigan Regional Militia, Tustin
Southern Michigan Regional Militia, Wayne County
Northern Michigan Regional Militia, Wolverine

MINNESOTA

Arrowhead Regional Militia, Duluth
Red Pine Regional Militia, Minneapolis
St. Cloud Metro Militia, Minneapolis

MISSISSIPPI

Mississippi Militia, Laurel

MISSOURI

Continental Militia, Crawford County
1st Missouri Volunteers, Des Peres
Missouri 51st Militia, Grain Valley

MONTANA

Militia Support Group, Eureka
Militia of Montana, Noxon

NEVADA

Nevada Volunteers, Carson City

NEW HAMPSHIRE

White Mountain Militia, Cornish
Rodgers Rangers, Haverhill
Hillsborough Troops of Dragoons, Hillsborough
Old Man and the Mountain Militia, Lincoln
Constitutional Defense Militia, Plainsfield

NEW JERSEY

Salem County Militia, Hancock's Bridge
Middlesex County Militia, Old Bridge
Warren County Militia, Warren County

NEW MEXICO

A Well Regulated Militia, Albuquerque
New Mexico Militia, Albuquerque
New Mexico Militia, Bernalillo County
New Mexico Militia, Mountainair

New Mexico Citizens Regulated Militia, Santa Fe

NEW YORK

2nd Amendment Militia, Binghamton
Citizens Militia of Chemung County, Chemung County
New York State Militia, Elmira
Patrick Henry Volunteers, Rochester

NORTH CAROLINA

Alamance Regulators Militia, Burlington
North Carolina Citizen Militia, Canton

OHIO

Mult-State Defense Force Unorganized Militia, Bellaire
Ohio Unorganized Militia, Belmont County
Ohio Unorganized Militia, Brown County
Ohio Unorganized Militia, Clark County
Ohio Unorganized Militia, Cermont County
Cuyahoga County Defense League, Cleveland
Cuyahoga Militia, Cleveland
Columbiana County Militia, Columbiana County
Mahoning Valley Militia, Columbiana County
Ohio Unorganized Militia, Columbiana County
Central Ohio Unorganized Militia, Columbus
Ohio Unorganized Militia, Coshocton County
Ohio Unorganized Militia, Dayton
Ohio Unorganized Militia, Delaware County
American Anti-Organized Crime Militia, Franklyn County
Ohio Unorganized Militia, Hamilton County
Ohio Unorganized Militia, Hilltop
Partisan Ranger, Lebanon
Ohio Unorganized Militia, Licking County
Ohio Unorganized Militia, Lucas County
Ohio Unorganized Militia, Marion County
Ohio Citizens Militia, Medina
Ohio Unorganized Militia, Medina County
Ohio Unorganized Militia, Morgan County
Mahoning Valley Militia, Mahoning, North Jackson
Mahoning Valley Militia, Stark County

Ohio Unorganized Militia, Stark County
Mahoning Valley Militia, Trumbill County
Ohio Unorganized Militia, Warren County
Ohio Unorganized Militia, Wayne County
Ohio Unorganized Militia, Williams County

OKLAHOMA

Oklahoma Citizens Militia, Eufala

OREGON

Eastern Oregon Militia, Baker City

PENNSYLVANIA

Proctor's Militia, Bedford
Militia of Blair and Bedford Counties, Bedford County
Militia of Blair and Bedford Counties, Blair County
Crawford County Militia, Crawford County
Bucktail Militia, Elk County
Greene County Militia, Greene County
Jefferson County Militia, Jefferson County
Bucktail Militia, McKean County
U.S. Free Militia, Millersburg
Pennsylvania Militia, Morrisville
Potter County Militia, Potter County
Bucktail Militia, Warren County
One Nation Under God American Militia, York

SOUTH CAROLINA

South Carolina Citizens Militia, Clearwater
South Carolina Civilian Militia, Pickens
South Carolina Civilian Militia, Spartanburg

SOUTH DAKOTA

American Constitutional Militia Network, Gregory
South Dakota Militia, Newell
Tri-State Militia, Rapid City
Tri-State Militia, Sioux Falls

TENNESSEE

1st Mississippi Light Artillery, Hixson
Jackson Militia, Jackson
Tennessee Volunteer State Militia, Knoxville
Tennessee Militia, Signal Mountain
Tennessee Volunteer People's Militia, Signal Mountain

TEXAS

Texas Militia Correspondence Committee, Arlington
Texas Light Infantry, Austin
Texas Constitutional Militia, Beaumont
Red River Militia, Bowie
Texas Constitutional Militia, Dallas
Red River Militia, Gilmore
Comal County Militia, Guadalupe Valley
1st Cavalry Reserve Militia, Houston
Montgomery County Militia, Houston
Texas Constitutional Militia, Houston
United States Special Forces National Militia, Houston
United States Civil Militia Organization, Kerrville
Red River Militia, Marshall
1st Light Infantry Regiment, Red Oak
North Texas Constitutional Militia, Richardson
Texas Constitutional Militia, San Antonio
Texas Militia Correspondence Committee, San Antonio
Red River Militia, Texarkana
Victoria County Constitutional Militia, Victoria
Freedom Fighters, Weslaco

UTAH

Sovereign Militia Patriots, Salt Lake City

VIRGINIA

Virginia Citizens Militia, Ashland
1st Virginia Freedom Civilian Militia, Bedford County
Virginia Citizens Militia, Roanoke

WASHINGTON

Lake Chelan Citizens Militia, Chelan
Washington State Constitutional Rangers, Chelan
Washington State Militia, Deming
Clark County Militia, Fargher Lake
Snohomish County Militia, Snohomish
Skamania Citizens Militia, Stevenson
Wenatchee Minutemen Militia, Wenatchee

WEST VIRGINIA

Mountaineer Militia, Clarksburg
West Virginia Militia, Wileyville

WISCONSIN

Waupaca County Militia, Manawa
Black Panther Militia, Milwaukee
Wisconsin Christian Freeman Militia, Milwaukee
Minutemen Militia, Slinger

Puerto Rican Groups

The term *transnational terrorism* refers to terrorism that extends
beyond national boundaries. Terrorists may originate in one country
and carry out attacks in another country, or they may carry out their
attacks in their own country in the name of a foreign government. In
the United States, émigré groups nursing old grudges or fighting for
the liberation of their homelands account for much of the transnational terrorism in the United States. Nowhere is this brand of terrorism
more active than with Puerto Rican groups.

Since the United States acquired Puerto Rico at the end of the
Spanish American War in 1898, small groups of nationalists have been
seeking independence for the former Spanish colony. Some of these
groups have resorted to violence to get their message across. In 1950,
for example, President Harry S. Truman escaped injury when two
Puerto Rican nationalists opened fire at Blair House, across the street
from the White House, killing a District of Columbia police officer.
Another attack 4 years later saw several nationalists open fire from the
gallery of the House of Representatives, wounding five Congressmen.

The individuals involved in these attacks spawned two organizations—the Commandos Armados de Liberación and the Movimento de Independenza Revolución en Armas—that were much sought after by the authorities during the late 1960s and early 1970s. Surviving members of these Puerto Rican terror organizations helped form in 1974 one of the most prolific terrorist groups of the 1970s, the Armed Forces of National Liberation (or FALN, after its Spanish acronym).

Nationalistic groups on the island have also been active in the commission of acts of terrorism. A majority of these actions have consisted of bombings and shootings. A few have even involved rocket attacks. Most of these actions, however, have been directed against U.S. government facilities and the personnel who staff them, particularly servicemen. During the latter half of the 1980s, these attacks occurred with such frequency that they accounted for more than half of all completed acts of terrorism in the United States and Puerto Rico.

Although over the years a variety of groups have claimed responsibility for their acts of terrorism, the overwhelming majority being committed by a few groups with ties to each other: FALN; Armed Forces of Popular Resistance; Guerrilla Forces of Liberation; Macheteros; Organization of Volunteers of the Puerto Rican Revolution; and Pedro Albizu Campos Revolutionary Forces. Of these six groups, however, only FALN and Macheteros have operated inside the continental United States.

Intensive police work against these terrorist groups has borne fruit. For example, authorities captured the leader of FALN, William Morales, in May 1983, and with his arrest and conviction in Mexico on a murder charge, all FALN-claimed bombings stopped. Despite this success, there is still no reason to believe that terrorist attacks inside Puerto Rico or on the mainland will stop in the foreseeable future. Only the granting of independence to Puerto Rico can lessen the threat of terrorism, assuming of course, that additional issues related to U.S. involvement do not surface. The groups listed below, though not heard from in years, can re-form at any given time as long as the desire for independence remains a burning issue with a significant portion of the island's population.

Antonia Martinez Student Commandos
Puerto Rico

Armed Forces of National Liberation (Fuerzas Armadas de Liberación
Nacional (FALN)
New York, Chicago, IL, northeastern states

Armed Forces of Popular Resistance (FARP)
Puerto Rico

Boricua Armed Anti-Imperialist Commandos
Puerto Rico

Boricua People's Army-Macheteros (Ejercito Popular Boricua-
Macheteros)
Puerto Rico

Boricua Revolutionary Front
Puerto Rico

Ejercito Popular
Puerto Rico

Guerrilla Column 29 September
Puerto Rico

Guerrilla Forces of Liberation (GFL)
Puerto Rico

Macheteros (Machete Wielders)
Hartford, CT

National Revolutionary Front of Puerto Rico
Puerto Rico

Organization of Volunteers for the Puerto Rican Revolution (OVRP)
Puerto Rico

Pedro Albizu Group Revolutionary Forces (Hostos del las Fuerza
Revolucionaries)
Puerto Rico

Pedro Albizu Campos, Pedro Albizu Campos Revolutionary Forces
(PACRF)
Puerto Rico

Popular Liberation Army
Puerto Rico

Provisional Coordination of the Labor Self-Defense Group
Puerto Rico

Star Group
Puerto Rico

Vieque Pro-Liberation Group
Puerto Rico

Right-Wing Extremist Groups

Today's right-wing extremist movement is a potpourri of the America Right, from neo-Nazis to Klan members, united in their hatred of blacks, Jews, gays, other minorities, and the federal government. Members in these groups come from all over this country and from all walks of life. They include Christian Identity believers, Christian Reconstructionists, militia members, Klan members, Freemen, skinheads, survivalists, Populists, gun enthusiasts, militant antiabortionists, secessionists, tax protesters, neo-Nazis, millennialists, white supremacists, home schoolers, common law court adherents, and Holocaust deniers, among others.

Members of these extremist groups share more than a few commonalities. They are almost always white, Christian males. They come together in their distinct groups, looking to express their similar beliefs about what they think America has become. They band together in groups usually representing some part of their twisted beliefs. But the fact is that they are joined together in their hatred in more ways than not.

Listed below for consideration are Christian Identity and neo-Nazi groups, as well as some other groups that are not quite a perfect fit. Common law court adherents, militia members, Klan members, and skinheads are discussed separately in this chapter even though they, too, fit under the heading of right-wing extremist groups.

Christian Identity

American Promise Ministries (APM)/Lord's Covenant Church
Sandpoint, OH

Christian Defense League (CDL)
Arabi, LA

Christian Patriots Defense League (CPDL)
Flora, IL

Covenant, Sword and the Arm of the Lord (CSA)
Missouri

Elohim City
Muldrow, OK

LaPorte Church of Christ
LaPorte, CO

Neo-Nazi

American Nazi Party (ANP)
Chicago, IL
LaPorte, IN

Aryan Brotherhood
California prison system

Aryan Nations
Bryans Road, MD
Burton, MI
Cambridge, MA
Columbus, OH
Fairdale, KY
Glendora, NJ
Hayden Lake, ID
Hereford, PA
Largo, FL
Lees Summitt, MO
Lexington, NC
Maquoketa, IA
Mariposa, CA
Merlin, OR
Mesa, AZ
Milwaukee, WI
Minden, LA
Minneapolis, MN
Mobil, AL
Murfreesboro, TN
Picayune, MS
Polson, MT
Salt Lake City, UT

Spokane, WA
Waterbury, CT
Winchester, IN

National Alliance
Alleghany, CA
Austin, TX
Charlotte, NC
Elon College, NC
Fond Du Lac, WI
Hagertown, MD
Hewit, NJ
Hillsboro, WV
Midland, MI
Orlando, FL
Parma, OH
Philadelphia, PA
Pomona, CA
Raleigh, NC
Reading, PA
Reno, NV
Silver City, NC

National Association for the Advancement of White People (NAAWP)
New Orleans, LA

New Order
New Berlin, WI
Milwaukee, WI

SS-Action Group
Dearborn Heights, MI
Morgantown, WV

White Aryan Resistance (WAR)
Catoosa, OK
Fallbrook, CA

Other

Arizona Patriots
Flagstaff, AZ

Prescott, AZ
Verde Valley, AZ

Phineas Priesthood
scattered throughout the United States

Posse Comitatus (Sheriff's Posse Comitatus)
decentralized, semiautonomous units scattered throughout the United
States

Skinheads

Skinheads have a distinctive appearance. Males usually shave
their heads or keep their hair closely cropped. They wear jeans with
thin suspenders, British-made combat-style boots (Doc Martens), and
black bomber jackets. Their bodies are usually tattooed with Nazi
symbols and slogans. Sometimes they disguise themselves by letting
their hair grow out and dressing in business attire.

A major aspect of skinhead life is devotion to "oi" music, a hard-
driving rock music with bigoted lyrics. Music is the greatest means of
attracting new recruits to the skinhead movement. Also central to the
skinhead scene is its magazines, called "skinzines" or "zines." The
zines promote skinhead ideology and at the same time advertise all
things popular with skinheads, such as oi music concerts, tattoo par-
lors, and the fashions of the day.

Those attracted to the movement are almost uniformly white
youths between the ages of 13 and 25. A high proportion of their
ranks come from broken homes or single-parent families. Their
gangs, which range in size from less than a dozen to several dozen
members, often serve as surrogate families for the members.

No single, national skinhead organization is known in the United
States. Instead, loosely-linked networks of skinhead gangs operate in
scattered communities. The gangs frequently change names and network affiliations. Individual gang member are highly mobile, often
with little to keep them tied to a particular location. It is not uncom-
mon for a group to leave one city to take up residence in another
because they were pressured to do so by law enforcement and the
community.

In recent years, skinheads have been aggressively courted by white
supremacist and neo-Nazi groups. They have happily participated in

Identity meetings and Klan rallies, as well as conducted joint paramilitary training sessions with other extremist groups. Today, skinheads number about 3,500 and are active in at least 40 states. Regrettably, the astonishing growth of the racist skinhead movement in America corresponds to a worldwide trend that currently claims the allegiance of more than 75,000 young people in no fewer than 33 countries. Of equal concern is the growth in their violence directed against blacks, Jews, gays, foreigners, and other minorities. Individual skinheads and groups have harassed, brutally beaten, and murdered in alarmingly increasing rates. Their violent acts are expected to increase during the next few years and to reach epidemic proportions in some parts of the country, particularly in the southwestern and western states.

ARIZONA

Fourth Reich, Lake Havasu City

CALIFORNIA

Extreme Hate, Anaheim
Nazi Low Riders, Antelope Valley
Sons of Odin, La Mesa
National Party, Los Angeles
United Bulldog Skins, San Bernardino
Mighty White Skinheads, Whittier

DELAWARE

Eastern Hammer Skins, Newark

FLORIDA

Confederate Hammer Skins, Jacksonville
Children of the Reich, Lakewood
South Miami Aryan Skinheads, Miami Beach

GEORGIA

Confederate Hammer Skins, Marietta

IDAHO

Northern Razor Skins, Nampa

ILLINOIS
Northern Hammer Skins, Midlothian

INDIANA
Northern Hammer Skins, Bristol

MASSACHUSETTS
Independent Skinheads of America, Cape Cod
Eastern Hammer Skins, East Cambridge
Angles of the Assault, Haverhill

MICHIGAN
American Front, Drayton Plains
Northern Hammer Skins, Rochester

MINNESOTA
Northern Hammer Skins, East St. Paul

MISSOURI
National Skinheads, Norwalk
Northern Hammer Skins, Stowe

NEW JERSEY
Aggravated Assault, Atlantic City

OHIO
Nationalist Skinheads, Norwalk

OKLAHOMA
Confederate Hammer Skins, Tulsa

OREGON
American Front, Salem

PENNSYLVANIA
Eastern Hammer Skins, Philadelphia

Church of the Western Deutch Skinheads, Phoenixville

TENNESSEE

Skinheads for White Justice, Knoxville

TEXAS

Confederate Hammer Skins, Dallas

UTAH

Army of Israel, Hurricane

WASHINGTON

Blood and Honor, Spokane

WISCONSIN

Northern Hammer Skins, Germantown

INTERNATIONAL GROUPS

In September 1997, the U.S. House of Representatives voted 396 to 6 to adopt an amendment to cut the budget of the U.S. Department of State by 2 percent for fiscal year 1998. House members took this punitive step to pressure the Department of State to name foreign terrorist organizations in accordance with the Antiterrorism and Effective Death Penalty Act of 1996. On October 8, 1997, after a 16-month delay, the Department of State complied. The designation of these organizations triggers the access and fund-raising restrictions of the federal statue passed in April 1996 and thereby makes it a crime to provide funds, weapons, or other types of material support to any designated organization. Moreover, members and representatives of these organizations are ineligible for visas to enter the United States and are subject to expulsion. Funds already raised by these organizations inside the United States will be frozen from leaving the country.

Prior to implementation of this legislation, members of known terrorist organizations were permitted to enter the United States as long as they had no direct link to an act of terrorism. The 1996 federal statute eliminates any member of a designated terrorist group from entering the United States. In addition, this legislation clearly ends any distinction between contributing to the military wing of a terrorist organization and donating to a hospital run by the same terrorist group.

Among the 30 groups listed as foreign terrorist organizations on October 8, 1997, are the following groups known to be active in the United States: Kach and Kahane Chai (Israel); Aum Supreme Truth (Japan); and the Abu Nidal Organization, Hamas, Hezbollah, and Palestine Islamic Jihad (Middle East).

Afghani Groups

The Afghani holy war, *jihad,* against the former occupying Soviets saw many sympathetic to the cause seek aid from the United States. Those who came here were not sent away empty-handed. Remember the saying, "The enemy of my enemy is my friend." After the Soviets retreated in 1989, the Afghan freedom fighters, the *mujahideen,* turned their attention to Israel, its supporters, and moderate Muslims in general. In addition to leftover U.S. military ordinance, including CIA-supplied Stinger missiles, the bases they set up in the United States to network and garner support for their cause also remained intact.

One such important organization was the Alkifah Refuge Center in Brooklyn, New York. Created by the Palestinian-born Abdullah Azzam when visiting the United States during the Afghan war, the center was used as a base of operations to send recruits off to fight the jihad. According to one expert, Azzam, his cousin Fayiz Azzam, and others sensing victory in Afghanistan turned their recruiting efforts at spreading their holy war throughout the United States, opening bases in such places as California, Michigan, and Texas. Once the war ended, a subversive network of meeting places for incendiary fundamentalist rhetoric existed to nurture criticism against moderate Muslims and Israel and its supporters, especially the United States.

Although no Afghani terrorist group is known to be inside the United States, Afghani nationals and their sympathizers are known to communicate with each other on a regular basis. Many of these individuals answered the call to jihad and earned their battle stars fighting alongside the Afghan freedom fighters. These battle-hardened veterans pose a formidable force if they should decide to target the United States.

Armenian Groups

Although the goals (revenge attacks against Turkey for past crimes against Armenians) and tactics (bombings and assassinations) are identical, ideological differences make it impossible for the Justice Commandos of the Armenian Genocide (JCAG) and the Armenian Secret Army for the Liberation of Armenia (ASALA) to act together. As a right-wing counterpart to the left-wing ASALA, JCAG members gain support for their terrorist activities from conservative elements in the Armenian communities in Europe and the United States. ASALA members have been particularly active in California.

ASALA and JCAG members, as well as splits within ASALA that have led to different radical segments, indicate that sporadic acts of terrorism may still be carried out by small cells within each of these two organizations. Still, the risk to Americans in the United States is small unless they happen to come between these groups and the target of their terrorist acts—usually the Turks.

Justice Commandos of the Armenian Genocide (JCAG)
Cambridge, MA
Los Angeles, CA
Philadelphia, PA
Sommerville, MA

Armenian Secret Army for the Liberation of Armenia (ASALA)
Los Angeles, CA

Cuban Groups

For more than two decades, expatriated Cubans have targeted the government of Fidel Castro and anyone supportive of his Marxist-Leninist regime. The oldest anti-Castro group, Alpha 66, named for the year of its founding, participated in the ill-fated Bay of Pigs invasion. Between 1968 and 1975, El Poder Cubano (Cuban Power) and the Cuban National Liberation Front gave the authorities in the United States fits as they bombed, assaulted, and assassinated their way to ignominy. Their demise led to the creation of Omega 7 in 1975.

Omega 7, made up of dissatisfied expatriated Cubans, committed at least 30 terrorist incidents in the late 1970s. Its members also engaged in selective assassinations of Cuban diplomats. Like no other Cuban group, the violent behavior of Omega 7 in New York, New Jersey, and Florida (Miami) effectively discouraged American citizens from engaging in business or personal relationships with the Cuban government.

During the early 1980s, aggressive law enforcement saw the arrest of the seven key members of Omega 7, including the group's infamous commander-in-chief, Eduardo Arocena (a.k.a. "Omar"). Most of the seven were convicted and sentenced to long prison terms. Arocena was sentenced to life plus 35 years in prison for ordering the murder of a Cuban diplomat and for masterminding a score of bombings in New York, New Jersey, and Florida (Miami). As Arocena was led from the courtroom, he shouted, "If to struggle for my country and sacrifice everything I have is to be a terrorist, then I am a terrorist."

Although the terrorist attacks committed by Omega 7 appear to have ended, Cuban émigré intimidation and violence continue in the United States, particularly in the Miami area. These individuals, acting alone or in concert, continue to discourage American citizens from engaging in business or personal relationships with the Cuban government. As long as Castro remains in power, future acts of terrorism by Cuban émigrés cannot be ruled out.

Omega 7
Miami, FL
New York, NY
Port Elizabeth, NJ
Union City, NJ

Irish Groups

The Irish Republican Army (IRA) is one of the oldest political terrorist organizations still in operation. In 1969, it reformed itself into the clandestine armed wing of *Sinn Fein* (Ourselves), a legal political movement dedicated to removing British forces from Northern Ireland and unifying Ireland. The Marxist orientation of the IRA caused some Irish Catholics to transfer their support to the IRA-Provos, or Provisional IRA (PIRA), which was also formed in 1969 by militant members of the IRA to protest the more moderate policies of the IRA. Relations between the two groups have not always been cordial, although fighting between them is rare.

The IRA, as well as other Irish terror groups, finds small, tightly knit cells the most effective for carrying out its clandestine operations. These cells are extraordinarily adept and innovative in bombing, assassinating, kidnapping, as well as a host of other criminal activities.

The IRA has received aid from a variety of groups and countries and considerable training and arms from Libya and, in the past, the Palestine Liberation Organization. The PLO even elicited the IRA's legendary bomb-making skills to sharpen its own terrorist operations. Another contributor to the IRA is the United States. Sometimes contributions come from the efforts of IRA operatives purchasing weapons in the United States. Such would have been the case had Noel Murphy, a native of County Kerry living in Boston, and Cairon Hughes, of Belfast, been able to ship to Ireland the 100 M-16 rifles, 5,000 rounds of ammunition, and Redeye surface-to-air missile they purchased back in 1986 from an undercover FBI agent. On other occasions, money is willingly donated to the IRA from Irish Americans who view IRA terrorists as carrying on a gallant fight to free the sacred soil of Ireland from seven centuries of occupation and domination by foreigners.

Irish American support for IRA activities is not a well-kept secret. St. Patrick's Day parades throughout the country have for the longest time showcased known IRA members. Sinn Fein leader Gerry Adams was so honored in 1996 as the Grand Marshall of the New York City parade. Along with the public displays of support comes an endless stream of monetary contributions. Not wanting to bite the hand that feeds it, the IRA has relegated its activities inside the United States to raising funds and purchasing weapons. Occasionally, it finances the latter activity, as do other terrorists groups, through drug trafficking.

IRA terrorist attacks in England continue to draw little attention stateside. The stigma associated with these horrendous acts seems not to label IRA terrorists the way it does Islamic fundamentalists. Not saddled with the terrorist label, IRA fund-raising activities in the United States will probably continue unabated. As with other terrorist groups, however, there is no guarantee that targets within the United States would not be selected, although this seems highly unlikely.

Irish Republican Army (IRA)
Boston, MA
New York, NY

Israeli Groups

Kach–founded by the late Rabbi Meir Kahane–and its offshoot Kahane Chai–founded by Kahane's son Binyamin following his father's assassination in the United States–are pledged to restoring the biblical state of Israel through a holy war of sorts. Since their inception, they have targeted Palestinians and other Arabs, as well as Israelis who have not supported the group's violent agenda.

In March 1994, the Israeli government declared Kach and Kahane Chai to be terrorist organization for remarks of their members in support of the Baruch Goldstein murder of 29 worshippers at the al-Ibrahimi Mosque (Goldstein was affiliated with Kach) and verbal attacks on the Israeli government. Nevertheless, these groups continue to organize protests against the Israeli government, harass and threaten Palestinians in Hebron, and threaten to attack Arabs, Palestinians, and Israeli government officials. Still, both groups receive financial support from sympathizers in the United States.

The stigma associated with Kach and Kahane Chai violence inside Israel, like IRA violence in Northern Ireland, though not nearly as widespread and violent, does not label these groups as violent as the militant Islamic fundamentalists. Not saddled with the terrorist label, these Jewish terrorist groups, like their Irish counterparts, will continue to raise significant funds in the United States from a sympathetic public. Also as with other terrorist groups, there is no guarantee that targets within the United States would not be selected, although this, too, seems highly unlikely.

Kach
New York, NY

Kahane Chai (Kahane Lives)
New York, NY

Japanese Groups

Established in 1987 by Shoko Asahara, the terrorist group Aum has as its stated goal the takeover of the world, with Japan as the first stop. Ironically, this cult was approved as a religious entity in 1989 under Japanese law but was disbanded as a religious organization under a different Japanese law in 1995. Clearly, the latter action was precipitated by the March 20, 1995, release of deadly Sarin gas onto Tokyo subway trains by Aum members that killed 12 persons and injured more than 5,000.

Over the years, Asahara seemed to have grown more reclusive and obsessed with danger. The religion he preaches, a hodgepodge of ascetic disciplines and New Age occultism, focuses on supposed threats from the United States, which he believes are under the influence of Freemasons and Jews bent on destroying Japan. If nothing else, the sense of crisis and impending doom that he imparts to his followers keep his followers in his thrall.

Aum members are indoctrinated by some fairly common cult practices, such as banning sex and limiting reading matter to Asahara's books, as well as to real rigors: self-starvation, immersion in hot and cold water, and drug ingestion. Aum also subscribes another classic, if not lucrative, cult practice—that of taking over its members' financial assets.

About 10,000 disciples of this doomsday cult have answered the call in Japan, and the cult has additional offices in Bonn and Sri Lanka, as well as in Moscow and New York. Some, like the one in New York, offer videotapes of Asahara's lectures to about 100 members. The cult even maintains a small presence on the campus of Columbia University in New York City. Aum claims about 40,000 members worldwide.

A 1995 Senate subcommittee hearing on the global proliferation of weapons of mass destruction uncovered the fact that the cult's main effort in the United States was not membership, but rather scientific-type equipment that would help them produce chemical weapons, biological weapons, and perhaps even nuclear weapons. Nevertheless, cult officials still operate out of a midtown New York apartment building, making Aum's presence unsettling.

Aum Supreme Truth (Aum) (a.k.a.: Aum Shrinrikyo)
New York, NY

Middle Eastern Groups

Middle Eastern terrorist organizations have developed significant support networks throughout the United States. Protected by a favorable economic environment, a system of democratic laws, and a sometimes sympathetic public, they have seen their assets rise in recent years. So-called political advisers from Middle Eastern terrorist organizations are seen presenting the party line on the evening news, as well as working the room at a White House function. They have been hard at work disguising their real terrorist intentions through their own words or those of a hired "spin doctor."

Ideological support for a terrorist cause is one thing; financial support is yet another. It is the stuff on which terrorist campaigns are built. Here is where Middle Eastern terrorist organizations excel. This should come to a halt with the access and fund-raising restrictions of the Antiterrorism and Effective Death Penalty Act of 1996, which makes it a crime to provide funds, weapons, or other types of material support to any designated terrorist organization. More important, however, this legislation clearly ends any distinction between contributing to the military wing of Hamas, for example, and donating to a hospital run by Hamas. Moreover, funds already raised by Hamas and other Middle Eastern terrorist groups for so-called charitable service will be frozen from leaving the country.

The down side to the access and fund-raising restrictions of the 1996 legislation is simply this: Stopped from raising money in a legitimate fashion, these terrorist groups may now be more willing to initiate criminal activities to raise capital for their activities both here and abroad. Expect more of the phony coupon schemes once used by the Abu Nidal Organization in St. Louis to raise significant sums of money. Or expect an increase in the exportation of drugs by Hezbollah to the United States from the Bekaa Valley region.

Financial matters aside, Middle Eastern terrorist groups, unlike other foreign terrorist organizations, have rattled their sabers on more than one occasion to threaten the United States for its policies in the Middle East and its treatment of Muslims throughout the world. Expect them to continue to do so unless an extraordinary shift occurs in U.S. foreign policy. Absenting that unlikely possibility, these groups and their supporters are still likely to call for a holy war against United States. The World Trade Center bombing, along with the other freelance terrorist attacks inside this country, does not bode well for tranquility in the future. Vigilance is in order when considering the potential for Middle Eastern terror in the United States.

Abu Nidal Organization (ANO)
Milwaukee, WI
St. Louis, MS

al-Gama´at al-Islamiyya (Islamic Group)
Jersey City, NJ
New York, NY

Hamas (Islamic Resistance Movement)
Detroit, MI
New York, NY
Richardson, TX

Hezbollah (Party of God)
New York, NY

Palestine Islamic Jihad (PIJ)
Tampa, FL

Pakistani Groups

Al-Fuqra (an Arabic word meaning "the impoverished") is an Islamic sect founded in the early 1980s that seeks to purify Islam through violence. The sect's U.S. birth is traced to Brooklyn in 1980, when a charismatic Muslim mystic from Pakistan, Sheik Mubarik Ali Jilani Hashemi, began preaching at what was the most influential black American mosque in the borough. Jilani later returned to his base in Lahore, Pakistan, but has traveled to the United States several times. Jilani disavows any connection to violence and denies the existence of any group called Al-Fuqra. He claims that he is a scholar who tries to instill discipline in the young men who enroll in branches of his Koranic Open University in Lahore; upstate New York, and at least three other sites in the United States.

Living communally in isolated rural compounds scattered through-out the United States from locations in South Carolina to the Colorado Rockies and the California desert, Al-Fuqra members, estimated between 1,000 and 3,000, most of them black, practice their faith while trying to insulate themselves from Western culture. Some of Al-Fuqra's America members received military training in Sudan in order to join Afghani mujahideen in their holy war against the former Soviet Union.

Al-Fuqra is organized into independent cells along the order of classically organized terrorist cells. During an operation, members are often kept in the dark about the identity of others in the cell and communicate with each other through pay telephones at predetermined times. The cells are known as "Soldiers of Allah." Each cell is assigned a "sector," or geographic region. Law enforcement authorities believe that five such cells are currently in operation. Al-Fuqra members have attacked numerous targets that they view as enemies of Islam. According to an FBI report, the sect's list of enemies includes the U.S. government, Israel, the Jewish Defense League, Hare Krishnas, Hindus, and even the Nation of Islam. Attacks during the 1980s and 1990s included several violent assaults on Hare Krishna temples, the murder of Muslim leaders in several states, the bombing of Hindu religious institutions, and murders in Kansas and Washington.

Al-Fuqra members have entered into a variety of criminal conspiracies to finance their violent activities. Their commitment to violence, coupled with their stealth, makes Al-Fuqra a significant terrorist threat. Anyone getting in their way is destined to experience their exceptional affinity for revenge.

Al-Fuqra
California
Colorado
Deposit, NY
South Carolina

Chapter 6

CHRONOLOGICAL SUMMARY
OF TERRORIST AND TERRORIST-RELATED
INCIDENTS IN THE UNITED STATES

Terrorists have been known to time their attacks to coincide with specific dates. Often, a date is an anniversary of a particular historical event or the birthday of someone special. Sometimes a date is the anniversary of a past terrorist or terrorist-related event. Terrorists do this because they like to wring almost every possible drop of publicity out of their dastardly deeds. Moreover, scheduling an operation on the anniversary of a past one almost certainly guarantees press coverage even if the new operation is a rather insignificant one.

The following list of terrorist and terrorist-related incidents provides the high-risk dates for years to come. Keep track of all of these and new terrorist events and mark them on your calendar to better understand the scope of the evil within.

Date	Location	Type of Incident	Group (or Individual)
1975			
1/24	New York, NY	Bombing of Fraunces Tavern; 4 killed and 60 injured	Armed Forces of National Liberation or Fuerzas Armadas de Liberación Nacional (FALN)
1/29	Washington, DC	Bombing of the U.S. Department of State to protest aid to South Vietnam	Weather Underground Organization (WUO)
2/1	New York, NY	Bombing of Venezuelan Consulate because of Venezuela's support for Fidel Castro	Omega 7

9/27	New York, NY	Pipe bombing of National Westminster Bank and First National City Bank in Financial District, two Chase Manhattan Banks in midtown area, and U.S. Mission to the United Nations; slight damage reported	Armed Forces of National Liberation (FALN)
9/27	Washington, DC	Pipe bombing of U.S. Department of State, slight damage reported	(same as above)
9/27	Chicago, IL	Pipe bombings of Continental Bank, Marina City, office buildings, and housing apartments; slight damage reported	(same as above)
10/4	Portland, ME	Robbery of Northeast Bank of Westbrook	United Freedom Front (UFF)
11/10	New York, NY	Bombings of buildings; little damage	Armed Forces of National Liberation (FALN)
11/10	Washington, DC	Bombings of buildings; little damage	(same as above)
11/10	Chicago, IL	Bombings of buildings; little damage	(same as above)
12/12	Augusta, ME	Robbery of Bank of Maine	(same as above)
12/29	Queens, NY	Bombing of crowded luggage area in the main terminal of La Guardia Airport near Gate 22 used jointly by Delta and Trans World Airlines; 14 killed and 70 injured	Croatian National Liberation Forces (CNLF) suspected

1976

2/14	San Simeon, CA	Bombing of the former Hearst estate, demands that parents of Patricia Hearst pay $250,000 to defense fund of Symbionese Liberation Army members Emily and William Harris within 48 hours or face more bombings	New World Liberation Front

4/1	New York, NY	Shots fired into Soviet Mission to the United Nation	Jewish Armed Resistance (JAR)
4/15	San Francisco, CA	Bombing of office building; slight damage reported	Red Guerrilla Family
4/22	Boston, MA	Bombing of Suffolk County Courthouse	United Freedom Front (UFF)
6/6	New York, NY	Bombing of Cuban delegation to the United Nations	Omega 7
6/21	Lowell, MA	Bombing of Middlesex County Courthouse	United Freedom Front (UFF)
7/2	Boston, MA	Bombings destroy airliner at Logan International Airport and 2 National Guard trucks at city armory	Fred Hampton People's Force and antibusing group
7/2	Newburyport, MA	Bombing severely damages Essex County Courthouse	(same as above)
7/4	Revere, MA	Bombing of First National Bank of Boston	(same as above)
9/10	New York, NY	Hijacking of TWA Flight 355 by 5 men and 1 woman	Croatian National Liberation Forces
9/16	Port Elizabeth, NJ	Bombing of the Soviet ship *Ivan Shepetkov*	Omega 7
9/21	Washington, DC	Car bomb kills Orlando Letelier, former foreign minister in Chilean government, and his female assistant	Commandos of the United Revolutionary Organization
12/12	Needham, MA	Bombing of Union Carbide Corporation	United Freedom Front (UFF)

1977

2/19	Seattle, WA	Bombing of federal building	Weather Underground Organization (WUO)
3/9	Washington, DC	134 hostages held in 3 buildings: International Headquarters of the B'nai B'rith, the Islamic Center, and the District Building (Washington, DC's city hall)	Hanafi Muslims

3/12	Marlboro, MA	Bombing of Ideal Roller and Graphics	United Freedom Front (UFF)
8/3	New York, NY	Bombing of Mobil Oil building and U.S. Department of Defense offices; 1 killed and 7 injured	Armed Forces of National Liberation (FALN)
9/8	Washington, DC	Two bombs shatter windows around Soviet Embassy and Aeroflot office and blow up flower pot near White House as President Carter and Latin American leaders gather for signing of Panama Canal treaties	Pedro Luis Boitel Commandos and El Condor
10/8	North Hollywood, CA	Bombing of the Beth Star Shalom Religious Center because of the temple's liberal stance against anti-Semitism	Jewish Armed Resistance (JAR)
10/19	Los Angeles, CA	Attempted bombing of the office of California State Senator John Briggs	Weather Underground Organization (WUO)

1978

2/15	Fairbanks, AK	Bomb blows a hole in the Alaska pipeline; thousands of barrels of oil spray on to the snow-covered tundra	El Condor
5/25	Evanston, IL	Bomb at Northwestern University injures a security guard	Unabomber
7/5	San Juan, PR	Ramon Gonzalez Ruiz, Chilean Consul, and Sergio Alejandro Nunez held hostage for more than 17 hours; kidnappers demand the release of prisoners convicted of wounding 5 congressmen on March 1, 1954, and the prisoner convicted of attempting to assassinate President Truman on November 1, 1950	Pablo Marcano Garcia and Nydia Cuevas Rivers
7/31	San Juan, PR	Two FBI agents are the intended victims of a bomb that explodes under a car in the parking lot of a federal building; no one is hurt	People's Revolutionary Commandos

8/24	Puerto Rico	Two Puerto Rican police officers ambushed; 1 killed	Suspected Puerto Rican terrorist elements
10/27	Wakefield, MA	Bombing of Mobil Oil Corporation offices	United Freedom Front (UFF)
10/27	Waltham, MA	Bombing of Mobil Oil Corporation offices	(same as above)
10/27	Eastchester, NY	Bombing of Mobil Oil Corporation offices	(same as above)
12/28	New York, NY	Bombing of Avery Fisher Hall at Lincoln Center and the Cuban Mission to the United Nations; no injuries	Omega 7

1979

3/25	New York, NY	Bomb explodes in a suitcase about to be loaded onto a Los Angeles-bound TWA flight, injuring 4 baggage handlers	Omega 7
3/25	Newark, NJ	Bombs explode at two New Jersey storefronts with Cuban links	(same as above)
5/9	Evanston, IL	Bomb at Northwestern University injures a student	Unabomber
8/31	San Diego, CA	Violence at Hare Krishna temple	al-Fuqra
10/17	Puerto Rico	Bombing of U.S. government installations island-wide, timed to coincide with a series of bombings in Chicago and New York	Armed Forces of National Liberation (FALN), Forces of Popular Resistance, and the Organization of Volunteers for the Puerto Rican Revolution (OVRP)
10/17	Chicago, IL	Time bomb explodes at a downtown office building, other bombs defused at the offices of the Republican Central Committee and the headquarters of a Democratic committee	(same as above)

10/17	New York, NY	Devices rigged to look like bombs but containing no explosives are found at a hotel in midtown Manhattan	(same as above)
10/21	Queens, NY	Violence at Islamic-Iranian temple	al-Fuqra
10/27	New York, NY	Bombing of Cuban Mission to the United Nations, windows blown out in the mission and surrounding buildings but no reported injuries	Omega 7
11/15	Chicago, IL	Bomb explodes on American Airlines Flight 444, 12 passengers treated for smoke inhalation	(same as above)
12/3	Sabena Seca, PR	Ambush of a bus in which 2 Navy personnel are killed and 10 others wounded	Macheteros, Armed Forces of National Liberation (FALN), and Organization of Volunteers for the Puerto Rican Revolution (OVRP)
12/7	New York, NY	Bombing of the Cuban Mission to the United Nations	Omega 7
12/11	New York, NY	Bombing of the Soviet Mission to the United Nations, no injuries reported	Suspected anti-Soviet terrorist element

1980

3/12	Puerto Rico	Armed assault of 2 U.S. Army officers and an enlisted man en route to the University of Puerto Rico	Suspected Puerto Rican terrorist elements
3/17	New York, NY	Bombing of a Yugoslav bank; no injuries but glass rained down from the 30th floor of the Yugobanka office	Suspected Croatian freedom fighters
3/18	Chicago, IL	Takeover of the Carter-Mondale presidential campaign office	Armed Forces of National Liberation (FALN)
3/18	New York, NY	Takeover of the Bush campaign office	(same as above)

3/25	New York, NY	Attempted bombing of the car of the Cuban ambassador to the United Nations, Raul Roa	Omega 7
6/3	Washington, DC	Bombing of the home of Yugoslavia's Minister Counselor Vladimir Sindjelic; no injuries	Suspected terrorist elements
6/3	Liberty (Bedloe's) Island, NY	Bombing of the museum section of the Statue of Liberty	Suspected Croatian freedom fighters
6/10	Lake Forest, IL	Mail bomb injures president of United Airlines, Percy Woods	Unabomber
9/12	Queens, NY	The Cuban embassy attaché, Felix Garcia Rodriquez, killed while driving along Queens Boulevard	Omega 7
9/14	Belleville, NJ	Attempted robbery	(same as above)

1981

1/12	Isla Verde, PR	Bombs blow up 9 military planes of the Puerto Rican National Guard at Muniz Airport	Macheteros
3/15	Puerto Rico	Attempted bombing of the convention center where former Secretary of State Henry Kissinger is to deliver a speech	Suspected Puerto Rican terrorist elements
3/21	Mobile, AL	Nineteen-year-old Michael Donald hit with a tree limb more than 100 times and hanged from a camphor tree	United Klans of America
6/25	New Britain, CT	Robbery of New Britain Bank & Trust	United Freedom Front (UFF)
10/8	Salt Lake City, UT	Bombing of University of Utah	Unabomber
10/20	Nyack, NY	$1.6 million Brinks' armored truck robbery; 2 police officers killed	May 19th Communist Organization (M19CO)

11/11	San Juan, PR	Bombing of Puerto Rico Electric Power Authority substations cutting power to San Juan's tourist area	Macheteros
11/27	San Juan, PR	Bombings of Puerto Rico Electric Power Authority substations black out the Condado beachfront hotel district, causing $2 million in damage, and a smaller facility less than 1 mile away, causing limited damage	(same as above)

1982

1/29	Los Angeles, CA	Assassination of the Turkish Counsel General Kemal Arikan	Justice Commandos of the Armenian Genocide (JCAG)
2/19	Washington, DC	Two bombs explode outside the Soviet airline Aeroflot, shattering glass doors; no injuries	Jewish Defense League (JDL)
2/19	Miami, FL	Attempted bombing of the Republica Publishing Company, which has supported economic trade with Cuba; no injuries	Omega 7
2/19	Miami, FL	Bombing in front of the Trans Cuba Inc. freight forwarding firm, which specializes in shipping packages to Cuba; no injuries	(same as above)
2/21	Rio Piedras, PR	Bombing outside a dormitory at the University of Puerto Rico; no injuries but some damage	Antonia Martinez Student Commandos
2/28	New York, NY	Bombing of Merrill Lynch headquarters; some damage but no injuries reported	Armed Forces of National Liberation (FALN)
2/28	New York, NY	Bombing at the New York Stock Exchange; some damage but no injuries reported	(same as above)

2/28	New York, NY	Bombing at the American Stock Exchange; some damage but no injuries reported	(same as above)
2/28	New York, NY	Bombing of Chase Manhattan Bank; some damage but no injuries	(same as above)
3/22	Cambridge, MA	Bombing of the office of the honorary Turkish consul general	Justice Commandos of the Armenian Genocide (JCAG)
4/2	Burlington, VT	Robbery of Chitteneden Trust Company	United Freedom Front (UFF)
4/5	Brooklyn, NY	Fire in Tripoli Restaurant kills 1 and injures 8	Jewish Defense League (JDL)
4/28	New York, NY	Twin bombings, one at the Lufthansa office and the other outside the Iraqi Mission to the the United Nations; no injuries but some damage	(same as above)
4/29	Bayamon, PR	Bombing of the Department of Natural Resources; no damage or injuries	Provisional Coordination of the Labor Self-Defense Group
4/29	San Juan, PR	Shooting at the home of the Communications Authority; doors shattered but no injuries	(same as above)
4/29	San Juan, PR	Bombing completely destroys power station	(same as above)
5/4	Somerville, MA	Assassination of the honorary Turkish Consul General Orham R. Gunduz	Justice Commandos of the Armenian Genocide (JCAG)
5/5	Nashville, TN	Bomb at Vanderbilt University injures 1 person	Unabomber
5/16	San Juan, PR	Shooting of U.S. sailors; 1 killed and 3 injured	Vieques Pro-Liberation Group jointly with the Boricua People's Army-Macheteros
5/17	Union City, NJ	Fire bombing	Omega 7

5/19	Rio Grande, PR	Shooting of police officer during storming of the Villa Sin Miedo; officer dies of his wounds	Boricua People's Army-Macheteros
5/20	Santurce, PR	Attempted bombing, bombs seized during storming of the Villa Sin Miedo	(same as above)
5/25	San German, PR	Assault	Star Group
5/30	San Juan, PR	Power station bombed, plunging several suburbs into darkness; no injuries	Provisional Coordinating Committee of the Self-Defense Labor Group
5/30	San Juan, PR	Assaults on the home of the head of the Communications Authority, front door of the Department of Justice, and the entrance of a field office of the Department of Natural Resources; no injuries	(same as above)
5/30	Los Angeles, CA	Attempted bombing of Air Canada building at Los Angeles International Airport	Armenian Secret Army for the Liberation of Armenia
6/10	Carolina, PR	Bombing	Armed Forces of Popular Resistance (FARP)
6/10	Carolina, PR	Bombing	(same as above)
6/10	Carolina, PR	Attempted bombing	(same as above)
6/25	Onondaga, NY	Robbery of Syracuse Savings Bank	United Freedom Front (UFF)
7/2	Berkeley, CA	Bomb at University of California injures Professor Diogenes Angelakos	Unabomber
7/4	Astoria, NY	Bombing of Yugoslav travel agency and nearby house	Croatian Freedom Fighters
7/4	New York, NY	Attempted bombing of Yugoslav Airlines office	(same as above)
7/5	New York, NY	Pipe bombing of Lebanese Consulate damages windows and doors at the French and Lebanese Consulates	Jewish Defense League (JDL)

7/5	New York, NY	Pipe bombing of French Consulate damages windows and doors	(same as above)
7/8	Phoenix, AZ	Pipe bomb damages a car parked outside the home of Rauf Diab, the son of a trustee of the Islamic Cultural Center in Tempe	al-Fuqra
8/20	San Juan, PR	Bombing	Boricua Armed Anti-Imperialist Commandos jointly with Guerrilla Column 29 September and Armed Forces of National Liberation (FALN)
9/1	San Juan, PR	Attempted armed robbery of Wells Fargo truck carrying more than $800,000	Boricua People's Army-Macheteros jointly with Star Group
9/1	Tempe, AZ	Pipe bombing of the Islamic Cultural Center; minor damage	al-Fuqra
9/2	Miami, FL	Attempted bombing of Nicaraguan Consulate	Omega 7
9/3	Miami, FL	Bombing of Venezuelan Consulate	(same as above)
9/8	Chicago, IL	Bombing	(same as above)
9/20	New York, NY	Bombing of Bankers Trust building on Park Avenue	Armed Forces of National Liberation (FALN)
9/25	Miami, FL	Attempted bombing of Nicaraguan Consulate	Omega 7
10/1	New York, NY	Eduardo Arocena, 39, leader of Omega 7, and 4 other men charged with conspiracy and interstate transport of weapons	(same as above)
10/15	Washington, DC	Attempted takeover of a mosque	Disassociated members of the Moslem Religion
10/22	Philadelphia, PA	Attempted bombing of home of honoree consul general of Turkey	Justice Commandos of the Armenian Genocide (JCAG)

11/4	New York, NY	Smoke bombing of Carnegie Hall Cinema; some damage but no injuries	Jewish Defense League (JDL)
11/16	Carolina, PR	Armed robbery of supermarket and $300,000 from a Well Fargo armored truck, killing an innocent bystander	Boricua People's Army-Macheteros
12/8	Washington, DC	Attempted bombing of Washington Monument with a van laden with explosives	Norman Mayer (antinuclear activist)
12/16	Elmont, NY	Bombing of South African Airways	United Freedom Front (UFF)
12/16	Harrison, NY	Bombing of IBM Building	(same as above)
12/21	New York, NY	Attempted pipe bombing of a diplomat's car at the Soviet Mission to the United Nations; no injuries	United Jewish Underground (UJU)
12/22	McLean, VA	Takeover of McLean office building by Libyan students; peaceful surrender and no injuries	People of Omar-Anti-Gadhafi Libyans
12/31	New York, NY	Bombing of police headquarters, 3 police officers injured	Armed Forces of National Liberation (FALN)
12/31	New York, NY	Bombing of a federal detention center; glass shatters but no injuries reported	(same as above)
12/31	New York, NY	Bombing of federal courthouse in Brooklyn; glass shatters but no injuries	(same as above)
12/31	New York, NY	Bombing of federal office building in lower Manhattan; glass shatters but no injuries	(same as above)

1983

1/11	Miami, FL	Bombing of Little Havana business in retaliation for U.S. Department of Justice probe of Omega 7	Omega 7

1/12	Miami, FL	Attempted bombing of Little Havana business in retaliation for U.S. Department of Justice probe of Omega 7	(same as above)
1/12	Miami, FL	Bombing of Little Havana business in retaliation for U.S. Department of Justice probe of Omega 7	(same as above)
1/28	Staten Island, NY	Bombing of FBI office	Revolutionary Fighting Group (RFG)
2/13	Medina, ND	Two U.S. marshals killed and 3 officers wounded trying to arrest Gordon Wendell Kahl	Posse Comitatus
2/15	Killeen, TX	A Rio Airlines flight hijacked and ordered to land in Nuevo Laredo, Mexico	Hussein Shey Kholifa
2/18	Washington, DC	Bombing outside Aeroflot Airlines; windows shatter but no injuries	Jewish Defense League (JDL)
2/23	Utica, NY	Robbery of Marine Midland Bank	United Freedom Front (UFF)
3/20	San Antonio, TX	Bombing of a vehicle owned by Rep. Bill Archer; car destroyed but no injuries	Republic of Revolutionary
4/26	Washington, DC	Bombing of National War College at Fort McNair and fire bomb thrown at Environmental Crimes Unit of U.S. Department of Justice, resulting in minor damage	Armed Resistance Unit (ARU)
4/27	Miami, FL	Attempted bombing	Suspected terrorist element
4/27	Miami, FL	Attempted bombing	(same as above)
4/27	Miami, FL	Attempted bombing	(same as above)
4/27	Miami, FL	Attempted bombing	(same as above)
4/29	Rio Piedras, PR	Attempted robbery	Boricua People's Army-Macheteros

5/12	Uniondale, NY	Bombing of Roosevelt Army Reserve Center	United Freedom Front (UFF)
5/13	Queens, NY	Bombing of Naval Reserve Center	(same as above)
5/27	Miami, FL	Bombing of Little Havana offices of Continental Bank	Omega 7
6/3	Smithville, AR	Gordon Wendell Kahl, 63, killed in a gun battle with state and federal authorities	Posse Comitatus
7/6	Rotterdam, NY	Robbery of Marine Midland Bank	United Freedom Front (UFF)
7/8	Miami, FL	Kidnapping of the wife of the former Salvadoran Ambassador Cecilia Sol de Quiones; she was held for $1.5 million ransom	Ejercito Revolucionario del Pueblo
7/15	Rio Piedras, PR	One killed in $600,000 robbery of Wells Fargo truck	Boricua People's Army-Macheteros
7/22	Miami, FL	Eduardo Arocena, 40, arrested and charged with masterminding a failed car bombing 3 years earlier apparently intended for the Cuban ambassador to the United States	Omega 7
7/28	Montgomery, AL	Fire bombing of the Klanwatch offices of the Southern Poverty Law Center; moderate damage	Members of the Ku Klux Klan
7/29	Portland, OR	Three pipe bombs explode in a 4th-floor room of the Hotel Rajneesh; 1 man seriously injured	Stephan P. Paster al-Fuqra
8/8	Canton, MI	Assassination of Ahmadiyya movement leader Dr. Mozaffar Ahmad	al-Fuqra
8/8	Detroit, MI	Fire bombing of an Ahmadiyya movement official's home; no injuries reported	(same as above)

8/9	Detroit, MI	Fire bombing destroys Ahmadiyya mosque; the suspected killer of Dr. Ahmad, William Cain, is killed while setting the fire	(same as above)
8/9	Springfield, MS	Metropolitan Community Church is burned for its support of gay rights	James Ellison and Bill Thomas (Covenant, Sword and the Arm of the Lord [CSA])
8/16	Los Angeles, CA	Takeover of foreign consulate	Individual Action
8/16	Bloomington, IN	Burned the Jewish community center	Bill Thomas (Covenant, Sword and the Arm of the Lord [CSA])
8/17	Washington, DC	Bombing of Computer Operations Center at Washington Navy Yard	Armed Resistance Unit (ARU)/FMLN
8/21	Bronx, NY	Bombing of J. Muller Army Reserve Center	United Freedom Front (UFF)
8/27	Washington, DC	Fire bombing of Philippine Embassy after assassination of Ninoy Aquino; no injuries reported	Suspected terrorist element
9/16	West Hartford, CT	$7.2 million in cash taken in armed robbery of Wells Fargo truck	Macheteros
10/5	Washington, DC	Bombing of the U.S. Capitol	Armed Resistance Unit (ARU) and Red Guerrilla Resistance (RGR)
10/12	Miami, FL	Fire bombing of El Titan market in Little Havana, moderate damage	Omega 7
10/18	Dewitt, NY	Robbery of Onondaga Savings Bank	United Freedom Front (UFF)
10/30	Hato Rey, PR	Bazooka attack aimed at the U.S. federal building, which housed an FBI office, in retaliation for the U.S.-led invasion of Grenada hit the deserted offices of the U.S. Department of Agriculture; 1 floor below	Boricua People's Army-Macheteros

11/2	Fulton, AR	Bombing of natural gas pipeline where it crosses the Red River; minimal damage	Bill Thomas, Richard Wayne Snell, and Stephen Scott (Covenant, Sword and the Arm of the Lord [CSA])
11/6	Washington, DC	Bombing of Senate side of Capitol Building; no injures	Armed Resistance Unit (ARU)
11/11	Texarkana, AR	Killing of pawnshop proprietor, mistakenly identified as Jewish	Covenant, Sword and the Arm of the Lord (CSA)
12/13	East Meadow, NY	Bombing of Navy recruiting office	United Freedom Front (UFF)
12/14	Queens, NY	Bombing of Honeywell Corporation	(same as above)

1984

1/29	Queens, NY	Bombing of Motorola Corporation	United Freedom Front (UFF)
2/23	Bronx, NY	Bombing of Soviet residential compound; bombs lobbed over fence, destroying 1 vehicle that had diplomatic plates	Jewish Direct Action (JDA)
3/16	Seattle, WA	Robbery of an armored truck; approximately $43,000 taken	Order
3/19	Harrison, NY	Bombing of IBM Building	United Freedom Front (UFF)
4/5	New York, NY	Bombing of an Israeli aircraft manufacturer; no injuries	Red Guerrilla Resistance (RGR)
4/20	Washington, DC	Bombing of Officers Club at Washington Naval Yard, no injuries	(same as above)
4/22	Seattle, WA	Attempted bombing of Embassy Theater (diversion for 4/23 robbery)	Order
4/23	Seattle, WA	Robbery of armored truck belonging to the Continental Armored Transport Service; more than $230,000 taken	(same as above)

4/26	Norfolk, VA	Robbery of First VA Bank of Tidewater	United Freedom Front (UFF)
4/30	Boise, ID	Congregation Ahavath Israel Synagogue is torched	Order
5/5	New York, NY	Bombing of an Israeli aircraft manufacturer	Red Guerrilla Resistance (RGR)
5/20	Washington, DC	Bombing of Navy Officers Club	(same as above)
5/23	Seattle, WA	Robbery of Continental Armored Transport Company	(same as above)
6/5	Norfolk, VA	Robbery of Sovean Bank	United Freedom Front (UFF)
6/16	Philadelphia, PA	Hare Krishna temple is firebombed	al-Fuqra
6/17	Seattle, WA	Vedanta Society temple and Integral Yoga Society are bombed	(same as above)
6/18	Denver, CO	Assassination of radio talk show host Alan Berg	Bruce Carroll Pierce, David Eden Lane, Frank Scutari, and Jean Craig (Order)
6/30	DeQueen, AR	Assassination of Louis Bryant, a black Arkansas state trooper	Richard Wayne Snell (Covenant, Sword and the Arm of the Lord [CSA])
7/19	Ukiah, CA	$3.6 million robbery of Brinks Armored Car Company; money is reputedly distributed to white supremacist groups across the country	Order
8/1	Seattle, WA	John Liczwinko, affiliated with the Seattle Vedanta Society, is attacked	al-Fuqra
8/1	Denver, CO	Hare Krishna temple is firebombed	(same as above)
8/1	Overland Park, KS	Hindu physician, Srinivasu Dasari, is kidnapped; victim remains missing	(same as above)

8/1	Tacoma, WA	Three East Indians are shot to death	(same as above)
8/22	Melville, NY	Bombing of General Electric Corporation	United Freedom Front (UFF)
9/26	New York, NY	Bombing of South African Consulate	Red Guerrilla Resistance (RGR)
9/27	Tarrytown, NY	Bombing of Union Carbide Corporation	United Freedom Front (UFF)
11/9	Newark, NJ	Eduardo Arocena, 41, leader of Omega 7, sentenced to life plus 35 years in prison for ordering the murder of a Cuban diplomat and masterminding a score of bombings in New York, New Jersey, and Miami	Omega 7
12/8	Whidbey Island, WA	Robert Jay Mathews, leader of the Order, killed in a firestorm while resisting arrest	Order
12/10	Mayaguez, PR	Attempted bombing at National Guard complex	Organization of Volunteers for the Puerto Rican Revolution (OVRP)
12/10	Levittown, PR	Bombing at the University of Puerto Rico	(same as above)
12/10	Rio Piedras, PR	Bombing of Army recruiting office; no injuries	(same as above)
12/10	Ponce, PR	Bombing of Army recruiting office	(same as above)
12/10	Cayey, PR	Attempted bombing of Army recruiting office	(same as above)

1985

| 1/25 | Old San Juan, PR | Light antitank weapon fired at the federal courthouse | Boricua People's Army-Macheteros/Organization of Volunteers for the Puerto Rican Revolution (OVRP) |
| 2/1 | Leetsdale, CO | Arson at power station | al-Fuqra |

2/23	New York, NY	Bombing of Patrolman's Benevolent Association	May 19th Communist Organization (M19CO)
4/13	Ridgedale, MO	Killing of 1 Missouri state trooper (Jimmie Linegar) and the wounding of another	Covenant, Sword and the Arm of the Lord (CSA)
5/3	Brooklyn, NY	Federal arrest warrant issued for Lal Singh and other Sikh terrorists for the conspiracy to assassinate a foreign official	Sikh terrorist
5/15	Northridge, CA	Bombing of the home of George Ashley, who claimed Holocaust never occurred; some damage but no injuries	Jewish terrorist element
5/15	Berkeley, CA	Bomb at University of California injures 1	Unabomber
6/13	Auburn, WA	Mail bomb sent to Boeing Company	(same as above)
6/22	Houston, TX	Islamic mosque attacked	al-Fuqra
6/24	Tigerton, WI	Law enforcement authorities confiscate property housed in illegal "township" and paramilitary camp called "Tigerton Dells"	Posse Comitatus
7/5	Rockford, IL	The Vat Thothikalam is attacked	al-Fuqra
8/15	Paterson, NJ	Pipe bombing of the home of Tscherin Soobzokov, alleged member of Waffen SS; victim dies	Jewish terrorist element
9/6	Brentwood, NY	Bombing of the home of Elmars Sprogis, reported to be a member of Hitler's SS; passerby seriously injured	(same as above)
10/11	Santa Anna, CA	Bombing at the office of the American Arab Anti-Discrimination Committee; Alex Odeh (leader of the Committee) died from his wounds	(same as above)

11/6	Bayamon, PR	Shooting of Army recruiting office near Fort Buchanan	Organization of Volunteers for the Puerto Rican Revolution (OVRP)
11/15	Ann Arbor, MI	Mail bomb sent to University of Michigan injures Professor James McConnell's research assistant	Unabomber
12/1	Rockford, IL	Laotian temple is attacked	al-Fuqra
12/11	Sacramento, CA	Bomb kills computer-store owner Hugh Scrutton	Unabomber
12/30	Seattle, WA	Ten members of a white supremacist gang are found guilty on federal racketeering charges for a series of crimes including murder, robberies, counterfeiting, and stockpiling illegal weapons; 12 other member had earlier pled guilty to the same charges	Order

1986

1/6	Cidra, PR	Bombing of U.S. post office; windows and doors shatter but no injuries	National Revolutionary Front of Puerto Rico
1/6	Guanica, PR	Bombing of U.S. post office; windows and doors damaged but no injuries	(same as above)
1/6	Santurce, PR	Bombing of U.S. post office; no injuries or damage reported	(same as above)
1/6	Toa Baja, PR	Attempted bombing of Army recruiting office	(same as above)
1/7	Coamo, PR	Attempted bombing of U.S. post office	Suspected Puerto Rican terrorist element
2/15	Philadelphia, PA	Dikran Sarkis Berberian convicted for the October 22, 1982, attempted bombing of home of honorary consul general of of Turkey	Justice Commandos of the Armenian Genocide (JCAG)

3/17	Ponce, PR	Attempted bombing of Esso service station	(same as above)
4/14	Rio Piedras, PR	An explosive device detonated in a women's restroom on campus of the University of Puerto Rico	Organization of Volunteers for the Puerto Rican Revolution (OVRP)
4/29	San Juan, PR	Assassination of Alejandro Gonzalez Malave, a former police officer, in a drive-by shooting in front of his mother's home	(same as above)
4/30	Seattle, WA	Richard Joseph Scutari pleads guilty for the July 19, 1984, armed robbery of an armored truck in Ukiah, California	Order
5/14	Phoenix, AZ	Sabotage of power lines that supply Palo Verde Nuclear Generating Station, Arizona; and California electric customers	Suspected terrorist element
5/28	Bathany, WV	Randell Gorby, who was linked to the Hare Krishna temple in Philadelphia, is attacked and injured	al-Fuqra
8/6	Hayden Lake, ID	Bomb sent to Gary Solomon, Jewish owner of trucking company	Order II
8/7	Kootenai County, ID	Pipe bombing of Fred Bower's Classic Auto Restoration	(same as above)
9/2	New York, NY	Tear gas grenade bombing of Soviet Union's Moiseyev Dance Company at the Metropolitan Opera; no injuries	Jewish terrorist element
9/15	Coeur d'Alene, ID	Home of Father William Wassmuth, pastor of St. Pious X. Roman Catholic Church and critic of Aryan Nations, fire bombed	Order II
9/18	Toa Baja, PR	Two incendiary devices are thrown through a plate glass window at Army recruiting office	El Movimiento Revolutionario Independentista (EMRI)

9/27	Fayetteville, NC	Attempted robbery of the local Pizza Hut	Wendell Lane (White Patriot Party [WPP])
9/29	Coeur d'Alene, ID	Bombing of New Era Telephone Company	Order II
9/29	Coeur d'Alene, ID	Bombing of Jax Restaurant	(same as above)
9/29	Coeur d'Alene, ID	Bombing of Beneficial Finance Company	(same as above)
9/29	Coeur d'Alene, ID	Attempted bombing of local federal building that houses the FBI's Resident Agency	(same as above)
9/29	Rathdrum, ID	Attempted robbery of the First National Bank of North Idaho	(same as above)
9/29	Post Falls, ID	Attempted robbery of the Idaho First National Bank	(same as above)
9/29	Post Falls, ID	Attempted robbery of the Idaho Army National Guard Armory	(same as above)
10/20	New York, NY	Fire bombing of Lincoln Center Concert Hall where the Moscow State Orchestra was scheduled to perform that evening; no injuries	Jewish terrorist element
10/24	Detroit, MI	Pipe bombing of Dimic's Restaurant and Bar that earlier that day served Yugoslavian delegation	Suspected terrorist element
10/23	Boston, MA	Noel Murphy, 26, native of County Kerry, and Cairon Hughes, 24, Belfast, found guilty in federal court for conspiracy to export arms without a license, conspiracy to export a Redeye missile without a license, and dealing in firearms	Irish Republican Army (IRA)

10/28	Fajardo, PR	Bombing of Navy recruiting office, 1 person, 1 truck destroyed	Boricua People's Army-Macheteros jointly with the Armed Forces of Popular Resistance (FARP), and the Organization of Volunteers for the Puerto Rican Revolution (OVRP)
10/28	Fort Buchanan, PR	Pipe bombing of Army Reserve base, 1 truck destroyed; 2 additional devices were found in the same area	(same as above)
10/28	Santurce, PR	Attempted bombing of Army Reserve recruiting office	(same as above)
10/28	Aguadilla, PR	Attempted bombing of Army Reserve center	(same as above)
10/28	Aguadilla, PR	Attempted bombing of Army recruiting office	(same as above)
10/28	Mayaguez, PR	Attempted bombing of National Guard Armory	(same as above)
10/28	Bayamon, PR	Attempted bombing of Army-Navy recruiting office	(same as above)
10/28	Cayey, PR	Attempted bombing of Army Reserve recruiting office	(same as above)
10/30	Chicago, IL	Jeff Fort, Melvin Mays, Alan Knox, and Tramell Davis indicted for allegedly plotting with the Libyan government to use hand grenades, rockets, and other weapons to destroy U.S. government targets	El Rukn
11/4	Puerta De, Tierra, PR	Attempted bombing of National Guard Armory	Boricua People's Army-Macheteros
11/27	Boston, MA	Federal District Judge A. David Mazzone sentenced Noel Murphy, 26, native of County Kerry, to 9 years and Cairon Hughes, 24, of Belfast, to 8 years for conspiracy to export arms without a license, conspiracy to export a Redeye missile without a license, and dealing in firearms	Irish Republican Army (IRA)

12/28	Yauco, PR	Bombing of a Puerto Rican National Guard truck; slight damage and no injuries	Suspected Puerto Rican terrorist element
12/28	Guayama, PR	Attempted bombing of a U.S. post office; no injuries	(same as above)

1987

2/13	Mobile, AL	A jury finds Klan group liable for the 1981 murder of Michael Donald and awards his mother, Beulah Mae Donald, $7 million in damages	United Klans of America
2/20	Salt Lake City, UT	Bomb found near computer store	Unabomber
3/2	Laguna Niguel, CA	Five explosive devices placed in the vicinity of the federal building; 4 of the devices detonated in a location adjacent to the federal building, which houses several IRS offices, and a fifth device was recovered on the roof of the building	Suspected terrorist element
4/16	Davis, CA	Fire set to the new Veterinary Medicine Research Building at the University of California at Davis, causing more than $3.5 million in damages	Animal Liberation Front (ALF)
4/19	Missoula, MT	A bomb detonated under a police vehicle at the Missoula Police Department	Aryan Nations (AN)
4/24	Fort Smith, AR	Ten white supremacists, including Louis Beam, Richard Butler, and Robert Miles, are indicted on seditious conspiracy charges	Various groups, such as the Order; Covenant, Sword and the Arm of the Lord (CSA), and Aryan Nations (AN)
5/1	Hialeah, FL	Pipe bomb detonated at the Almacen El Español, a business that sends medicine and other supplies to Cuba from Miami; slight structural damage	Suspected Cuban terrorist element

5/2	Miami, FL	Pipe bomb detonated against the front door of Cubanacan, a pharmacy supply house that ships pharmaceuticals to Cuba	(same as above)
5/25	Miami, FL	Pipe bombing of Cuba Envios, a business that ships medicine and packages to Cuba	(same as above)
5/25	Mayaguez, PR	Pipe bombing of the Western Federal Bank	Guerrilla Forces of Liberation (GFL)
5/25	Caguas, PR	Pipe bombing of department store	(same as above)
5/25	Ponce, PR	Pipe bombing of U.S. Customs Service building	(same as above)
5/25	Aibonito, PR	Pipe bombing of U.S. Postal Service mailbox in front of post office building	(same as above)
5/25	Mayaguez, PR	Attempted pipe bombing of Citibank	(same as above)
5/25	Carolina, PR	Attempted pipe bombing of a Bank of Boston branch office	(same as above)
5/25	Cidra, PR	Attempted pipe bombing of U.S. post office	(same as above)
7/14	Washington, DC	Mohammad Said Rashid indicted by a federal grand jury and charged with 9 criminal violations in regard to the bombing of Pan Am Flight 830 en route from Tokyo, Japan, to Honolulu, Hawaii, resulting in the death of a Japanese teenager and injuries to 15 other passengers	The 15 May Organization
7/30	Miami, FL	Pipe bomb explodes in front of Machi Community Services, a business that sends packages and airline tickets to Cuba	Suspected Cuban terrorist element
8/27	Hialeah, FL	Pipe bomb explodes next to Va Cuba, a business that ships packages and medicine to Cuba	(same as above)

10/9 (approx)	Flagstaff, AZ	Malicious destruction of property	Evan Mecham Eco-Terrorist International Conspiracy (EMETIC)
10/24	Richford, VT	Walid Nicholas Kabbani detained after illegally crossing the Canadian border into the United States	Syrian Social Nationalist Party
11/5	Burlington, VT	Walid Nicholas Kabbani, 36; Walid Mojib Mourad, 38; and Georges Fouad Younan Nicolas, 45, charged with illegal interstate and foreign transfer of firearms and explosives	(same as above)
11/7	Flagstaff, AZ	Malicious destruction of property; over $20,000 in damage by destroying bolts that anchor the power lines on the lift at Fairfield Snow Bowl ski resort	Evan Mecham Eco-Terrorist International Conspiracy (EMETIC)
11/17	Denver, CO	Verdict handed down in the trial of the 4 persons accused of violating the civil rights of the late Alan Berg (a Denver radio talk-show host murdered on June 18, 1984); David Lane and Bruce Pierce convicted, whereas Richard Scutari and Jean Craig acquitted	Aryan Nations, KKK and other white supremacist elements.
11/24	Chicago, IL	Jeffrey Fort, Alan Knox, Leon McAnderson, and Roosevelt Hawkins convicted of purchasing a light antitank weapon (LAW rocket) to be used in the commission of a terrorist act in the United States in order to obtain funding from the government of Libya	El Rukn
11/28	Livermore, CA	A vehicle of a Lawrence Livermore National Laboratory employee was blown up at the parking lot directly across the street from the laboratory	Nuclear Liberation Front (NLF)

1988

1/4	Fayetteville, NC	Frazier Glenn Miller pleads guilty to 1 count of possessing illegal hand grenades and to having mailed a declaration of war and death threats against Morris Dees	White Patriot Party (WPP)
1/12	Rio Piedras, PR	Firebombing	Pedro Albizu Campos Revolutionary Forces (PACRF)
1/12	Rio Piedras, PR	Firebombing	(same as above)
4/7	Fort Smith, AK	An all-white jury finds 10 white supremacists, including Louis Beam, Richard Butler, and Robert Miles, indicted on seditious conspiracy charges, not guilty	Various groups, such as the Order; Covenant, Sword and the Arm of the Lord (CSA); and Aryan Nations (AN)
4/12	New Jersey Turnpike, NJ	Yu Kikumura arrested by New Jersey State Trooper Robert Cieplenski at Vince Lombardi Service Area; his car contained 3 powerful pipe bombs, tools and material to make more bombs, and a false passport	Japanese Red Army
5/26	Coral Gables, FL	Bombing at the home of an executive for the Cuban Studies Institute; $3,000 damage reported	Organization Alliance Cuban Intransigence (OACI)
7/22	Gaguas, PR	Pipe bombing	Ejercito Popular Boricua-Macheteros
9/17	Augusta, GA	Doctor shot to death in front of Humana Hospital	al-Fuqra
9/19	Los Angeles, CA	Bombing of garage beneath 6th story of the City National Bank building; no injuries	Up the IRS, Inc.
9/25	Grand Canyon, AZ	Destruction of power lines leading to uranium mines owned by Energy Fuels Nuclear	Evan Mecham Eco-Terrorist International Conspiracy (EMETIC)

10/25 or 10/26	Flagstaff, AZ	Malicious destruction of property	(same as above)
11/1	Rio Pedras, PR	Pipe bombing of General Electric company office; no injuries but heavy damage reported	Pedro Albizu Campos Revolutionary Forces (PACRF)
11/4	Rio Pedras, PR	Attempted pipe bombing	(same as above)
11/11	Norwalk, CT	Pipe bomb placed in the bushes of U.S. Surgical Corporation near the parking spot reserved for Leon Hirsh, the company's founder	Animal rights activist Fran Stephanie Trutt
11/13	Portland, OR	Mulugeta Seraw, an Ethiopian, is beaten to death	Skinheads
11/29	Newark, NJ	Yu Kikumura found found guilty of unlawful transport of explosive materials, possession and transport of unregistered firearms, use and misuse of a passport, and fraud in obtaining a visa	Japanese Red Army

1989

2/7	Newark, NJ	U.S. District Court Judge Alfred Lechner sentences Yu Kikumura to 30 years in prison	Japanese Red Army
4/3	Tucson, AZ	Thousand lab animals released from the University of Arizona and 2 campus buildings set afire: the Pharmacy Microbiology Building and the Office of the Division of Animal Resources	Animal Liberation Front (ALF)
5/30	Wenden, AZ	Training for an attack on nuclear facilities in Arizona, California, and Colorado	Evan Mecham Eco-Terrorist International Conspiracy (EMETIC)
6/19	Bayamon, PR	Pipe bombing of Bank of Boston Branch; no injuries but slight damage	Boricua People's Army-Macheteros

6/19	Bayamon, PR	Pipe bombing of Army recruiting office; no injuries but slight damage	(same as above)
7/3 or 7/4	Lubbock, TX	Laboratory animals released, lab equipment destroyed, records and data for lab experiments stolen, and animal rights slogans painted on walls of the Health Sciences Center at Texas Tech University	Animal Liberation Front (ALF)
10/4	Washington, DC	Fawaz Younis sentenced to concurrent terms of 5 years for conspiracy to commit air piracy, 30 years for taking American hostages, and 25 years for aircraft piracy	Islamic Amal

1990

1/12	Santurce, PR	Pipe bombing of Navy recruiting office; windows shatter but no injuries	Brigada Internacionalista Eugenio Maria De Hostos de las Fuerza Revolucionarias Pedro Albizu Campos (Eugenio Maria de Hostos International Brigade of the Pedro Albizu Campos Revolutionary Forces)
1/12	Carolina, PR	Pipe bombing of Westinghouse Electric Company; no injuries	(same as above)
1/31	Tucson, AZ	Rashid Khalifa, controversial Muslim leader, is stabbed to death	al-Fuqra
2/22	Los Angeles, CA	An explosive device detonated in a vehicle parked within 60 feet of the Olympic Plaza Building containing offices of the IRS	Up the IRS, Inc.
3/30	Quincy, MA	The Islamic center is attacked	al-Fuqra
4/22	Santa Cruz County, CA	Two power poles sawed in half, disrupting electrical power for 4 hours	Earth Night Action Group

5/27	Mayaguez, PR	Two Puerto Rican Army National Guard (PRANG) vehicles set on fire, which results in the destruction of 1 vehicle and considerable damage to the other	Suspected Puerto Rican terrorist element
8/7	Pittsburgh, PA	James Wickstrom, 47, sentenced to 38 months in prison for conspiracy to distribute $100,000 in counterfeit money and pass bad checks to finance an underground guerrilla army	Posse Comitatus
9/7	Washington, DC	Marilyn Jean Buck, Laura Jane Whitehorn, and Linda Sue Evans plead guilty to charges relating to the 1983 bombing in the Washington, DC, area	May 19 Communist Organization (M19CO)
9/17	Arecibo, PR	Bombing of Citibank branch; small damage and no injuries	Pedro Albizu Campos Revolutionary Forces (PACRF)
9/17	Vega Baja, PR	Bombing of Harvey Hubber electric plug factory; damage reported but no injuries	(same as above)
10/22	Portland, OR	Tom Metzger, 52; his son John, 22; and 2 skinheads, Ken Mieske and Kyle Brewster, found liable for the 1988 beating death of Mulugeta Seraw, an Ethiopian, $12.5 million in damages awarded	White Aryan Resistance (WAR)
11/5	New York, NY	Assassination of Rabbi Meir Kahane	El Sayyid Nosair

1991

1/2	Chicago, IL	The "liberation" of rabbits and guinea pigs from Hektoen Lab, a Cook County Hospital research laboratory	Animal Liberation Front (ALF)
1/11	San Diego, CA	Islamic Cultural Center is attacked	al-Fuqra

2/3	Mayaguez, PR	Two Puerto Rican Army National Guard (PRANG) vehicles set afire	Popular Liberation Army (PLA)
2/18	Sabana, Grande, PR	Two Puerto Rican Army National Guard (PRANG) vehicles set afire	(same as above)
3/17	Carolina, PR	Arson of A-7D combat jet at Air Force National Guard base	Suspected Puerto Rican terrorist element
3/31	Fresno, CA	Bombing of National Treasury Employee Union; no injuries	Up the IRS, Inc.
4/1	Fresno, CA	Pipe bombs explode in parking lot and on roof of IRS building; no injuries but several cars damaged	(same as above)
7/6	Punta Borinquen, PR	Bombing of a Hercules C-130 aircraft; front portion of fuselage burns	Popular Liberation Army
9/11	Yauco, PR	Pipe bomb explodes in front of the U.S. post office, causing moderate damage	Unknown individuals or group
11/14	Washington, DC	Two Libyan intelligence operatives indicted by a federal grand jury for their involvement in the terrorist bombing of Pan American Flight 103 over Lockerbie, Scotland, on December 20, 1988, which claimed 270 lives	Terrorists with ties to Iran, Syria, and Libya
12/21	New York, NY	Egyptian-born Muslim, El Sayyid Nossair, 36, found guilty of assault, coercion, and weapons charges but innocent of the 1990 killing of Rabbi Meir Kahane and of attempted murder stemming from a gunfight with police after the rabbi's slaying	Radical Islamic terrorist element

1992

1/29	New York, NY	Justice Alvin Schlesinger sentences El Sayyid Nossair, found guilty of assault, coercion, and weapons charges but innocent of the 1990 killing of Rabbi Meir Kahane, to 7 1/3 to 22 years in prison	Radical Islamic terrorist element
2/2	East Lansing, MI	Fire is started at Mink Research Facility at Michigan State University	Animal Liberation Front (ALF)
4/5	New York, NY	Five MEK members forcibly enter and seize control of the Iranian Mission to the United Nations; no injuries result, and all 5 members are subsequently arrested	Mujahedin-E-Khalq (MEK)
8/21	Ruby Ridge, ID	Eleven-day siege with the separatist Weaver family; 3 killed, including a federal agent	Randall Weaver
11/19	Urbana, IL	Attempt at firebombing the Levis Faculty Center (LFC), located at the University of Illinois, where the conference "Latin America 2000" was taking place with academics and corporate personnel from throughout the United States, Mexico, and South America in attendance	Mexican Revolutionary Movement (Movimiento Revolucionario Mexicano)
12/10	Chicago, IL	Car fire and attempted pipe bombing of Marine recruiting office	Boricua Revolutionary Front (2 incidents)

1993

1/17	Chicago, IL	Three Molotov cocktails cause a fire at the Serbian National Defense Council (SNDCA); threatening telephone calls were received	Suspected terrorist element

1/25	Langley, VA	Shooting outside CIA headquarters, 2 victims killed–Frank Darling, 28-year-old covert for the CIA, and Lansing Bennett, 66-year-old physician and intelligence analyst–and 3 injured as they sat in their cars in rush hour traffic	Mir Aimal Kasi
2/26	New York, NY	Car bombing of the World Trade Center kills 6 people, injures more than 1,000, and does more than $500 million in damage	International Radical Terrorism (IRT)
2/28	Waco, TX	51-day siege begins at Branch Davidian compound	David Koresh and followers
4/19	Waco, TX	51-day siege ends at Branch Davidian compound; 92 killed, including 4 federal agents	(same as above)
6/22	Tiburon, CA	Mail bomb injures Charles Epstein, geneticist at University of California, San Francisco	Unabomber
6/24	New Haven, CT	Mail bomb injures Yale University professor David Gelernter	(same as above)
7/15	Los Angeles, CA	Eight suspects are arrested in a plot to start a race war by assassinating prominent black and Jewish leaders	A variety of skinhead and neo Nazi groups, including White Aryan Resistance (WAR)
7/20	Tacoma, WA	Pipe bombing and fire bombing of NAACP building	American Front Skinheads (AFS)
7/22	Tacoma, WA	Bombing of Elite Tavern gay bar	(same as above)
9/16	New York, NY	Mohamed Salameh, Nidal Ayyad, Mahmoud Abouhalima, and Ahmed Ajaj go on trial for conspiracy to bomb targets in the United States, the bombing of the World Trade Center, and the use of explosive devices	International Radical Terrorism (IRT)

| 11/27-11/28 | Chicago, IL | Fire bombings (9 incidents), 4 left small fires at Saks Fifth Avenue, Marshall Field's, Carson Pirie Scott, and forced the evacuation of Neiman Marcus; no injuries reported in all bombings | Animal Liberation Front (ALF) |

1994

1/5	New York, NY	Two explosive devices found outside buildings housing Jewish American organizations that actively support the Middle East peace process	Suspected terrorist element
3/1	New York, NY	Rashid Baz, Lebanese immigrant, shoots at car carrying Jewish rabbinical students on Brooklyn Bridge and injures 4; Aaron Haberstam dies of his wounds	Possible ties to Middle Eastern terror group
3/4	New York, NY	Mohamed Salameh, Nidal Ayyad, Mahmoud Abouhalima, and Ahmed Ajaj convicted on all 38 counts against them, including conspiracy to bomb targets in the United States, the bombing of the World Trade Center, and the use of explosive devices	International Radical Terrorism (IRT)
5/25	New York, NY	Mohamed Salameh, Nidal Ayyad, Mahmoud Abouhalima, and Ahmed Ajaj are each sentenced to 240 years in prison and are fined $250,000 for conspiracy to bomb targets in the United States, the bombing of the World Trade Center, and the use of explosive devices	(same as above)
5/25	Miami, FL	Alain Daniel Mesili, sought by U.S. and Bolivian governments in connection with a bomb and automatic weapons attack on the U.S. Marine Security Guard in La Paz, is arrested and later returned to Bolivia to stand trail	Comision Nestor Paz Zamora (CNPZ)

7/26	St. Louis, MO	Tawfiq Musa, Saif Nijmeh, and Luie Nijmeh plead guilty for violating 1 felony count of the Racketeer Influenced and Corrupt Organizations (RICO) Act by conspiring to participate in a terrorist organization known as ANO	Abu Nidal Organization (ANO)
9/27	Pascua Yaqui Reservation, AZ	Rod Coronado arrested for involvement in the 1992 arson at Michigan State University's mink facilities and later accepts plea agreement for aiding and abetting the arson	Animal Liberation Front (ALF)
10/21	St. Louis, MO	U.S. District Judge Donald J. Stohr sentences Tawfiq Musa, Saif Nijmeh, and Luie Nijmeh to 21 months in prison for violating 1 felony count of the Racketeer Influenced and Corrupt Organizations (RICO) Act by conspiring to participate in a terrorist organization known as ANO	Abu Nidal Organization (ANO)
12/6	Chicago, IL	Claude Daniel Marks and Donna Jean Willmott, wanted for assisting in an escape plan to liberate Oscar Lopez of the FALN from a U.S. penitentiary, surrender to the FBI	Armed Forces of National Liberation (FALN) and the Prairie Fire Organizing Committee (PFOC)
12/10	North Caldwell, NJ	Mail bomb kills Thomas Mosser of Young and Rubicam	Unabomber

1995

1/9	New York, NY	Jury selection begins in the trial of Sheik Omar Abdel Rahman and 9 other defendants charged with seditious conspiracy and other crimes in a June 1993 plot to bomb major landmarks in New York City and assassinate prominent politicians and foreign leaders	International Radical Terrorism (IRT)

2/28	Minneapolis, MN	Jury convicts Douglas Allen Baker and Leroy Charles Wheeler for the manufacture and intended use of ricin, a highly toxic biological substance, with the intent to kill law enforcement officers	Minnesota Patriot Council
3/9	Chicago, IL	Melvin Edward Mays, indicted in 1986, arrested and charged with conspiracy to conduct terrorist activities on behalf of Libya	El Rukn
3/11	Lakewood, CA	Threatening telephone calls made to First Data Corporation	Benjamin Ruiz Valencia, supporter of Zapatista National Liberation Army (EZLN)
3/12	Tucson, AZ	Michael "Mixie" Martin pleads guilty to 1 count of violating Title 18, U.S.C., Sec. 371, Conspiracy to Obtain Munitions and Weapons	Provisional Irish Republican Army (PIRA)
4/19	Oklahoma City, OK	Bombing of the Alfred P. Murrah Federal Building, killing 168 and wounding hundreds of others	Individuals (Timothy McVeigh and Terry Nichols) and perhaps others unknown
4/19	Varner, AR	Execution of Richard Wayne Snell, who murdered a black police officer and a businessman who he mistakenly thought was Jewish	Snell was a member of the Covenant, Sword and the Arm of the Lord (CSA)
4/21	Oklahoma City, OK	Timothy James McVeigh charged with violating Title 18, U.S. Code, Section 844{f} and 2, maliciously damaging and destroying a building by means of explosives	Timothy McVeigh, Terry Nichols, and others unknown
4/24	Sacramento, CA	Mail bomb kills timber-industry lobbyist Gilbert Murray	Unabomber
5/9	Chicago, IL	Claude Daniel Marks and Donna Jean Willmott plead guilty to a plot to use explosives to help Oscar Lopez escape from U.S. penitentiary in Leavenworth, Kansas in 1985	Supporters of the Prairie Fire Organizing Committee and the Armed Forces of National Liberation (FALN)

5/11	Oklahoma City, OK	Terry Lynn Nichols charged with violating Title 18, U.S. Code, Section 844{f} and 2, maliciously damaging and destroying a building by means of explosives	Individuals and others unknown
5/31	Lancaster, OH	Larry Wayne Harris, 44, charged with placing an illegal mail order for freeze-dried bubonic plague bacteria	Ties to white supremacist groups
6/25	Monroe County, OH	Michael Hill, a 50-year-old militia member, is shot and killed by a police officer after he exits his car, carrying a .45 caliber pistol in his waistband, and additional weapons and ammunition are found in his truck	Ohio Unorganized Militia
6/28	Los Angeles, CA	Bomb threat slows traffic at Los Angeles International Airport	Unabomber
6/30	Tucson, AZ	Kevin McKinley and Seamus Moley sentenced to 19 months in prison for placing explosives on a motor vehicle and possession of property, and aid of foreign government	Provisional Irish Republican Army (PIRA)
7/3	East Lansing, MI	Rodney Coronado pleads guilty to arson charges relating to a 1992 fire at the Mink Research Facility in Michigan	Animal Liberation Front (ALF)
7/25	Jamaica, NY	Mousa Mohammed Abu Marzook, 44, detained by Immigration and Naturalization Service at Kennedy International Airport after his name surfaces in a terrorist watch list; held for possible extradition to Israel	Suspected political leader of Islamic Resistance Movement (Hamas)
8/3	New York, NY	Eyad Ismoil, returned by Jordanian authorities to the United States on August 2, 1995, is charged with bombing and conspiracy violations in connection with the 1993 World Trade Center bombing	International Radical Terrorism (IRT)

8/10	Oklahoma City, OK	A federal grand jury in the Western District of Oklahoma indicts co-conspirators McVeigh and Nichols on 1 count of conspiracy to use a weapon of mass destruction to kill persons and to destroy federal property; 1 count of using a weapon of mass destruction to kill persons; 1 count of malicious destruction of federal property; and 8 counts of first-degree murder	Individuals and others unknown
9/19	Washington, DC	At the request of of Attorney General Janet Reno and FBI, and with the concurrence of the *New York Times*, the *Washington Post* publishes the unaltered 35,000-word manifesto of the serial bomber known as the Unabomber	Suspected serial bomber known as the Unabomber
10/1	New York, NY	Sheik Omar Abdel Rahman convicted of seditious conspiracy, solicitation to murder Egyptian President Hosni Mubarak, conspiracy to murder President Mubarak, solicitation to attack a U.S. military installation, and conspiracy to conduct bombings	Sheik Rahman is affiliated with al-Gama´at al-Islamiyya
10/1	New York, NY	Clement Hampton-El, Amir Abdelgani, Fares Khallafalla, Tarig Elhassan, Fadil Abdelghani, Mohammed Saleh, and Victor Alvarez found guilty with Sheik Rahman of seditious conspiracy, bombing conspiracy, and attempted bombing	International Radical Terrorism (IRT)

10/1	New York, NY	In the only acquittals in the Rahman trial, Ibrahim El-Gabrowney and El Sayyid Nosair are found not guilty of the bombing conspiracy; however, Elgabrowney is found guilty of seditious conspiracy and other charges, including possession of false documents, and Nosair is also convicted of seditious conspiracy, as well as the earlier murder of Rabbi Meir Kahane (charged under a federal provision that does not constitute double jeopardy)	(same as above)
10/9	Hyder, AZ	Derailment of Amtrak's Sunset Limited, killing 1 and injuring more than 100	Sons of the Gestapo
10/25	Minneapolis, MN	Jury convicts Richard John Oelrich and Dennis Brett Henderson for the manufacture and intended use of ricin, a highly toxic biological substance	Minnesota Patriot Council
11/11	Vernon, OK	Ray Willie Lampley, Cecilia Lampley, and John Dare Baird arrested for conspiring to build and possess a destructive device for use against civil rights offices, abortion clinics, and federal agencies	Militia ties
12/18	Reno, NV	Thirty-gallon plastic drum packed with 100 pounds of ammonium nitrate and fuel oil found in the parking lot of the IRS building	Joseph Martin Bailie and Ellis Edward Hurst are suspected
12/20	Onia, AR	Thomas Lewis Lavy, 50, arrested for trying to smuggle 130 grams of ricin, a poisonous white powder distilled from castor beans, across Alaska's border with Canada in 1993	Ties to right-wing survivalist groups

1996

2/20	Oklahoma City, OK	Judge Richard P. Matsch of federal court moves the McVeigh and Nichols trials to Denver in an effort to ensure a fair hearing	Timothy McVeigh, Terry Nichols, and others unknown
3/25	Jordan, MT	Authorities arrest Leroy Schweitzer in connection with bogus checks, prompting an 81-day standoff between FBI and members of antigovernment extremists	Montana Freemen
4/3	Lincoln, MT	After nearly two decades, 16 package bombs, 3 killed, and 23 wounded, Theodore John Kaczynski is detained by federal agents as a suspect in the Unabomb case	Suspected serial bomber known as the Unabomber
4/6	Spokane, WA	Pipe bombing of suburban office of *The Spokesman-Review* newspaper	Phineas Priesthood
4/6	Spokane, WA	Bombing and robbery of Spokane Valley Bank; building damaged but no injuries	(same as above)
4/10	New York, NY	U.S. Department of State expels a Sudanese diplomat at the Sudanese Mission to the United Nations who had ties to the conspirators planning to bomb the UN and other targets in New York in 1993	Sudanese Government
4/12	Sacramento, CA	Pipe bomb found near post office	Unknown group leaving note stating "Timothy McVeigh lives-on"
5/20	Laredo, TX	Bomb is detonated outside building where FBI offices are located	Suspected terrorist element
6/13	Jordan, MT	Peaceful end of 81-day standoff between FBI and members of antigovernment extremists	Montana Freemen

7/1	Phoenix, AZ	A dozen members of a militia-type organization are arrested for allegedly planning to blow up 7 government buildings in Phoenix, including the Phoenix Police Department and National Guard Headquarters	Viper Militia
7/17	South Jordan, UT	Clinton Ellerman, 21-year-old Kevin Dexter Clark, and several others jump a fence and open door to the mink buildings and cages, as well as spray-paint "ALF" and "blood money" on buildings	Animal Liberation Front (ALF)
7/27	Atlanta, GA	A crude pipe bomb detonates at 1:25 A.M., spraying nails and screws at Centennial Olympic Park, killing 1 and wounding more than 100 people	Unknown group (at 1:06 A.M. a male with no discernible accent calls 911 and warns of an impending explosion in Centennial Park in 30 minutes)
9/5	New York, NY	Ramzi Ahmed Yousef and Abdul Hakim Murad found guilty in plotting to bomb U.S. air carriers transiting the Far East	Conspiracy with Wali Khan Amin
10/11	Stonewall, Lewis County, Fairmont, Lavalette, WV; Maple Heights and Cleveland, OH; and Waynesburg, PA	Seven members of a West Virginia militia group arrested for allegedly planning to blow up an FBI complex in Clarksburg, West Virginia	West Virginia Mountaineer Militia
10/25	Oklahoma City, OK	Judge Richard P. Matsch orders separate trials for McVeigh and Nichols	Timothy McVeigh, Terry Nichols, and others unknown
11/8	Wheeling, WV	Seven men are indicted by a federal grand jury in connection with an alleged plot to blow up the FBI fingerprint center in Clarksburg, West Virginia	West Virginia Mountain Militia

12/5	New York, NY	Wali Khan Amin Shah convicted for plotting to bomb U.S. air carriers transiting the Far East	Conspiracy with Ramzi Ahmed Yousef and Abdul Hakim Murad

1997

1/2-3	Washington, DC	Letter bombs found in the Washington area (4 bombs sent to the Arabic-language newspaper *Al-Hayat*, located in the National Press Club, and 1 in a Washington-area post office)	Suspected Middle East terrorist element
1/2-3	Fort Leavenworth, KS	Letter bombs sent to the federal prison where a key figure in the World Trade Center bombing, Mohammed Salameh, is serving a life sentence	(same as above)
1/13	New York, NY	Letter bomb found at the United Nations bureau of the Arabic-language newspaper *Al-Hayat*	(same as above)
1/16	Sandy Springs, GA	Bomb shatters southwest corner of an abortion clinic; more powerful bomb programmed to detonate last explodes in a trash container outside the northwest corner of the building, injuring 6 people	Army of God is suspected
2/15	Wilmington, OH	Shootout with Ohio police following a traffic stop	Patriot adherents Chevie Kehoe and Cheyne Kehoe; Chevie wanted for federal firearm charge and for questioning in connection with June 1996 murder of Arkansas gun dealer and his wife and 8-year-old daughter
2/19	Philadelphia, PA	Mark Thomas, 47-year-old former head of the Pennsylvania Ku Klux Klan and current head of the Commonwealth's Aryan Nations chapter pleads to charges involving several midwestern bank robberies	Aryan Republican Army

2/22	Atlanta, GA	Bombing of the Otherside Lounge nightclub catering primarily to gays and lesbians	Army of God suspected
2/24	New York, NY	An English teacher from the Gaza Strip fires a gun into a crowd on the Empire State Building's 86th-floor observation deck, killing 1 and injuring 6 others	Ali Hassan Abu Kamal, 69-year-old Palestinian with a note declaring his hatred for Zionists
2/25	Jacksonville, FL	Harry Shapiro, 31, charged with planting a bomb at a Conservative Jewish synagogue on February 13 only hours before Shimon Peres, the former prime minister of Israel, spoke to 1,500 people there	Radical Jewish element
4/3	Phoenix, AZ	Dean Pleasant, 28, who allegedly narrated a videotape on how to destroy federal Buildings, sentenced to 71 months in prison for conspiring to use explosives	Viper Militia
4/23	Lancaster, OH	Former white supremacist Larry Wayne Harris, 46, who pleads guilty to illegally obtaining 3 vials of lethal bubonic plague germs, given 18 months' probation and 200 hours of community service	Ties to white supremacy groups
4/27	Fort Davis, TX	Start of a week-long standoff at remote area where a separatist group led by Richard McLaren, wanted on charges of avoiding a federal contempt citation, abducted Joe and Margaret Ann Rowe	Republic of Texas
5/3	Fort Davis, TX	End of the week-long standoff between Richard McLaren and 4 followers; a sixth separatist, Richard F. Keyes, 22, was later arrested	(same as above)

5/28	New York, NY	Mohammad Aboulalima, 33, found guilty of helping his brother Mahmud Aboulalima flee to Saudi Arabia following the February 1993 bombing of the World Trade Center	No terrorist affiliation
5/30	Wheeling, WV	A West Virginia militia group member, Edward F. Moore, 52, and Jack A. Phillips, 57, plead guilty in connection with the alleged plot to bomb the FBI's fingerprint complex in West Virginia in 1996	Mountaineer Militia
5/30	New York, NY	Government of Jordan agrees to accept Abu Marzook, the political director of Hamas held in a federal holding facility for possible extradition to Israel, on "humanitarian grounds"	Hamas
6/2	Denver, CO	Timothy James McVeigh is convicted on 1 count of conspiracy to use a weapon of mass destruction, 1 count of the use of a weapon of mass destruction, 1 count of destruction by an explosive, and 8 counts of causing the death of 8 federal law enforcement agents	Timothy James McVeigh
6/6	Atmore, AL	Henry Francis Hays, former Klansman convicted of 1981 lynch-style killing of black teenager Michael Donald put to death in Alabama's electric chair	United Klans of America
6/13	Denver, CO	Jury recommends a death sentence for Timothy James McVeigh	Timothy James McVeigh
6/13	Wheeling, WV	Floyd "Ray" Looker, 56, found guilty of conspiracy to engage in manufacturing of and dealing in explosives without a license in the plot to destroy the FBI's fingerprint complex in West Virginia in 1996	Mountaineer Militia

6/16	Colville, WA	Cheyne Kehoe, wanted for a videotaped shootout with Ohio police after a traffic stop, surrenders in his hometown of Colville	Ties to right-wing extremist groups
6/17	Cedar City, UT	Chevie Kehoe, wanted for a videotaped shootout with Ohio police after a traffic stop, arrested at traffic stop	(same as above)
6/18	Fairfax, VA	Mir Aimal Kansi, wanted for killing 2 and injuring 3 outside CIA headquarters in Virginia, turned over to U.S. officials by Afghan individuals	Reputed to have wanted to make statement against CIA and U.S. foreign policy
6/18	Washington, DC	Hani Abdel Rahim Hussein al-Sayegh extradited from Canada in connection with a bombing that killed 19 U.S. airmen in Saudi Arabia in 1996	Possible links to Saudi Shiite groups and Iran
6/23	Phoenix, AZ	Federal jury convicts Viper Militia member Charles Knight of a conspiracy charge stemming from the group's paramilitary explosives exercises in the desert	Viper Militia
6/26	Jacksonville, FL	Harry Shapiro, 31, sentenced to 10 years in prison for planting a bomb at a Conservative synagogue where Shimon Peres, the former prime minister of Israel, spoke on February 13, 1997	Radical Jewish element
7/23	Fort Hood TX	Seven men and a women are arrested in connection with a plot to use antipersonnel bombs and other weapons at Fort Hood army base	Elements of the Southern Kansas Regional Militia
7/30	Washington, DC	Hani Abdel Rahim Hussein al-Sayegh indicted for conspiring during 1994 and 1995 to kill Americans residing in Saudi Arabia, but he backs out of the plea agreement and pleads not guilty; the U.S. Department of Justice announces in September that it is dropping the charge because it lacks the evidence to bring Sayegh to trial	Possible links to Saudi Shiite groups and Iran

7/31	Brooklyn, NY	Two suspects, Ghazi Ibrahim Abu Maizer and Lafi Khalil, are arrested as they allegedly plan a suicide bombing attack of the New York subway system	Possible links to the Islamic resistance movement (Hamas)
8/13	Tampa, FL	Emilio Ippolito, 72, his daughter, Susan Mokdad, 41, and 5 men were found guilty of threatening U.S. and state judges and jurors in Florida and California	Constitutional Common Law Court
8/14	Denver, CO	Judge Richard P. Matsch sentences Timothy James McVeigh to death	Timothy James McVeigh
8/26	Wheeling, WV	Firefighter James Roger, 41, becomes the first person to be convicted under the 1995 federal antiterrorism law, when jury finds him guilty of giving photographs of blueprints of the FBI complex in West Virginia to a self-described paramilitary leader	No suspected terrorist connection
8/30	Brooklyn, NY	A federal jury returns a 4-count indictment against Gazi Ibrahim Abu Maizer and Lafi Khalil, accused of plotting suicide bombings in the New York City subway system	Possible links to the Islamic resistance movement (Hamas)
9/30	Spokane, WA	Four Idaho men—Verne Jay Merrell, 51; Charles Barbee, 45; Robert S. Berry, 43; and Brian Ratigan, 38, convicted of federal charges stemming from 3 pipe bombings—*The Spokesman-Review* newspaper, Planned Parenthood, and a branch of a U.S. bank—and 2 bank robberies	Phineas Priesthood
11/4	Alpine, TX	Richard McLaren, leader of Texas separatist movement, sentenced to 99 years in prison; his top lieutenant, Robert Otto, gets 50 years for the April 27 abduction of Joe and Margaret Ann Rowe that led to a week-long standoff with police	Republic of Texas

11/10	Fairfax, VA	Mir Aimal Kasi, 33, found guilty of capital murder for killing 2 and wounding 3 outside CIA headquarters	Reputed to have wanted to make a statement against CIA and U.S. foreign policy
11/11	Sacramento, CA	Theodore John Kaczynski goes on trial in the Unabomb case	Suspected serial bomber known as the Unabomber
11/12	New York, NY	Ramzi Ahmed Yousef, mastermind of the plot to blow up the World Trade Center; and Eyad Ismoil, the driver of the bomb-laden van, were found guilty of 10 charges, including participating in a plot to topple the twin towers through explosives, transporting explosives, and other related crimes	A terrorist conspiracy among Sheik Omar Abdel Rahman, Ramzi Ahmed Yousef, Eyad Ismoil, Mohammed Salameh, Ahmed Ajaj, Nidal Ayyad, and Mahmud Abouhalima
12/18	Salt Lake, UT	Clinton Colby Ellerman sentenced to a 2-year jail term and fined $14,594 for his role in releasing thousands of minks from a South Jordan mink farm	Animal Liberation Front (ALF)
12/23	Denver, CO	After deliberating 41 hours over 6 days, jury finds Terry Lynn Nichols guilty of conspiracy to use a weapon of mass destruction and involuntary manslaughter with regard to causing the deaths of 8 federal law enforcement agents	Terry Lynn Nichols

1998

1/8	New York, NY	Ramzi Ahmed Yousef is sentenced by Federal Judge Kevin Duffy to 240 years for his role in the bombing and a life sentence for his role in blowing up a Philippines airliner; both sentences to be served in solitary confinement	A terrorist conspiracy among Sheik Omar Abdel Rahman, Ramzi Ahmed Yousef, Eyad Ismoil, Mohammed Salameh, Ahmed Ajaj, Nidal Ayyad, and Mahmud Abouhalima

1/22	Sacramento, CA	Theodore John Kaczynski, 55-year-old mathematics professor-turned-hermit, pleads guilty to being the serial bomber who killed 3 and avoided detection for nearly 20 years in exchange for a sentence of life in prison without parole	Unabomber
1/23	Fairfax, VA	Judge J. Howe Brown sentences Mir Aimal Kasi, 33, to death for the 1993 shooting deaths of 2 CIA analysts outside the agency's Langley, Virginia, headquarters	Freelance terrorist
1/29	Birmingham, AL	Head nurse and counselor of the New Women All Women Clinic, Emily Lyons, 41, is severely injured and off-duty Police Officer Robert D. Sanderson, 34, moonlighting at the clinic as a security guard, is killed in what is believed to be the first fatal abortion clinic bombing in U.S. history	Army of God
2/20	Las Vegas, NV	Larry Wayne Harris, 46, and William Job Leavitt, Jr., 47, charged by federal agents for possession of a toxin believed to be anthrax	Harris has ties to white supremacist groups
2/23	Las Vegas NV	All biological weapons charges dropped against Larry Wayne Harris and William Job Leavitt, Jr., arrested on February 20, 1998, for possession of anthrax, when tests showed the material they possessed was a harmless anthrax veterinary vaccine	(same as above)
3/6	East St. Louis, IL	Group of white supremacists, including Dennis Michael McGriffen, 35; Wallace Scott Wetcherding, 64; and Ralph P. Block, 27, plotted to bomb public buildings and to kill Morris Dees, head of SPLC in Montgomery, Alabama, FBI agent Jason Thompson testifies at a hearing	The New Order

| 3/6 | Columbus, OH | Larry Wayne Harris, arrested last month in the Las Vegas anthrax scare and jailed after being accused of violating probation was ordered released by a federal magistrate | Ties to white supremacy groups |

Chapter 7

ORGANIZATIONS TO CONTACT FOR INFORMATION ON TERRORIST AND EXTREMIST

THE SENTINELS

A variety of organizations monitor the activities of terrorist and extremist groups operating within the United States. All have information available to the public, some free and some not. Some even make this information available on their Web sites. Listed below are reference services, depositories, and publishers that also provide data on terrorists and extremists, usually at a modest cost. Consult the organization or service for a price list.

The following list was compiled close to the date of publication of this book; names, addresses, telephone and fax numbers, and e-mail/Internet addresses may change. Be aware that many organizations take several weeks or longer to respond to inquires.

American Jewish Committee (AJC)
The Jacob Blaustein Building
165 East 56th Street
New York, NY 10022
(212) 751-4000
Fax: (212) 751-4019
e-mail: *ajc@compserv*
Web site: *http://www.ajc.org*

Founded in 1906, the American Jewish Committee is the oldest human relations agency in the United States. The agenda of the AJC is devoted to fighting anti-Semitism and bigotry, promoting pluralism and intergroup relations, and protecting democratic traditions. Its research department tracks white supremacist groups and militias.

The AJC has issued many reports, such as *Skinheads: Who They Are and What to Do When They Come to Town* and *Militias: A Growing Danger.*

Anti-Defamation League (ADL)

823 United Nations Plaza
New York, NY 10017
(212) 490-2525
Fax: (212) 867-0779
Web site: *http://www.adl.org*

The Anti-Defamation League was formed in 1913 to fight bigotry, racism, and anti-Semitism. It advocates the adoption of penalty-enhancement laws and antiparamilitary training statutes as a means to fight hate crimes and terrorism. The ADL publishes the quarterly *Facts* magazine, the monthly *On the Frontline* newsletter, and the occasional *Terrorism Update.* It also distributes reports such as *Armed and Dangerous: Militias Take Aim at the Federal Government, Beyond the Bombing: The Militia Menace Grows,* and *The ADL Anti-Paramilitary Training Statute: A Response to Domestic Terrorism.*

American Society of Industrial Security (ASIS)

1625 Prince Street
Alexandria, VA 22314
(703) 519-6200
Fax: (703) 519-6299
Web site: *http://www.asisonline.org*

The American Society of Industrial Security is an international organization for security professionals, with more than 25,000 members worldwide. ASIS is dedicated to increasing the effectiveness and productivity of security professionals by developing educational programs and materials that address broad security issues such as terrorism. ASIS has a standing committee on terrorism and conducts educational sessions at its annual meetings. Its monthly publication *Security Management* is often devoted to terrorism and related security issues.

Center for Democratic Renewal (CDR)

P.O. Box 50469
Atlanta, GA 30302
(404) 221-0025

Fax: (404) 221-0045

e-mail: *cdr@igc.apc.org*

The Center for Democratic Renewal, formerly the National Anti-Klan Network, monitors hate group and white supremacist activity in the United States. It publishes the magazine *The Right Unmasked* and the annual report *The Monitor*. The CDR also publishes such reports as *Militias: Exploding Into the Mainstream* and *Paramilitary Right Moves Center Stage*.

Center for Hate and Extremism

Richard Stockton College of New Jersey

Jim Leeds Road

Pomona, NJ 08240

(609) 652-4719

Fax: (609) 748-5559

The Center for Hate and Extremism was created to study hate crime and to track the spread of antigovernment extremist movements throughout the United States. It shares its findings with researchers and students, as well as releases media alerts and holds press conferences to warn of particular trends in extremist behavior.

Coalition for Human Dignity (CHD)

P.O. Box 40344

Portland, Oregon 97240

(503) 281-5823 or

(206) 233-9775 in Seattle

Fax: (503) 281-8673

e-mail: *chdpx@aol.com*

The Coalition for Human Dignity, founded in 1989, is dedicated to opposing organized bigotry. It works to strengthen democracy and oppose racism, anti-Semitism, and homophobia through research, public education, networking, and organizing. The CHD publishes a quarterly journal, *The Dignity Report,* and reports such as *Against the New World Order: The American Militia Movement* and *Guns and Gavels: Common Law Courts, Militias, and White Supremacy.*

Federal Aviation Administration (FAA)

U.S. Department of Transportation

800 Independence Avenue, SW

Washington, DC 20591

(202) 267-3484

Since 1986, the FAA's Office of Civil Aviation Security has published an annual report entitled *Criminal Acts Against Civil Aviation.* This report is a compilation of criminal incidents against civil aviation aircraft and interests worldwide. Beginning with the 1993 edition, each subsequent issue also contains feature articles and geographic overviews. Incidents are summarized in the overviews, and the feature articles focus on specific aviation-related issues or case histories. Copies of these reports may be obtained from the National Technical Information Service (NTIS), U.S. Department of Commerce, 5285 Port Royal Road, Springfield, VA 22151. Write or call the NTIS for a price quotation: (703) 487-4650.

Federal Bureau of Investigation (FBI)

Terrorist Research and Analytical Center (TRAC)

935 Pennsylvania Avenue, NW

Washington, DC 20535

(202) 324-2680

Fax: (202) 324-4746

Web site: *http://www.fbi.gov*

In 1977, the Federal Bureau of Investigation began issuing annual reports on terrorism. Today, these annual editions, known as *Terrorism in the United States,* are compiled by a specialized antiterrorist research section—the Terrorist Research and Analytical Center (TRAC). TRAC publishes an annual edition that describes international and domestic terrorist activity occurring inside the United States. It also reports on other politically-oriented violence committed in the United States and comments on foreign events that affect domestic extremist activities.

General Accounting Office (GAO)

Box 37050

Washington, DC 20013

(202) 512-6000

Fax: (202) 512-6061

e-mail: *dispatch@gao.gov*

Web site: *http://www.gao.gov*

The General Accounting Office was established in 1921 to audit independently government agencies. The GAO offers a range of products to communicate the results of its work. Product types include testimony, oral briefings, and written reports. All of GAO's unclassified reports are available to the public unless a requester desires to postpone release of a report for up to 30 days. The GAO can be consulted for reports relating to terrorism, such as the 112-page report entitled *Combating Terrorism: Federal Agencies' Efforts to Implement National Policy and Strategy* (GAO/NSIAD-97-254).

The Heritage Foundation
214 Massachusetts Avenue, NE
Washington, DC 20002
(202) 546-4400
Fax: (202) 546-8328
e-mail: *dicksonj@heritage.org*
Web site: *http://www.nationalsecurity.org*

The Heritage Foundation is a conservative, nonprofit, public-policy organization that advocates a strong national defense, free enterprise, and limited government. It provides a variety of position papers dealing with national defense and international and domestic terrorism issues. Its Web site provides links with a wide variety of defense issues related to intelligence and counterterrorism.

Institute for Alternative Journalism (IAJ)
77 Federal Street
San Francisco, CA 94107
(415) 284-1420
Fax: (415) 284-1414
e-mail: *alternet@alternet.org*
Web site: *http://www.mediademocracy.org*

The Institute for Alternative Journalism monitors the activities of groups with conservative and far right agendas. Its Web site provides information on militias in America and an on-line guide to promoting greater understanding and tolerance in America, "Democracy Works."

International Association of Chiefs of Police (IACP)
515 North Washington Street
Alexandria, VA 22314
(800) 843-4227
Fax: (703) 836-4543

Web site: *http://www.theiacp.org*

The International Association of Chiefs of Police is the world's oldest and largest nonprofit membership organization of police executives. Established in 1893, the IACP currently has more than 16,000 members in the United States and 94 other countries. The IACP studies all issues relating to contemporary law enforcement, including terrorism. The work of the IACP's Committee on Terrorism is made available to law enforcement professionals throughout the world. The association's monthly publication, *Police Chief,* devotes theme issues to terrorism and related topics.

International Association of Counterterrorism and Security Professional (IACSP)
P.O. Box 10265
Arlington, VA 22210
(703) 243-0993
Fax: (703) 243-1197
Web site: *http://www.securitynet.net*

The International Association of Counterterrorism and Security Professionals was founded in 1992 to form a center of information and educational services for counterterrorism professionals. The IACSP holds an annual Terrorism Trends & Forecast Symposium. It publishes the quarterly magazine *Counterterrorism & Security* and the bimonthly newsletter *Counterterrorism & Security Report.*

Militia Watchdog
P.O. Box 12606
Columbus, OH 43212
(614) 488-9141
Fax: (614) 487-9174
e-mail: *sparky@militia-watchdog.org*
Web site: *http://www.militia-watchdog.org*

The Militia Watchdog was created to monitor and disseminate information about the militia and patriot movements, including common law courts and tax resistors. It keeps an up-to-date list of Internet resources on these movements. The Militia Watchdog makes these resources, as well as "the Neo-Militia News," available to all who visit its Web site.

Montana Human Rights Network (MHRN)
P.O. Box 1222
Helena, MT 59624
(406) 442-5506
Fax: (406) 442-5589
e-mail: mhrn@initco.net

The Montana Human Rights Network is a watchdog group devoted primarily to exposing the activities of right-wing and other extremist groups operating in Montana. It provides research and monitoring, accountability and lobbying, and community organizing. The MHRN publishes a quarterly newsletter, *The Human Rights Network News*; the *News Flash*, a news update; and occasional research reports, such as *The Season of Discontent: Militias, Constitutionalists, and the Far Right in Montana* and *No More Wacos*.

National Institute of Justice (NIJ)
National Criminal Justice Reference Service (NCJRS)
Reference Department
P.O. Box 6000
Rockville, MD 20850
(301) 251-5500
Fax: (301) 251-5212
e-mail: *askncjs@ncjs.aspensys.com*
Web site: *http://www.ncjrs.org*

Established in 1977, the National Criminal Justice Reference Service has more than 140,000 volumes in its collection. Its entire holdings are abstracted and available on CD-ROM at a variety of university and public libraries throughout the United States. Anyone interested in information on terrorism, extremism, and related topics can request a customized search of the NIJ/NCJRS database.

Northwest Coalition Against Malicious Harassment (NWC)
P.O. Box 16776
Seattle, WA 98116
(206) 233-9136
Fax: (206) 233-0611
e-mail: *ncamh@aol.com*

Formed in 1987, the Northwest Coalition Against Malicious Harassment now includes more than 250 organizations and groups from Colorado, Idaho, Montana, Oregon, Washington, and Wyoming. The purpose of the NWC is to address the problem of malicious harassment and violence based on race, religion, gender or sexual orientation, and national origin and ancestry. The NWC newsletter *Northwest Beacon* is published four times a year. *What to Do When the Militia Comes to Town* is another of its publications.

Political Research Associates (PRA)

120 Beacon Street, Suite 202
Somerville, MA 02143
(617) 661-9313
Fax: (617) 661-0059
e-mail: *publiceye@igc.apc.org*
Web site: *http://www.publiceye.org*

Founded in 1981, Political Research Associates is a think-tank-type organization that researches, analyzes, and publishes on the political Right. Specifically, PRA tracks the entire right-wing movement in the United States, from the right wing within the electorate to paramilitary organizations such as the armed citizen militias. The PRA provides support for organizing efforts, especially among immigrants, welfare recipients, people of color, homosexuals and lesbians, and other targets of right-wing scapegoating. The PRA publishes *The Public Eye*, a quarterly newsletter devoted to unmasking the political Right. Its research analysts also publish such works as *Too Close for Comfort: Right-Wing Populism, Scapegoating, and Fascist Potentials in U.S. Political Traditions* and *Eyes Right! Challenging the Right Wing Backlash.*

Raoul Wallenberg Center for Civil Justice

1666 Connecticut Avenue, NW, Suite 500
Washington, DC 20009
(800) 636-0159
Fax: (800) 636-0159
e-mail: *wallenberg@earthlink.net*
Web site: *http://home.earthlink.net/~wallenberg*

The Raoul Wallenberg Center for Civil Justice was established to address the civil rights of victims of terrorism in the United States and abroad. The center maintains a network of lawyers, researchers, journalists, investigators, and government officials to aid in this effort.

Religious Movement Resource Center
629 South Howes
Fort Collins, CO 80521
(970) 490-2032
The Religious Movement Resource Center is a service of United
Campus Ministry at Colorado State University and Interfaith of Fort
Collins, Colorado. The center monitors extremist group activity per-
taining to religious intolerance, especially within Colorado.

Simon Wiesenthal Center (SWC)
9760 West Pico
Los Angeles, CA 90035
(310) 553-9036
Fax: (310) 210-0665
e-mail: *wiesenthal.com*
Web site: *http://www.wiesenthal.com*
The library and archives of the Simon Wiesenthal Center contain
information on racism, anti-Semitism, and related issues. SWC
resources are available to researchers, the media, students, and the
public. The SWC publishes a quarterly magazine called *Response*, as
well as reports such as *Racism, Mayhem, and Terrorism: The Emergence of
an Online Subculture of Hate.*

Southern Poverty Law Center (SPLC)
400 Washington Avenue
Montgomery, AL 36104
(334) 264-0286
Fax: (334) 264-8891
Web site: *http://www.splcenter.org*
The Southern Poverty Law Center litigates civil cases to protect the
rights of poor people threatened by extremist groups. The center's
Klanwatch Project was formed in 1979 to monitor white supremacist
and hate crime activity throughout the United States. It publishes the
Klanwatch Intelligence Report, a bimonthly newsletter updating develop-
ments in white supremacist activity and hate violence. In 1994, the
Klanwatch Project created the Militia Task Force to monitor developments in the antigovernment patriot movement. The SPLC publishes
numerous books and reports, including *False Patriots: The Threat of
Antigovernment Extremists, The Ku Klux Klan: A History of Racism and*

Violence, and *Law Enforcement Strategy: Effective Responses to Hate Groups.*

Studies in Conflict & Terrorism
Taylor & Francis
1900 Frost Road, Suite 101
Bristol, PA 19007
(800) 821-8312 (ext. 16)
Fax: (215) 885-5515
e-mail: *ssullivan@tandfpa.com*
   Studies in Conflict & Terrorism (formerly *Terrorism: An International Journal*) is a bimonthly journal devoted to the study of terrorism. Although the focus of the journal is international in scope, many articles deal with issues that have a direct impact on terrorism in America. The journal also has a book review section.

Terrorism and Political Violence
Frank Cass, c/o ISBS
5804 NE Hassalo Street
Portland, OR 97213
(800) 944-6190
Fax: (503) 280-8832
e-mail: *orders@isbs.com*
Web site: *http://www.frankcass.com*
   Terrorism and Political Violence is a British quarterly devoted to the academic study of all aspects of terrorism and political violence. It serves as the scholarly counterpart in Europe to the American journal *Studies in Conflict & Terrorism.* Like its sister journal, it contains a wide variety of articles devoted to issues that relate to terrorism in America. The publisher of the journal, Frank Cass and Company Limited, also offers additional publications devoted to the study of terrorism.

University Microfilms International (UMI)
300 North Zeeb Road
Ann Arbor, MI 48106
(313) 761-4700
Fax: (313) 973-1464
e-mail: *library_sales@umi.com*
Web site: *http://www.umi.com*
   University Microfilms International is a depository of more than

1.5 million dissertations from educational institutions throughout the United States, Canada, and the rest of the world. Major public and university libraries offer a hardbound listing of its holdings, *Dissertation Abstracts International.* A search of its computerized Datrix Research system can yield information on terrorism and related subject matter.

U.S. Department of State
Bureau of Public Affairs
Office of Public Communication
Washington, DC 20520
(202) 647-6575

Each year, the U.S. Department of State publishes a summary of international terrorist activity, *Patterns of Global Terrorism.* These annual reports contain data on terrorist activities aimed against Americans living and visiting abroad. The reports also contain information on groups that target the United States.

Western States Center (WSC)
522 SW 5th Avenue, # 1390
Portland, OR 97204
(503) 228-8866
Fax: (503) 228-1965
Web site: *http://www.igc.org/westernstates/*

The Western States Center, founded in 1987, provides research and policy analysis to Western leaders, the press, and the public in eight Western states: Alaska, Idaho, Montana, Nevada, Oregon, Utah, Washington, and Wyoming. The center trains grassroots organizers and community leaders in advocacy skills and public policy, as well as consults on education and organizing campaigns and strategy. It publishes *Western States News,* as well as reports such as *Extremists and the Anti-Environmental Lobby: Activities Since Oklahoma City, Eyes Right! Challenging the Right Wing Backlash,* and *Covert Crusade: Religious Right and Politics in the West.*

REFERENCES

Abu Toameh, K. (1993, week ending March 11). Intifada on a shoestring. *Jerusalem Post International Edition,* pp. 24-26.

Adams, J. (1986). *The financing of terrorism: How the groups that are terrorizing the world get the money to do it.* New York: Simon & Schuster.

American Heritage College Dictionary of the English Language (3rd ed.). (1996). Boston: Houghton Mifflin.

Anti-Defamation League (ADL). (1994). *Armed and dangerous: Militias take aim at the federal government.* New York: Author.

Arendt, H. (1951). *The origins of totalitarianism.* New York: Harcourt Brace.

Atkins, S. E. (1992). *Terrorism: A reference handbook.* Santa Barbara, CA: ABC-CLIO.

Bell, J. B. (1975). *Transnational terror.* Washington, DC: American Enterprise Institute.

Burghart, D., & Crawford, R. (1996). *Guns and gavels: Common law courts, militias, and white supremacy.* Portland, OR: Coalition for Human Dignity.

Chaliand. G. (1987). *Terrorism: From popular struggle to media spectacle.* Atlantic Highlands, NJ: Saqi Books.

Chomsky, N. (1986). *Pirates and emperors: International terrorism in the real world.* New York: Claremont.

Claridge, D. (1996). State terrorism? Applying a definitional model. *Political Violence and Terrorism, 8,* 47-63.

Clark, R. P. (1983). Patterns in the lives of ETA members. *Terrorism: An International Journal, 6,* 423-454.

Cline, R. S., & Alexander, Y. (1984). *Terrorism: The Soviet connection.* New York: Crane, Russak.

Clutterbuck, R. (1994). *Terrorism in an unstable world.* New York: Routledge.

Combs, C. (1997). *Terrorism in the twenty-first century.* Upper Saddle River, NJ: Prentice Hall.

Copper, H. A. A. (1977). What is a terrorist: A psychological perspective. *Legal Medical Quarterly, 1,* 16-32.

Cooper, H. A. A. (1978). Terrorism: The problem of the problem definition. *Chitty's Law Journal, 26,* 105-108.

Cooper, J. (1995, May). Cooper's corner. *Guns & Ammo,* pp. 105-106.

Crenshaw, M. (Ed.). (1983). *Terrorism, legitimacy, and power.* Middletown, CT: Wesleyan University Press.

Crenshaw, M. (1990). The logic of terrorism: Terrorist behavior as a product of strategic choice. In W. Reich (Ed.), *Origins of terrorism* (pp. 7-24). Cambridge, UK: Cambridge University Press.

Dale, S. F. (1988). Religious suicide in Islamic Asia: Anticolonial terrorism in India, Indonesia, and the Philippines. *Journal of Conflict Resolution, 3,* 37-59.

Emerson, S., & Del Sesto, C. (1991). *Terrorist: The inside story of the highest ranking Iraqi terrorist ever to defect to the West.* New York: Villard Books.

Emerson, S. (Producer). (1994). *Jihad in America* [Videotape]. (Available from PBS Video).

Emerson, S. (1998). Terrorism in America: The threat of militant Islamic fundamentalism. In H. W. Kushner (Ed.), *The future of terrorism: Violence in the new millennium* (pp. 33-54). Thousand Oaks, CA: Sage.

Esposito, J. L. (1992). *The Islamic threat: Myth or reality?* New York: Oxford University Press.

FBI Terrorist Research and Analytical Center. (1990). *Terrorism in the United States: 1989.* Washington, DC: U.S. Department of Justice.

FBI Terrorist Research and Analytical Center. (1991). *Terrorism in the United States: 1990.* Washington, DC: U.S. Department of Justice.

FBI Terrorist Research and Analytical Center. (1992). *Terrorism in the United States: 1991.* Washington, DC: U.S. Department of Justice.

FBI Terrorist Research and Analytical Center. (1993). *Terrorism in the United States: 1992.* Washington, DC: U.S. Department of Justice.

FBI Terrorist Research and Analytical Center. (1994). *Terrorism in the United States: 1993.* Washington, DC: U.S. Department of Justice.

FBI Terrorist Research and Analytical Center. (1996). *Terrorism in the United States: 1995.* Washington, DC: U.S. Department of Justice.

Ferracuti, F., & Bruno, F. (1981). Psychiatric aspects of terrorism in Italy. In I. L. Barak-Glanmtz & C. R. Huff (Eds.), *The mad, the bad, and the different: Essays in honor of Simon Dinitz* (pp. 199-213). Lexington, MA: Lexington Books.

Fleming, P., & Stohl, M. (1988). The theoretical utility of typologies of terrorism: Lessons and opportunities. In M. Stohl (Ed.), *The politics of terrorism* (pp. 157-170). New York: Marcel Dekker.

Golan, G. (1990). *Gorbachev's "new thinking" on terrorism.* New York: Praeger.

Goldstein, B. (1981, July 9). Israel needs no enemy state at its borders. *New York Times,* p. A22.

Goren, R. (1984). *The Soviet Union and terrorism.* Winchester, MA: Allen & Unwin.

Gross, F. (1990). *Political violence and terror in 19th- and 20th-century Russia and Eastern Europe.* New York: Cambridge University Press.

Gurr, T. R. (1970). *Why men rebel.* Princeton, NJ: Princeton University Press.

Hacker, F. J. (1976). *Crusaders, criminals, and crazies: Terror in our time.* New York: Norton.

Hanle, D. (1989). *Terrorism: The newest face of warfare.* Washington, DC: Pergamon-Brasseys.

Harris, J. W. (1987). Domestic terrorism in the 1980s. *FBI Law Enforcement Bulletin, 53,* 5-13.

Herman, E. (1983). *The real terror network.* Boston: South End Press.

Heskin, K. (1984). The psychology of terrorism in Ireland. In Y. Alexander & A. O'Day (Eds.), *Terrorism in Ireland* (pp. 88-105). New York: St. Martin's Press.

Hiro, D. (1987). *Iran under the ayatollahs.* London: Routledge & Kegan Paul.

Hutman, B. (1996, week ending March 9). Attack with car kills 1, injures 22. *Jerusalem Post International Edition,* p. 1.

Jenkins, B. (1985). *International terrorism: The other world war.* Santa Monica, CA: Rand.

Kaplan, A. (1978). The psychodynamics of terrorism. *Terrorism: An International Journal, 1,* 237-254.

Katz, S. M. (1993). *Israel versus Jibril: The thirty-year war against a master terrorist.* New York: Paragon House.

Kelman, H. (1983). Conversations with Arafat. *American Psychologist, 70,* 203-216.

Kidder, R. M. (1993). "Terrorism": A term notoriously difficult to pin down. In B. Schechtermann & M. Slann (Eds.), *Violence and terrorism* (3rd ed., pp. 9-10). Guilford, CT: Duskin.

Kupperman, R., & Kamen, J. (1989). *Final warning: Averting disaster in the new age of terrorism.* New York: Doubleday.

Laqueur, W. (1987). *The age of terrorism.* Boston: Little, Brown.

Laqueur, W., & Alexander, Y. (Eds.). (1987). *The terrorism reader: A historical anthology.* New York: Meridian.

The letter: My restless aspiration to murder. (1997, February 26). *New York Times,* p. B3.

Lippman, T. W. (1990). *Understanding Islam: An introduction to the Muslim world* (rev. ed.). New York: Mentor.

Livingstone, N. C., & Arnold, T. E. (Eds.). (1986). *Fighting back: Winning the war against terrorism.* Lexington, MA: Lexington Books.

Lodge, J. (1981). *Terrorism: A challenge to the state.* Oxford, UK: Martin Robertson.

Macdonald, A. (1978). *The Turner diaries.* Arlington, VA: National Alliance.

Macdonald, A. (1989). *Hunter.* Arlington, VA: National Alliance.

McCauley, C. R., & Segal, M. E. (1987). Social psychology of terrorist groups. In C. Hendrick (Ed.), *Annual review of social and personality psychology: Volume 9. Group processes and intergroup relations* (pp. 231-256). Newbury Park, CA: Sage.

Mickolus, E. F., Sandler, T., & Murdock, J. M. (1989). *International terrorism in the 1980s: A chronology of events.* Ames: Iowa State University Press.

Miller, J. (1994, November/December). Faces of fundamentalism. *Foreign Affairs, 73,* 123-142.

Miller, J. (1996). *God has ninety-nine names.* New York: Simon & Schuster.

Moore, K. G. (1991). *Airport, aircraft, and airline security* (2nd ed.). Stoneham, MA: Butterworth-Heinemann.

Moosa, M. (1988). *Extremist Shiites: The Ghulat sects.* Syracuse, NY: Syracuse University Press.

Morf, G. (1970). *Terror in Quebec.* Toronto: Irwin.

Netanyahu, B. (1986). *The terrorism reader.* New York: Meridian.

Netanyahu, B. (1995). *Fighting terrorism: How democracies can defeat domestic and international terrorism.* New York: Farrar, Straus & Giroux.

Office of Combating Terrorism. (1984). *Terrorist bombings.* Washington, DC: U.S. Department of State.

Olson, N. (1997). Citizen militias defend liberty. In C. Cozic (Ed.), *The militia movement* (pp. 10-18). San Diego: Greenhaven.

Post, J. M. (1984). Notes on the psychodynamic theory of terrorist behavior. *Terrorism: An International Journal,* 7, 241-256.

Pratt, L. (1995). *Safeguarding liberty: The Constitution and citizens militias.* Franklin, TN: Legacy Communications.

Presser v. Illinois, 116 U.S. 252(1886).

Ross, J. I. (Ed.). (1995). *Controlling state crime.* New York: Garland.

Ross, J. I. (1996). A model of the psychological causes of oppositional political terrorism. *Journal of Peace Psychology,* 2, 129-141.

Sadler, A., & Winters, P. A. (Eds.). (1996). *Urban terrorism.* San Diego: Greenhaven Press.

Schamis, G. J. (1980). *War and terrorism in international affairs.* New Brunswick, NJ: Transaction Books.

Schmid, A. P. (1983). *Political terrorism: A research guide to concepts, theories, data bases and literature.* New Brunswick, NJ: Transaction Books.

Schmid, A. P. (1988). *Political terrorism: A new guide to actors, authors, concepts, data bases, theories and literature.* Amsterdam, The Netherlands: North-Holland.

Sederberg, P. C. (1998). Defining terrorism. In B. Schechtermann & M. Slann (Eds.), *Violence and terrorism* (4th ed., pp. 8-10). Guilford, CT: Duskin.

Silke, A. (1996). Terrorism and the blind men's elephant. *Terrorism and Political Violence,* 8, 12-28.

Simon, J. D. (1994). *The terrorist trap: America's experience with terrorism.* Bloomington: Indiana University Press.

Smith, B. L. (1994). *Terrorism in America: Pipe bombs and pipe dreams.* New York: State University of New York Press.

Southern Poverty Law Center (SPLC). (1996). *False patriots: The threat of antigovernment extremists.* Montgomery, AL: Author.

Stern, K. (1995). *Militias: A growing danger* (Background Report, Vol. 5, No. 1). New York: American Jewish Committee.

Strong language from both sides. (1998, January 9). *Newsday,* p. A3.

Taheri, A. (1987). *Holy terror.* Bethesda, MD: Adler & Adler.

Taylor, M., & Ryan, H. (1988). Fanaticism, political suicide, and terrorism. *Terrorism,* 11, 91-111.

Terrorist Activity: International Terrorism. Hearings before the Subcommittee to Investigate the Administration of the Internal Security Act and Other Internal Security Laws of the Committee on the Judiciary, 79th Cong., 1st Sess. (1975). (testimony of Brian Crozier).

Thornton, T. P. (1964). Terror as a weapon of political agitation. In H. Eckstein (Ed.), *Internal war* (pp. 71-99). New York: Free Press.

The truth must be told [Editorial]. (1996, March 3). *Jerusalem Post,* p. 6.

U.S. denies FBI head's visit linked to Abu Marzook deal. (1997, week ending March 1). *Jerusalem Post International Edition,* p. 6.

U.S. Department of State. (1991). *Patterns of global terrorism: 1990.* Washington, DC: Author.

U.S. Department of State. (1992). *Patterns of global terrorism: 1991.* Washington, DC: Author.

U.S. Department of State. (1993). *Patterns of global terrorism: 1992.* Washington, DC: Author.

U.S. Department of State. (1994). *Patterns of global terrorism: 1993.* Washington, DC: Author.

U.S. Department of State. (1997). *Patterns of global terrorism: 1996.* Washington, DC: Author.

Vetter, H. J., & Perlstein, G. R. (1991). *Perspectives on terrorism.* Pacific Gove, CA: Brooks/Cole.

Wardlaw, G. (1989). *Political terrorism: Theory, tactics, and counter-measures.* New York: Cambridge University Press.

Weinberg, L., & Davis, P. B. (1989). *Introduction to political terrorism.* New York: McGraw-Hill.

Weiner, T. (1998, January 24). Killer of two at C.I.A. draws death sentence. *New York Times,* p. A11.

White, J. R. (1991). *Terrorism: An introduction.* Pacific Grove, CA: Brooks/Cole.

Wilkinson, P. (1974). *Political terrorism.* New York: Wiley.

Wright, R. (1986). *Sacred rage.* New York: Touchstone.

AUTHOR INDEX

Adams, J., 18
Alexander, Y., 8, 15
Atkins, S. E., 3
Bell, J. B., 6
Bruno, F., 5
Burghart, D., 65
Chaliand, G., 5
Chomsky, N., 5
Claridge, D., 5
Clark, R. P., 5
Cline, R., 15
Clutterbuck, R., 9
Combs, C., 3, 8
Cooper, J., 5, 8, 56
Crawford, R., 65
Crenshaw, M., 4, 6, 7
Crozier, B., 4
Davis, P. B., 6
Del Sesto, C., 12
Emerson, S., 12, 13, 40, 41
Esposito, J., 27
Ferracuti, F., 5
Fleming, P., 7
Ford, H., 60
Golan, G., 16
Goren, R., 5, 15
Gross, F., 7
Gurr, T. R., 6
Hacker, F., 6
Hanle, D., 5
Harris, J., 57
Herman, E., 5
Heskin, K., 5
Hutman, B., 34
Jenkins, B., 3
Jibril, A., 8
Kamen, J., 12, 13
Kaplan, A., 6

Katz, S., 8
Kelman, H., 5
Kidder, R. M., 3
Kupperman, R., 12
Laqueur, W., 4, 16
Livingstone, N., 4
Lodge, J., 4
McCauley, C. R., 5
Miller, J., 26
Moore, K. G., 8
Morf, G., 5
Netanyahu, B., 4
Perlstein, G., 3, 8, 11, 13, 57
Post, J. M., 5
Ross, J. I., 5, 6
Ryan, H., 33
Sadler, A., 3
Schamis, G. J., 5
Schmid, A., 3, 4, 7, 8
Sederberg, P. C., 3
Segal, M. E., 5
Simon, J. D., 7
Smith, G. L. K., 60
Smith, B., 5, 12, 13
Stern, K., 57
Stewart, P., 8
Stohl, M., 7
Taheri, A., 25
Taylor, M., 33
Thompson, L., 59
Thornton, T. P., 4
Trochmann, J., 58
Vetter, H., 3, 8, 11, 13, 57
Wardlaw, G., 4, 8, 9
Weinberg, L., 6
White, J. R., 3, 8, 12, 13, 57
Wilkinson, P., 6
Winters, P. A., 3

SUBJECT INDEX

A

Abu Nidal Organization, 35 (*see also* Terrorists, U.S.-based)
  U.S. coupon clipping scam, 36
Afghanistan
  Soviet invasion and buildup of Islamic response to holy war, 28, 136
  Alkifah Refuge Center, Brooklyn, NY
  CIA support, 28
  sanctuary of international terrorists, 11, 28–29
  Stinger antiaircraft missile availability, 30–31
  terrorist boot camps, 28–29, 30–32
Alfred P. Murrah Federal Building, Oklahoma City, OK
  domestic terrorism, 56–59
Animal Liberation Front, 91, 100, 115
Anti-Defamation League
  monitor of hate groups, extremists, paramilitary groups, 57
Antigovernment extremists' identity sketch, 79–83
Antigovernment movement, 57–59 (*see also* Christian Identity movement)
  Aryan Nations, 60–62, 72–74, 79
  Brady Bill passage, 59
  Christian Identity movement, 59–64, 79, 81–83
  Internet usage to disseminate information, 77–79
    cyberspace version of Paul Revere's ride, 77
    Stormfront web site, 78, 91
    web sites for organizations monitoring activity, 194–204
  leaderless resistance and phantom cells, 73, 92
  militias, 57–59, 79, 81
  National Alliance, 68–71 (*see also* Pierce, William)

Oklahoma City, OK bombing, 56–59
Posse Comitatus movement, 64–68
Ruby Ridge, 58
significance of April 19 to patriot groups, 58
skinheads, 62, 63, 69–70, 72–73, 79, 81
targets of violence, 82
Waco, TX, and Branch Davidians, 58–59
Antiterrorism and Effective Death Penalty Act, 135
  identification of foreign terrorist organizations, 135–44
Arab nationalism, 20
Arafat, Yasir (*see also* Palestine Liberation Organization)
  alliance with Iraq during Persian Gulf War, 17–19
    financial impact, 18
  ideological differences between PLO and Hamas, 19–20
  Middle East peace talks, 21–22
  political activities, historical overview, 20–22
  transcript of conversation with Gromyko, 15–16
Aryan Brotherhood, 61
Aryan Nations group, 60–62, 72–74, 79

B

Baz, Rashid, 45–46
Beach, Henry L.
  Blue Book of antigovernment ideas, 64, 68
  Posse Comitatus movement, 64–68
Beam, Louis R., 72–74
  Aryan Nations Liberty Net, 74–79
  assassination point system, 72
  heir apparent to Aryan Nations, 74
  Ku Klux Klan involvement, 72–74
  leaderless resistance and phantom cells, 73, 78, 92

New Right movement, 72–74
The Seditionist, 72, 73, 91
Black, Stephen D., Stormfront web site, 78, 91
Blue Book (*see* Beach, Henry L.)
Butler, Richard G.
    Aryan Nations group, 60–62
        recruitment of skinheads, 62
    California Rangers paramilitary group, 60
    prison ministry and Aryan Brotherhood, 61

C

Carlos the Jackal, terrorist activities, 29–30
Christian Defense League, 63
Christian Identity movement, 59–64
    antigovernment movement, 57–59
    Elohim City, OK compound, 62
    right-wing extremists affiliation, 63
Common law courts, 66–67, 101–2
Coupons, redemption scam, 36, 141–42
Cuba
    actions of Omega 7 against Castro, 12, 137–38
    Dept. of State list of terrorist states, 27
    support of U.S. left-wing extremist groups, 114

D

Department of State, 9, 12–13
    countries supporting terrorism, 27
    terrorism definition, 9–10
Domestic terrorism, 56–85, 100–44
    animal rights and environmental groups, 100
    antigovernment extremists' identity sketch, 79–83
    antigovernment movement, 57–59, 79–83
        Brady Bill passage, 59
        militias, 57–59, 81, 116 (*see also* Domestic terrorism, group listings)
        Oklahoma City, OK bombing, 56–59, 88–89
        Ruby Ridge, 58, 89
        significance of April 19 to patriot groups, 58
        Waco, TX, and Branch Davidians, 58–59, 89

Christian Identity movement, 59–64, 81, 129
    Anglo-Israelism, 59
    anti-Semitic, anti-color, 60
    neo-Nazis and skinheads, 62, 63, 69–70, 72–73, 79, 81, 130, 132–33
    common law courts, 66–67, 101–2
    criminal gangs, 108
    international terrorist groups, 135–44
    Internet use for communications, 77–79, 91
    left-wing extremist groups, 114
    Puerto Rican transnational terrorism, 126–27
    right-wing extremist groups, 129, 132–33
    terrorism definitions, 3–10, 86–87
    violence targets, 82
    web site and mail addresses for terrorism activity monitors, 194–204
    World Wide Web, 74–79
        importance of Internet for dissemination of communications, 77–79, 91
Domestic terrorism, group listings
    animal rights and environmental groups, 100–1
    common law courts (by state), 101–7
    criminal gangs, 108
    Israeli groups, 140
    Japanese groups, 140–41
    Jewish groups, 109–10
    Ku Klux Klans (by state), 110–14
    left-wing extremist groups, 114–15
    Middle Eastern groups, 141–43
    militias (by state), 116–26
    Pakistani groups, 143–44
    Puerto Rican groups, 127–29
    right-wing extremists, 129–35
        Christian Identity groups, 129–30
        neo-Nazi groups, 130–32
        skinheads, 132–35
    international terrorist groups
        Afghani groups, 136
        Armenian groups, 137
        Cuban groups, 137
        Irish groups, 138–39
        Israeli groups, 140
        organizations active in U.S., 136
Duke, David
    Ku Klux Klan involvement, 68, 72, 78

E

Egypt
  terrorist activities of Islamic Group, 27
E-mail, 75
Emry, Sheldon, 63
Endnotes, 10, 53–55, 83–85

F

Father Holy War, 8 (*see also* Jibril, Ahmed)
Federal Building, Oklahoma City, OK (*see*
    Alfred P. Murrah Federal Building)
Federal Bureau of Investigation
  international radical terrorists label for
      freelancers, 12–13, 49–53, 87
  terrorism definition, 9
  Terrorist Research and Analytical Center
      reports, 12–13, 49–51
Freedom Fighters
  actions against unarmed victims, 9
Freelancing terrorists (*see also* Terrorist-relat-
    ed U.S. incidents)
  international radical terrorism (IRT),
      12–13, 49–53, 87
  Islamic fundamentalists
    religious, political, and military views,
        19–20, 22–25, 26–27, 88–89
    Shiite martyrdom and suicide mis-
        sions, 23–25, 32–33
  law enforcement difficulties, 95–98
  organization and activities within U.S., 11,
      43–53, 92–98
    Ali Hassan Abu Kamal, Empire State
        Building murders, 46–47, 51, 92,
        96
    Gazi Ibrahim Abu Maizer, attempted
        subway attack, 47–48, 51, 92, 97
    Lafi Khalil, attempted subway attack,
        47–48, 51, 92, 97
    Mir Aimal Kasi, CIA murders, 43–45,
        51, 92
    Rashid Baz, assault on Hasidic stu-
        dents, 45–46, 51, 92, 96
  retaliation on U.S. citizens for punishment
      of terrorists, 51–53

G

Gadhafi, Moammar, 18, 108 (*see also* Libya)
Gale, William P., 64, 66

Germany, impact of reunification, 17
Gun Owners of America (GAO), 74, 85

H

Hamas (Islamic Resistance Movement)
  ideological differences from PLO, 19–20
  Islamic Association for Palestine, 38–40
  Islamic fundamentalism, 20
  religious zealotry in terrorism, 19
  terrorist activities, 27
  U.S. funding, 38–40
  web site, 91
Hamideh, Ahmed, 34
Hezbollah (Party of God), 22
  organization and mission, 22
  martyrdom and suicide missions, 23–25
  terrorist activities, 22–24, 27
Hussein, Saddam, 18, 42

I

Internet
  Aryan Nations Liberty Net, 74–79
  browsers, 76
  dissemination of extremist communica-
      tions, 77–79, 91
    cyberspace version of Paul Revere's
        ride, 77
  e-mail, 77
  home page, 76
  hypertext markup language (html), 76
  search engines, 77
  Stormfront web site, 78, 91
  system requirements and use explanation,
      74–77
  Usenet, 75–76
  web site addresses for terrorism activity
      monitors, 194–204
  World Wide Web, 76
Iran
  Ayatollah Ruhollah Khomeini, 22
  Dept. of State list of terrorist states, 27
  Hezbollah, terrorist activities, 22–24
  Shiism, religious point of view, 22–25
    martyrdom and suicide missions,
        23–25, 32–33
Iraq
  Arafat alliance during Persian Gulf War,
      17–19
  Dept. of State list of terrorist states, 27

Irish Republican Army, 12, 14, 138–39
    Sinn Fein, 138
IRT (*see* Federal Bureau of Investigation)
Islamic Association for Palestine
    activities and funding for Hamas, 38–40
    web site, 91
Islamic fundamentalist groups
    activities and funding for Hamas, 38–40
    Islamic influence in terrorist boot camps,
        31–32
    militant activities and foundation, 88–89
    religious, political, and military views,
        19–20, 22–25, 26–27, 88–89
    Sharia, source of law and conduct, 88–89
    Shiite martyrdom and suicide missions,
        23–25, 32–33
Islamic Group, 27
Islamic Jihad, 23–25, 27, 136
Islamic Resistance Movement (*see* Hamas)
Islamic Salvation Front (FIS), 27
Israel, 13, 19
    Hamas' activities, 19
    Middle East peace talks, 21–22
    Mossad, 21
    suicide bombings, 32–33

J

Japanese Red Army, 12, 14
Jewish Defense League, 109
    web site, 109
Jibril, Ahmed, 8

K

Kahl, Gordon W., 66–68
Kamal, Ali Hassan Abu, 46–47, 51
    quoted from suicide note, 47, 93
Karim, Abdul Basit Mahmoud Abdul (see
    Yousef, Ramzi Ahmed)
Kasi, Mir Aimal, 28, 43–45, 51
    CIA murders, 43–45
    quoted at sentencing, 92
    retaliation against U.S. citizens for convic-
        tion, 51–52
Kaczynski, Theodore J., 95
Khalil, Lafi, 47–48, 51
    attempted attack on subway, 47
Ku Klux Klan, 14, 72–74, 81–82
    groups by state, 110–14

Kuwait
    protectionist alliance with PLO, 18

L

Lebanon
    Beirut bombings, 23–25
    terrorist activities of Hezbollah and
        Islamic Jihad, 22–24
Libya, 17
    Dept. of State list of terrorist states, 27

M

Maizer, Gazi Ibrahim Abu, 47–48, 51
    attempted attack on subway, 47
Marzook, Musa Mohammed Abu, 38–40
Mathews, Robert J., 69–70
McVeigh, Timothy (*see also* Alfred P. Murrah
    Federal Building)
    domestic terrorism, 56–59, 89–90
Middle East, 14, 15
    peace talks, 21–22
    Persian Gulf War, 17–19
    suicide bombers, 23–25
Militia Day, April 19, 74
Militias, 57–59, 79, 81, 116
    groups by state, 117–26
Millar, Robert G.
    Elohim City, OK founder, 62
Mossad, 21 (*see also* Israel)
Muslims (*see also* Islamic fundamentalist
        groups)
    activities and funding for Hamas, 38–40
    acts of martyrdom and suicide missions,
        23–25
    militant activities and foundations, 88–89
    Islamic influence in terrorist boot camps,
        31–32
    religious, political, and military views,
        19–20, 22–25, 26–27
    Shiite martyrdom and suicide missions,
        23–25, 32–33

N

Nasser, Gamal Abdel, 20
National Islamic Front, 28
Neo-Nazis, 62, 63, 69–70, 72–73, 79, 81 (*see
    also* Domestic terrorism)

Nichols, Terry (*see also* Alfred P. Murrah Federal Building)
  domestic terrorism, 56–59, 89–90
North Korea
  Dept. of State list of terrorist states, 27

O

Oklahoma City, OK, Federal Building (*see* Alfred P. Murrah Federal Building)
Omega 7, 12, 137–38

P

Palestine, 13
  Hamas, 19–20
  Patrice Lumumba University school of terrorism, 14
Palestine Islamic Jihad (PIJ), 21, 27, 37 (*see also* Islamic Jihad)
Palestine Liberation Organization (PLO), 14 (*see also* Arafat, Yasir)
  Abu Nidal Organization (ANO) activities, 21
  Arafat, Yasir
    alliance with Iraq, 17–19
    political activities overview, 20–22
  Hamas, ideological differences, 19–20
  Middle East peace talks, 21–22
  protectionist alliance with oil states, 18
  Soviet support of terrorist activities, 14–15
  terrorist training camps, 14
    list of terrorist organizations, 14
  transcript of Arafat-Gromyko conversation, 15–16
Persian Gulf War, 17–19 (*see also* Iraq)
  Arafat alliance with Iraq, 17–19
Peters, Peter J., 63, 74
Pierce, William
  ideologic basis for antigovernment extremists, 68–72
  National Alliance movement, 68–71
  periodical publications, 69
  racist comic books, 69
  Turner Diaries, 69, 90
PLO (*see* Palestine Liberation Organization)
Posse Comitatus movement, 64–68
  Blue Book, 64, 68
  Montana Freemen Justice Township, 66
  Tigerton Dells, WI common law township, 65

R

Rabin, Yitzhak, 21 (*see also* Israel)
Rahman, Omar Abdel
  retaliatory action against Luxor, Egypt tourists, 52
  terrorist activities, 32, 33, 43, 52, 89
Repressive terrorism, 6
Revolutionary terrorism, 6
Roberts, Archibald E., 68
Rushie, Salman, 108

S

Saudi Arabia
  protectionist alliance with PLO, 18
Shallah, Ramadan Abdullah, 37 (*see also* World and Islam Studies Enterprise)
Silver Shirts, 60, 64, 84
Skinheads, 62, 63, 69–70, 72–73, 79, 82, 132
  groups, 132–35
Southern Poverty Law Center
  monitor of militia movements, 57–59
Soviet Union
  actions of Omega 7, 12
  condemnation of terrorist activities, 16
  conditional support of terrorist activities, 15
  disintegration of Soviet state, 16–17
  efforts to destabilize the West, 15–16
  Patrice Lumumba University school of terrorism, 14
  political history of national liberation wars' support, 13–17
  terrorism as indirect aggression, 15
  transcript of Gromyko-Arafat conversation, 15–16
Stinger antiaircraft missile
  availability in Afghanistan and Sudan, 30–31
Subrevolutionary terrorism, 6
Sudan
  Dept. of State list of terrorist states, 27
  Khartoum conference and manifesto, 26
  National Islamic Front, 28
  religious, political, and military views, 25–27, 30–32
  sanctuary of terrorists, 30
  terrorist boot camps, 27–28, 30–32
Suicide bombings, 23–25, 32–33, 47
Swift, Wesley,

Christian Identity, anti-Semitic movement, 59–60
Syria, 17
   Dept. of State list of terrorist states, 27

T

Terrorism (*see also* Terrorists; Domestic terrorism)
   activity monitors
      web site and mail addresses for reference sources, 194–204
   definitions, 3–10, 86–87
      political end vs. criminal activity, 4
      psychological, 5–6
      state control of citizenry, 5
      warfare, 4–5
   definitive elements, 9
   freelancers, 43–53, 87
   ideologies, 7, 30–32, 86–92
   international radical terrorism, 12–13, 49–53, 87, 132–44
   militant Islamic fundamentalists, 88–89
      activities and funding for Hamas, 38–40
      Islamic influence in terrorist boot camps, 27–28, 30–32
      Jihad, 21, 27, 37
      religious, political, and military views, 19–20, 22–25, 26–27
      Shiite martyrdom and suicide missions, 23–25, 32–33
   motivations, 6–7, 30–32, 87–92
      authorized, 6
      criminal, 6
      endemic, 6
      psychotic, 6
      revolutionary, 6
      vigilante, 6
   tactics, 7, 30–32
   typology of actions
      repressive, 6
      revolutionary, 6
      subrevolutionary, 6
Terrorist-related U.S. incidents (*see also* Domestic terrorism)
   chronological summary (1975–98), 145–93

international terrorism freelancer incidents
   Ali Hassan Abu Kamal, Empire State Building murders, 46–47, 51, 92, 96
   Gazi Ibrahim Abu Maizer, attempted subway attack, 47–48, 51, 92, 97
   Lafi Khalil, attempted subway attack, 47–48, 51, 92, 97
   Mir Aimal Kasi, CIA murders, 43–45, 51, 92
   Rashid Baz, assault on Hasidic students, 45–46, 51, 92, 96
Terrorists (*see also* Domestic terrorism)
   boot camps, 27–32
      Islamic influence in zealotry, 31
      organization and activities of groups, 31–32, 92
   decline of state sponsored attacks, 42–43
   freelance terrorists, 33–35, 42, 43–53, 92–98
      organization and activities within U.S., 43–53, 92
      retaliation for U.S. imprisonment of terrorists, 51–52
   influence of religious leaders, 33, 92
   PLO training list, 14
   Soviet trained vs. Sudan-Afghan trained, 30–32
   U.S.-based groups, 35–37
Turabi, Hassan Abdallah, 25–27
Turkey
   terrorist groups, list, 14
Turner Diaries, William Pierce, 69, 90

U

Unabomber, 95 (*see also* Kaczynski, Theodore J.)
Underdeveloped countries
   use of terrorism as warfare, 4–5
United Association of Studies and Research, 39, 40 (*see also* Hamas)
United States (*see also* Terrorist-related U.S. incidents)
   absence of rampant terrorism, 11–12
   Beirut bombings, 23–25
   freelance terrorists' activities, 43–53

Hamas presence, 40–41
Hezbollah presence, 40
Islamic Jihad presence, 40
militant Islamic fundamentalists' retalia-
    tion activities, 19–20, 22–25, 26–27,
    88–89
networking of terrorist groups, 40–41
vigilance against internal terrorism, 13
University of South Florida
    activities of WISE, 37
Usenet, 75–76
U.S.S.R. (*see* Soviet Union)

V

Victims, unarmed, 9
Violence
    motivational, 4
    targets of Christian Identity movement,
        82

W

War Sports Group (WSG), 14 (*see also* Neo-
    Nazis)
Warner, James K., 63
White Patriot Party, 70–71
Wickstrom, James P., 65
World and Islam Studies Enterprise (WISE)
    terrorist activities and funding, 37
World Trade Center
    plan and plot for international radical ter-
        rorist act, 49–50

sanctuary of terrorists, 43
sodium cyanide, 11
terrorists' actions and training, 11, 28, 43,
    49–53
World Wide Web, 76
    Aryan Nations Liberty Net, 74–79
    browsers, 76
    dissemination of extremist communica-
        tions, 77–79, 91
        cyberspace version of Paul Revere's
            ride, 77
    e-mail, 77
    home page, 76
    hypertext markup language (html), 76
    Internet, 74–76, 91
    search engines, 77
    Stormfront web site, 78, 91
    system requirements and use explanation,
        74–77
    Usenet, 75–76
    web site addresses for terrorism activity
        monitors, 194–204

Y

Yassin, Ahmed, 19 (*see also* Hamas)
Yousef, Ramiz Ahmed, 11, 28, 43, 49–50 (*see
    also* World Trade Center)
    quoted at sentencing, 53, 89, 93, 94–95
Yu Kikumura, 12